THROUGH THE
BRAZILIAN WILDERNESS

Colonel Roosevelt and Colonel Rondon at Navaïté on the River of Doubt

The Lakeside Classics

THROUGH THE
BRAZILIAN WILDERNESS

by Theodore Roosevelt

EDITED BY
DAIN BORGES

The Lakeside Press

R. R. DONNELLEY & SONS COMPANY
December 2016

PUBLISHER'S PREFACE

THIS YEAR, WITH the eyes of the world turned to Brazil, the first South American country to host the Olympics, it seemed appropriate to select Theodore Roosevelt's *Through the Brazilian Wilderness* as our Lakeside Classic.

After failing to recapture the presidency in 1912, Colonel Roosevelt, his preferred name, was looking for adventure. He decided to follow a lecture tour in Latin America with a scientific journey through the Amazon under the sponsorship of The American Museum of Natural History. The plan became more ambitious when the Brazilian government suggested that he join the famed Brazilian explorer Colonel Cândido Rondon in a voyage down an untraced river—the Rio Dúvida, or River of Doubt.

The Rondon-Roosevelt Scientific Expedition began as an enjoyable trek across the interior of Brazil, hunting and collecting specimens. But when it finally started down the River of Doubt, it became a harrowing journey. The expedition suffered mightily from insects and starvation. They planned to supplement their rations with local foraging but found insufficient edible vegetation or wildlife. The rapids were frequent and dangerous, requiring arduous portages and resulting in not only the loss of canoes and supplies, but also the loss of lives.

Fevers, infections, and injuries plagued the men. Colonel Roosevelt bruised his leg against a boulder, developed an abscess, and became dangerously ill. Although, as was his style, he makes little of this in his narrative, he was so seriously ill that his survival was in doubt. He lost more than fifty pounds and never really regained his health after the journey, dying only five years later at the age of sixty.

All of the talents of Teddy Roosevelt come through in this narrative: his love of adventure, his skill as a writer, his progressive ideology, his devotion to nature, and his commitment to conservation. While reveling in the adventure of the hunt, he kills only for food or scientific specimens and eloquently proposes that the time for collecting will soon end and the future of the naturalist lies in studying animals living in their native habitats. We think you will find this somewhat abridged text of Roosevelt's narrative a great read.

We are extremely pleased to publish, for the first time, colored versions of many of the photographs taken by members of the expedition. These lantern slides were found by our editor in the library of the American Museum of Natural History. We are deeply grateful to the museum and its staff for their gracious assistance and their generosity in allowing us to use them.

We also thank Dain Borges, Assistant Professor of History at the University of Chicago, for serving as our historian and linguist. His essay and footnotes will enable our readers to better understand the geography, politics, and people of the Amazon. With his assistance, we were also able to clarify and modernize many of the Portuguese terms and locations.

*   *   *

AS THEODORE ROOSEVELT'S gripping account of his journey down the River of Doubt was first reaching an audience in 1914, RR Donnelley was both observing its 50th anniversary and planning a departure of its own. This journey would follow a much more thoroughly charted course than Roosevelt's leap into the unknown. The company's careful planning came to fruition a century ago as RR Donnelley spun off its publishing operations to create a separate corporation. The spinoff carried with it the scale, expertise, intellectual capital, and financial resources to quickly become an industry leader. As two separate businesses, RR Donnelley and the newly formed publisher could even better focus their capital expenditures, product development, and other strategic resources on their respective segment's needs.

After the spinoff, RR Donnelley continued to grow organically—through innovation and geographic expansion, as well as via acquisitions, which dramatically broadened the range of solutions that the company could provide to its customers.

That growth allowed RR Donnelley, on the centennial of that previous spinoff, to execute another carefully mapped separation, this time to create two new independent publicly traded companies, each again with the scale, expertise, intellectual capital, and financial resources to be a leader in its respective industries. As with RR Donnelley, each spinoff is now even better positioned to focus its resources and capabilities to take advantage of emerging opportunities.

This year saw the debut of spinoffs Donnelley Financial Solutions, which serves clients' financial communications and language solutions needs, and LSC Communications, which serves the needs of publishers, catalogers, and retailers worldwide. RRD, which retained the formal and legal name of R. R. Donnelley & Sons Company, continues to create, manage, deliver, and optimize its customers' multichannel communications strategies globally.

* * *

DONNELLEY FINANCIAL SOLUTIONS serves capital markets and investment management clients internationally, providing one-stop content creation, collaboration, management, and distribution capabilities. While the company draws on deep experience in financial printing, its diverse resources includes a range of proprietary and commercial data management and analytics services, virtual data rooms, translations and language solutions, e-delivery, and more.

For example, to help clients meet their financial

reporting needs, the company offers FundSuiteArc® document management platform. The elements of this suite, ArcReporting, ArcProspectus, ArcFiling, and ArcMarketing, individually and seamlessly together help clients who manage funds electronically create compliant fact sheets, shareholder communications, and prospectuses for filing with the Securities and Exchange Commission.

Across the board, Donnelley Financial Solutions is expanding conventional offerings to do much more for clients. Its translations offering, for instance, has grown to encompass *transcreation*. Transcreation ensures that messaging makes the leap into different languages in a way that resonates correctly with each audience . . . and avoids the sorts of translation disasters that provide fodder for comedians. It helps to recast a brand's promise in a way that is tailored to how people think, feel, and respond to messages in a particular language.

Donnelley Financial Solutions will continue to invest in new technology and workflow solutions, focus on content collaboration and data analytics, and help clients adapt quickly to changing regulatory requirements.

LSC Communications derives its name from the long-standing Lakeside Classics series, the latest volume of which you hold in your hands. The Lakeside Classics book series has long been a symbol of the ability to use emerging technologies to cost-effectively deliver products and services of exceptional quality and enduring value.

With manufacturing operations across the United States, Mexico, and Europe, LSC Communications serves customers by producing and distributing periodicals, catalogs, retail inserts, books, office products, and directories.

The operations that comprise LSC Communications produce more than twenty billion pages annually. These are the pages that you turn as you curl up with a new volume by a favorite author, read to a child, study a textbook, or contemplate a religious text. They are the pages you carry as you settle into an airline seat with a magazine, scan ads in circulars to plan a shopping trip, leaf through the catalogs that inspire you, or look for a 24-hour plumber to fix that sudden leak in the basement. LSC Communications has more than three thousand innovative organization solutions and office products for school, work, home, and everything in between. You see them on display as you shop for popular brands of materials, such as legal pads, organizers, binders, presentation folders, and more in stores and online.

Though LSC Communications has an unparalleled heritage spanning three different centuries, its gaze continues to be firmly forward-looking. For example, it offers book publishers a comprehensive set of digital book-printing operations that use high-speed inkjet presses and inline binding units to cost-effectively produce titles on demand. The acquisition of Courier Corporation in June of 2015 enhanced LSC Communications' content management and customization capabilities.

All of these production resources are linked to sophisticated inventory management and digital workflow systems to create an Automatic Replenishment Program (ARP) that helps publishers respond quickly to surges in demand, to keep making their back titles (books published in years past) or end of life titles available to customers, and to reduce on-hand inventory, minimize warehousing costs, and decrease the potential for new title obsolescence.

Tight integration with LSC Communications makes this process seamless for publishers. These capabilities were enhanced this year as the company announced that it was teaming with Context Labs (CXL) to pursue leading-edge blockchain-enabled technology for its global publishing customers. This technology has great potential to deliver extended consumer reach for publishers while reducing their supply chain costs and providing them with deep, direct, and secure relationships with the consumers who purchase their products.

LSC Communications unveiled another innovative way to serve customers this year with an even more comprehensive supply chain management offering. One publisher, for example, is drawing on LSC Communications as its single source procurement, manufacturing, warehousing, distribution, and inventory management provider for one of its extensive line of educational products.

LSC Communications has a strong heritage, experienced professionals in every role, wonderful long-term and new-customer relationships, and a deep commitment to delivering exceptional quality and value.

*   *   *

WITH THE SPINOFFS successfully launched, RRD is focusing on providing customized multichannel communications management products and services internationally. These resources, tightly integrated, can take the form of digital and creative solutions, business-process outsourcing, logistics services, packaging and related products, direct mail, personalized printed and online statements, labels, forms, commercial and digital print, and supply chain management services.

The ability to tie a diverse mix of capabilities together allows customers to work with RRD in entirely new ways. One is called "centralized production." Here is how it works: A customer provides RRD with a set of brand guidelines (describing how its logo, colors, and other branding elements should be used), as well as its promotional campaign strategy. This campaign strategy will be brought to life in a variety of individual promotions, showing up in its customers' mailboxes, on their computer screens, in store aisles, and more. RRD executes these promotions across a broad number of media, adapting the campaign in print, video, and digital messaging. Providing centralized production draws on RRD's creative design and strategic services, its editorial and interactive support, its range of print production capabilities, and its distribution expertise to manage brand guidelines and deliver with consistency across all media channels for our customers.

During 2016, RRD announced a further enhancement to its already robust information technology resources by entering into a strategic relationship with Adobe to integrate Adobe Marketing Cloud into its technology platform. This added resource will allow RRD to even more effectively help customers use big data, which is all of that information that organizations collect as we surf the Internet, create transactions, and interact with computers and smart phones. RRD will use this enhanced capability to create highly personalized marketing in print and through its Digital Solutions Group (DSG). DSG's comprehensive offering includes photography and videography; creative and editorial; digital media/interactive services; digital publishing; cloud-based automated marketing; prepress and art production; and workflow solutions.

This year RRD also continued to enhance its ability to provide customers with a range of products that include RFID capabilities. You see RFID—radio frequency identification—tags and labels on a variety of products. They are somewhat like barcodes, in that they convey information to a computer via a reader. However, where a barcode reader like the one that scans your groceries must "see" the barcode, RFID signals do not have to be "seen" by the reader. A direct line of sight is not required to activate them. RFID might, for example, be embedded into packaging of an item on a retail shelf, for inventory-control purposes and to assist in preventing shoplifting.

RRD has been a leader in producing printed electronic antennas that are used in RFID tags and labels, which RRD also produces. This year RRD entered into an agreement to jointly market RAIN-enabled tags and labels. RAIN is next-generation Radio Frequency Identification initiative, designed to allow tags and labels to communicate via the Internet. This will allow RRD to provide customers RAIN inlays that use two distinct components that do not need to be adhered together. This permits RRD's customers to simplify their RFID-compliance needs by making all their product tags, labels, and packaging RFID-ready and then enabling them on an as-needed basis.

You may see how RRD creates customized communications in the billing and informational statements that you receive, and not necessarily just through the mail. RRD can do much more than just receive "print ready" files from a telecommunications provider or a utility and then use those files to create a statement and mail it to you.

Thanks to RRD's sophisticated information technology resources, a customer may actually authorize RRD to assume control of select applications and perform document composition with the customer's raw data files. Once the applications are running on the RRD platform, enhancements such as color, targeted messages, and more can be added. Then, completed statements can be sent to individual consumers via mail, email, or text.

RRD's continuing vision is to create, manage, deliver, and optimize individualized and branded communications strategies for a broad array of customers; to provide integrated logistics, supply chain management, and workflow solutions; and to complement these capabilities by helping our customers to manage related analytics and employ leading-edge digital services.

WITH SINCERE THANKS

Since 1996, Susan M. Levy has served as the Lakeside Classics editor, researching and recommending titles for publication, engaging scholars to write historical introductions, editing the texts themselves, choosing the maps, photographs, and illustrations, and helping to shepherd the volumes to completion. As you read this volume, we are deeply appreciative for all she has done, particularly in expanding the diversity of the voices brought to life through the Lakeside Classics series.

In October, Thomas J. Quinlan III, who had served

RR Donnelley as its President and Chief Executive Officer and also served on the RR Donnelley Board of Directors since 2007, became LSC Communications' Chairman and Chief Executive Officer. Daniel L. Knotts assumed the role of RRD's Chief Executive Officer, having served the company for thirty years in a number of capacities, most recently as its Chief Operating Officer. Daniel N. Leib assumed the role of Chief Executive Officer of Donnelley Financial Solutions, having served the company for more than ten years in a number of financial management capacities, most recently as RRD's Executive Vice President and Chief Financial Officer.

We are grateful to the members of the RR Donnelley Board of Directors, whose independent governance and wise counsel is always valued, and which played an important role in the successful execution of the spinoff transactions this year: John C. Pope – Chairman, Susan M. Cameron, Richard L. Crandall, Susan M. Gianinno, Judith H. Hamilton, Jeffrey G. Katz, Richard K. Palmer, Michael T. Riordan, and Oliver R. Sockwell.

This volume itself is designed to be an expression of our sincerest wishes for you to enjoy the blessings for the holiday season and a happy, safe, and peaceful New Year.

THE PUBLISHER
December 2016

Contents

Illustrations

Illustrations

Illustrations

Colonel Rondon and Colonel Roosevelt in campaign dress

The route of the Roosevelt-Rondon Scientific Expedition

Historical Introduction

ON FEBRUARY 27, 1914, Theodore Roosevelt and Brazil's great military frontiersman Colonel Cândido Rondon set their expedition on a one-way river trip down the Rio da Dúvida, called the River of Doubt because its course went through entirely unexplored territory of the Amazon forest. They hoped for a vigorous downriver paddle of several weeks, with stops to take navigational fixes and to collect specimens for the American Museum of Natural History. Instead of weeks, it took them two months, often making progress of no more than a mile or two a day. Instead of paddling downriver, they often had to haul their heavy wooden dugouts over roller tracks they laid through the forest and across granite canyon edges. Three men were lost, and Roosevelt nearly died of malaria fever and an infected leg. Roosevelt's twenty-five-year-old son Kermit, a strong construction engineer, was wracked with fever, too. All of them nearly starved to death. Roosevelt lost 55 pounds. They did it for science–when Roosevelt had to divide the party, he sent away the photographer and kept with him the veteran naturalist who was collecting bird specimens. They did it for adventure, for a publicity stunt and a thrill. And they did it for the wonder of exploring.

Who could resist a river named Doubt? The Rio da Dúvida had known headwaters on the high central plateau where Rondon was building a transcontinental telegraph line. But none of the friendly Indians living in that region knew or would tell where it went. Everyone knew that it must be a tributary of the Amazon, but rivers in this part of the Amazon River valley bend in hooks, elbows, and oxbows. It probably entered the Madeira River, the greatest tributary of the upper Amazon. The best guess, which turned out to be right, was that it dropped due north into the Aripuanã River, which flows into the Madeira. But some of the officers on Rondon's survey argued it bent west to join the Ji-Paraná before the Madeira, and others thought it must turn east, far into the Tapajós River. Nothing was mapped for about 150 miles in any direction, a territory the size of West Virginia, and not much was mapped in a zone as big as Spain. As it turned out, the River of Doubt descended through a completely unknown range of low mountains that squeezed it into narrow gorges and rapids.

By 1914, the days of epic exploration were over, and an ambivalent imperialist writer like Joseph Conrad had long ago made fun of his boyish desire to enter "blank spaces on the map," to probe the Heart of Darkness, and discover lost cities in the jungle.[1] Most leftover places to explore involved dangerous journeys toward futile goals. They were fictional zero points like the North Pole, not new trade routes to great kingdoms. Around the time

that Roosevelt and Rondon's expedition pushed off
downriver, Ernest Shackleton received 5,000 letters
applying to join his South Pole expedition on the
Endurance. It turned out that Shackleton's expedition is known for just that, endurance. At the end
of 1914, his men used magnesium floodlights to take
the famous photograph of their ship being crushed
in the Antarctic ice while they camped outside it.
They then spent two years hunkered down in improvised shelter and building a small boat to look
for rescue.[2]

To be honest, Roosevelt's South American trip
had been planned as a vacation and an adventure.
Having just lost his third-party Bull Moose campaign for the presidency that split the Republican
vote and allowed the Democrat Woodrow Wilson
to win office, Roosevelt needed to get away from the
United States. Invitations to lecture on his controversial imperialist policies in Buenos Aires, Montevideo, and Santiago de Chile focused his attention
on South America. He also needed to get outdoors,
but he didn't want to repeat anything that might be
mocked, like his controversial African hunting safari of 1909. Instead, he persuaded the American
Museum of Natural History to commission him to
take two of its best naturalists—the veteran George
Cherrie and the younger Leo Miller—to collect bird
and mammal specimens across the center of South
America. An old acquaintance, Father John Zahm,

a dean of Notre Dame University and a popular adventure writer, talked him into their going together as a demonstration of American broadmindedness. Teddy Roosevelt, the Rough Rider hero of the Spanish American War, the former president of the United States, the model of Protestant vigor, would circle through the heart of the South American continent with Father Zahm, a manly Catholic priest. Two adventurous Americans would retrace the journeys of the Spanish explorers. And indeed, Father Zahm made it on the long first leg of their trip, taking steamboats up the Paraná and Paraguay Rivers into the high central plateau of Brazil. But Roosevelt would not let him continue on the exploration of the River of Doubt. Sometimes a wise decision is made in anger. Roosevelt was annoyed at Father Zahm's impracticality—Zahm had supposedly asked for bearers to carry him in a chair on one of their treks—and wisely ordered him to turn back. Father Zahm, unfazed, made the best of it and finished his own journeys through the interior of South America, visiting abandoned Catholic missions and the routes of the Spanish (Catholic) conquistadors. He wrote a popular travel book on his own discovery of the Americas' heroic Catholic heritage.

The rub was that the original Catholic-Protestant buddy stunt had been diverted into another, more risky scheme. Brazil's Minister of Foreign Relations,

Lauro Müller, had known of Roosevelt's plan to visit South America and had added Rio de Janeiro to the itinerary of lecture stops. He knew Roosevelt would be a lightning rod for complaints about American imperialism. As president, Roosevelt had extended the Monroe Doctrine, saying that the United States would intervene if any Latin American government "invited" European intervention by disorder, or by not paying its foreign debt. Roosevelt had maneuvered Panama to secede from Colombia so that the United States could get the canal concession. His great project, the Panama Canal, was scheduled to open in 1914, and Roosevelt hoped he could inoculate South American opinion against accusations of imperialism by preaching pan-American partnership.

Müller figured out a way that Brazil could upstage Argentina, Uruguay, and Chile. He invited Roosevelt, the great hunter and conservationist outdoorsman, to form a Brazilian-American partnership, a joint expedition into the heart of the continent, going down the unmapped River of Doubt. This hooked Roosevelt. Rather than merely collect specimens along the well-mapped Tapajós River, they would truly explore, truly discover. From Müller's point of view, it couldn't hurt that the approach to the River of Doubt would run close by the Acre Territory that Brazil had only recently acquired from Bolivia. Müller envisioned a new

Colonel Roosevelt (front row center) with Dr. Lauro Severiano Müller, foreign minister of Brazil (front row right), in Rio de Janeiro, 1913

duo: an American outdoors President and a Brazilian military frontiersman, Colonel Cândido Rondon, Brazil's hero of the exploration and mapping of the West. When Müller met Roosevelt with his proposal (the expedition had been outfitting for almost a year before Müller's offer), he had already telegraphed Colonel Rondon, urgently ordering him to return to Rio de Janeiro from the Mato Grosso frontier.

For Rondon, Müller's summons to Rio was a distraction. He was in the middle of his own publicity stunt. Since 1907, he had commanded the military unit that was building the Strategic Telegraph Line that would stretch from the colonial capital of Brazil's western Mato Grosso state, Cuiabá, almost 700 miles to the newest rubber boomtown on the Bolivian frontier, Porto Antonio da Madeira (today, Porto Velho, the capital of Rondônia). The line was almost entirely symbolic rather than strategic. There were, to say the least, few clients for transcontinental telegram service in Porto Velho. There was little prospect of a border war that would require military communications, and some of Rondon's rivals in the army refused to call service in that unit hazardous duty. But the telegraph line had immense symbolic importance as a survey line, like the Mason-Dixon Line[3] in North America. Colonel Rondon's companies cut a three-hundred-foot-wide right of way northwest through the forest, marking the land as Brazilian. They sang the national anthem and raised the Brazilian flag in villages where it had never been seen before.

Securing national borders was a single-minded obsession of Rondon—who had been orphaned in the midst of a Paraguayan invasion—and the stated mission of the Brazilian army. Colonel Rondon's Brazilian patriotism matched Colonel Roosevelt's American patriotism. And he was even something of a Brazilian imperialist—though not quite in the same way that Roosevelt was an American imperialist. Rondon wanted Brazil to be strong inside its borders and to peacefully integrate the Indians of the West into the nation.

Rondon was a complex, proud man. Whether he or his parents could be considered Indians depended on the way his grandparents, who were of Terena, Bororo, and Guaná origins, had crossed an unwritten line between behaving like "Brazilians" (getting baptized and married in the Catholic Church, speaking Portuguese, wearing shirts and shoes, drinking coffee, living in a single cabin) or behaving like "Indians" (dancing pagan dances, wearing body paint, hunting with bow and arrow, living in a collective long house). In Mato Grosso, Brazilian and Indian neighbors alike farmed in the indigenous way, by burning a clearing in the forest and planting the root crops adapted to the land. Rondon's parents were certainly well over the "Brazilian" side of the line. After they both died young—his mother died among the refugees fleeing the Paraguayan surprise attack on Mato Grosso at the beginning of the Paraguayan War of 1864-70[4]—Cândido was brought up as an orphan and a Brazilian on his uncle's ranch in Mato Grosso.

After schooling in Cuiabá, he went to the big city, Rio de Janeiro, where he worked his way through the military academy. The officer training school was the place for poor boys to rise, the only place they could get an engineering education and a career. Rondon was the classmate of Lauro Müller, who was also born poor, the grandson of humble German homesteaders, and the son of a small-town shopkeeper in Santa Catarina, in the south of Brazil. Like Rondon, Müller too had been helped by an uncle slightly better off than his parents.

At the military academy, cadets took math, science, and engineering courses, while the students at the elite law schools wore tailcoats to classes in rhetoric and political theory. Many of the cadets were swept away by their patriotic, altruistic geometry professor, Benjamin Constant Botelho de Magalhães, who taught them Auguste Comte's social theory of Positivism[5] as part of "geometry." Almost all of the cadets in that generation passed through a phase in which they became thoroughgoing Positivists, seeing the world around them through Comte's theory of three stages of human history. According to their Comtean reading of Brazil, the nation was just emerging from a "theological stage" like the European Middle Ages, had barely skipped into the "metaphysical stage" of the French Revolution and abstract political thought, and had a good chance to enter the "positive stage" of scientific government—if some true men of science took charge. Many officers had felt that they were the men to take charge of Brazil ever since their victory in the Paraguayan War. Only a few of the cadets, like Cândido Rondon, went beyond social philosophy to join Comte's new-age Religion of Humanity. Its temple in Rio de Janeiro was a Greek-Revival–style curiosity, where images of Gutenberg and Aristotle took the place of the Catholic saints, and sermons preached political order, industrial progress, and altruistic love.

The cadets and officers were reformers as well as engineers. In the 1880s, while Theodore Roosevelt was beginning his career as an anti-corruption reformer in the New York State Assembly, Cândido Rondon and Lauro Müller got caught up in the movement for the abolition of slavery in 1888. In 1889, like most of the cadets, they joined the military coup to overthrow the constitutional monarch of Brazil, Dom Pedro II,[6] and establish a republic. In the 1890s, while Roosevelt was making his name as the reformist police commissioner of New York City and colonel of the volunteer Rough Riders cavalry regiment in the Spanish-American War, Ron-

O PEQUENO PARRIBA, ÍNDIO DA TRIBU DOS ARI-KEMES, HABITANTES DO ALTO JAMARY. (1915)

1915

O ENTÃO 1.° TE-NENTE CANDIDO RONDON EM 1890, QUANDO INICIOU SEUS TRABALHOS DE ENGENHARIA NO SERTÃO DE MATTO-GROSSO, CO-MO CHEFE D'UMA COMMISSÃO MIXTA

1890

*Lower left: 1st Lt. Candido Rondon as a young engineer in 1890;
upper right: Parriba, an Indian lad who, as Rondon's ward, was
educated in Rio de Janeiro*

don and Müller were rising in an atmosphere of tough conspiratorial politics. Rondon survived both the dictatorship of field marshal Floriano Peixoto[7] and an 1893-95 civil war,[8] by accepting unpopular, dangerous postings to frontier telegraph projects. While remaining in ranks, Müller prospered by jumping into electoral politics and fighting in the civil war. Rondon made his reputation by his competence in building telegraph lines, finally getting the government to back his patriotic, nationalistic mission of occupying and mapping the Brazilian West. At the time that Foreign Minister Müller ordered Rondon to report to Rio, both were army colonels of the 1912 cohort, Müller with a month of seniority. On the day that Rondon and Roosevelt emerged from the river, Müller was promoted to brigadier general.

A man like Rondon was only one of the brilliant team of diplomats, mapmakers, historians, and lawyers who helped Brazil to win every one of its territorial claims on disputed frontiers: against French Guiana and British Guiana to the north, Argentina and Paraguay to the south, and Bolivia and Peru to the west. Brazilian territory expanded not by war but by negotiation, and notably, by winning settlements before international arbitration committees that accepted Brazil's case made by better maps and by the effective occupation of much disputed territory. Europeans and South Americans had uneasily accepted the United States Panama Canal Zone concession as an act of force, but they recognized Brazil's annexation of secessionist Acre as the outcome of an equitable settlement with Bolivia. The Strategic Telegraph Line from Cuiabá to Porto Velho was a key part of Brazil's diplomatic machine, a way to help the government defend and consolidate its claims. Rondon had jumped into that role as a self-sacrificing, hard-working, stern, but fair commander. When Roosevelt ended his second presidency in 1909, Rondon was two years into his great feat.

In the course of his Telegraphic Commission work, Rondon had also made a special decision that has made him one of Brazil's national heroes. Despite being a military disciplinarian who could sacrifice men's lives and health for the mission, Rondon was a Positivist pacifist, a believer in harmony and the incorporation of outcasts. Rather than meet Indians with gunshots—and sometimes he was working through lands where the custom of Indians and Brazilians alike was to shoot at strangers on sight—he ordered his soldiers to hold their fire. "Die if you must, but never kill," became his slogan.

The journey down the Rio da Dúvida was by no means the first time that Rondon had prepared for a tense meeting with unknown Indians. But it was especially complicated because now he had no intermediaries. None of the neighboring Indian peoples who had come to an accommodation with the Telegraphic Commission soldiers—the Paresi, the Nhambiquara—knew the Cinta Larga ("Broad Sash") people who lived in the area of the Rio da Dúvida. Nobody knew their language, nobody had old stories about raiding them, and nobody knew how aggressive they were on meeting strangers. "Die if you must, but never kill" was a rule primarily for first contact, and it was only the first of a set of methods for maintaining a nonviolent encounter: to leave irresistibly good gifts like fish hooks, glass beads, and machetes hanging from trees; to always make a loud noise when approaching a camp; to speak gently; to accept pilfering; to offer jobs and, where possible, schools. Almost all the forest Indian bands lived in some kind of wary rivalry or family feud with neighboring bands, raiding each other periodically to "steal wives" or claim hunting grounds. Poison arrows were to be expected. Peace took patient, continuing demonstrations of good will.

Rondon's Commission usually had friendly relations with the Paresi Indians around its permanent telegraph stations, and one Paresi, Antonio, came on the trip. Rondon did what he could to get along with the Nhambiquara, who could frustrate outsiders with their stubborn, passive postures, their stark nakedness, their slyness. And the Paresi and Nhambiquara did what they could to tolerate Rondon's

Paresi woman and children in front of a home

soldiers, who were often disciplinary cases who had been posted to the Commission because it was considered a penal battalion, hazardous service at hard labor.

Rondon's orders had been so successful in avoiding warfare on the line that the Brazilian government awarded him authority over all of Brazil's Indians as director of a newly created bureau of Indian affairs. The Service for the Protection of Indians (Serviço de Proteção aos Índios, SPI), founded in 1910, replaced the government's reliance on subsidized Catholic mission villages to "pacify" and acculturate Indians. The missionaries had sometimes done well enough with people like Rondon's grand-parents, but any official partnership with the Catholic Church violated the spirit of the 1891 Constitution's separation of church and state. As a Positivist, Rondon himself was scornfully anti-Catholic. The real challenge of Indian protection would be less in remote forests of the Amazon than in São Paulo, the agribusiness heartland of Brazilian coffee and sugar production, where bounty gangs hired by railroad and land speculators were carrying out systematic massacres in places like Baurú. The real test of Rondon's policy was whether the SPI posts for the Kaingang Indians near Baurú, established about 1911-17, would work; but unfortunately, they did not. Epidemics carried off many of the Kaingang refugees who took shelter from the bounty hunters at the posts. However, this test of the SPI's policies of tutelage and incorporation lay in the future. In 1910, the government had appointed Cândido Rondon as first head of the SPI, while he continued to work the line. Several of the future leaders of the SPI, such as Amilcar Botelho de Magalhães, were still young officers in the Commission. In a sense then, the Roosevelt-Rondon expedition helped the government to legitimize and publicize its reformist turn in Brazil's Indian policy.

Indian affairs—the relations between forest Indians and other Brazilians—also mattered greatly in the Amazon River region, which had become the center of a worldwide boom in the rubber business. Like the Klondike gold rush in the Yukon, skyrocketing rubber prices had brought hundreds of thousands of wealth-seeking rubber tappers, merchants, and promoters into the Amazon. Brazilians, and before them Indians, had long known how to tap white latex sap from rubber trees. After Goodyear's invention of vulcanization in 1839, rubber became more than a local novelty. And since 1890, the popularity of the bicycle and automobile, and specifically the invention of inflatable rubber tires, had more than tripled demand. Every river filled up with camps and cabins of rubber tappers, who walked a trail through their trees, cutting the bark, placing clean taps and buckets, collecting the full buckets to bring back to their shed and smoke on a spit into a fifty-pound ball. An industrious tapper could hope to make $900 in a good year, selling one thousand pounds of rubber.

Until a profitable year came, someone would stake him credit. The tappers usually wound up in debt to traveling riverboat peddlers and to the owner of their bit of forest, who took the lion's share of their earnings. In fact, everything up and down the Amazon had run on credit for long before this boom. What was new was the gigantic magnitude of the rubber business, which dwarfed older trades like Brazil nuts, medicinal barks, small-scale gold

A Brazilian man smoking a ball of rubber over a fire

panning, cotton farming, and ranching. As older rubber trails on rivers near the Atlantic were all claimed and exploited to their limits, tappers had moved far inland, up the rivers of the Amazon valley, even into Peru and Bolivia. The great Madeira River, for example, had always had a few Catholic missions, a few fishing villages and military posts, a few gold prospectors. It had been a sleepy trade route between backlands of Bolivia and Brazil. But starting in the 1880s, rubber trade had become big business there, big enough to justify the construction of the costly Madeira-Mamoré Railroad.

So, while Roosevelt and Rondon worked down the River of Doubt, the river valleys parallel to them were all being worked by rubber tappers and by traveling salesmen in their barges and canoes. The tappers tended to stop advancing wherever rapids made river transportation too expensive or where higher elevations made rubber trees too scarce. At river mouths on the great highway of the Amazon River, populations were denser. The city of Manaus, at the meeting of the Negro and Amazon Rivers, was a magnetic boomtown, like Dawson City in the Yukon or San Francisco in the California gold rush. Manaus boosters built a spectacular wooden opera palace with lacy Victorian woodwork, and they hired the best opera companies of Europe to tour there, not out of vanity or the love of Caruso, but out of scheming calculation. Opera was a loud demonstration that their city had arrived. They wanted big merchant houses, shipping lines, and bankers to relocate, away from the city of Belém at the mouth of the Amazon, upriver to their new heart of the rubber boom.

To the east of the River of Doubt, on the Tapajós River, thousands of tappers and merchants were doing a million dollars a year in business. To the west, on the upper Madeira, the business was worth millions a year. And all of that business could be funneled through Manaus. Two years before the Roosevelt-Rondon Expedition, the Madeira-Mamoré (Mad-Ma, or "Mad Maria") Railway Company had concluded five years of construction of a two-hundred-mile line running parallel to the rockiest parts of the Madeira River. The Madeira-Mamoré Railroad bypassed river rapids and water-falls. It should have opened the upper Madeira zone, including parts of Amazonian Bolivia, to a new scramble for rubber wealth.

Theodore Roosevelt and his expedition might have traveled up the Amazon to the glorious city of Manaus, steamed up the Madeira River to the Porto Antonio terminus, ridden the brand-new Madeira-Mamoré Railroad to the ridge where Rondon was cutting the telegraph line, taken trucks, mules, and oxcarts to the headwaters of the River of Doubt, and started downriver from there. It would have saved them time and expense, but that would perhaps have looked too much like taking a cable car to the top of a mountain and sledding downhill. Or maybe traveling on the Madeira-Mamoré railroad, built by the Farquhar Syndicate, an American holding company that owned mega-projects all over Brazil, including the Southern Brazil Railway on which Kermit had worked as a construction supervisor, would have looked too imperialistic.

The stated reason for not entering through Manaus and the railway was that Roosevelt's voyage should be a grand internal circle, a sweep through the heart of the South American continent. He would start from the south, the great cities of Montevideo and Buenos Aires at the mouth of the Paraná River system. He would go north upriver by steamboats of the heavily navigated Paraná-Paraguay River system. Then he would trek across Brazil's continental divide, the high plateau and ridges where Rondon was cutting the telegraph line. He would explore downriver by the River of Doubt, continue from whatever major river it belonged to, until it joined the Amazon, then out to the Atlantic Ocean and New York. If Father Zahm had stuck with him, it would have been Catholic and Calvinist, retracing the routes of the Spanish explorers. George Cherrie and Leo Miller would have been able to collect bird and animal specimens along a spectrum of South American environments, from south to north.

Indian rubber gatherers on the upper Amazon, Brazil

Another reason to avoid the Madeira-Mamoré Railroad was the reputation the upper Amazon zone was getting for violent neo-slavery. In the first phase of the Amazon rubber boom, tappers had naturally concentrated on the Hevea tree, which can be tapped sustainably for years and yields the fine-quality latex. Most of the tappers were indebted sharecroppers, but they were fiercely independent indebted sharecroppers, and they took the rainy season off to farm for themselves or live in town. In a second phase, as demand grew, the rubber trade had pushed farther into the upper Amazon River valley, into the regions of the Caucho trees, from which a mediocre rubber can be obtained year-round by chopping trees into pieces and boiling out their sap.

In the caucho regions, especially the Putumayo River of Peru, rubber business was built on year-round enslavement of Indians who were kept in chains for punishment, hunted down, flogged, and branded if they tried to escape their "debts," and in fact were nearly exterminated.

In 1910, the British government sent in Roger Casement, who had made his name in 1890, exposing the slavery and violence of the rubber trade of the Belgian King Leopold II's "free state" in the Congo. In the Putumayo, Casement found systematic coercion and atrocities. The Casement report largely exempted Brazilian officials and pointed to Peruvian and Bolivian connivance in the caucho-zone slavery. But, on this trip, Roosevelt was trying to avoid any association with violent imperialism, just as he was trying to downplay his safari hunting.

Colonel Rondon and Colonel Roosevelt would personify Pan-American cooperation at the moment of the opening of the Panama Canal. Just as they were heading into the River of Doubt, Roosevelt had news of difficulty in the United States' relations with the rival governments of revolutionary Mexico. As they were reaching Manaus, in April 1914, he had telegrams about the U.S. Marines' occupation of Veracruz. The press wanted to hear what he recommended to his adversary, President Wilson. Even as a retired, private citizen, a former president on a scientific exploration in the middle of the jungle, Roosevelt embodied American interests. His shy pride in accepting that the Rio da Dúvida be renamed Rio Teodoro Roosevelt, but preferring that it be called "Rio Teodoro," is significant.

British motives in exposing atrocities in the rubber trade of the Peruvian Amazon were not altogether pure. For generations, the British government had encouraged expeditions to obtain rubber tree seeds and break the Brazilian monopoly on rubber. By 1910, they had succeeded. Rubber seeds, grown into Hevea trees at the Royal Botanic Gardens, Kew, in London, had been transplanted to the British colony of Malaysia. Plantation trees, grown in close rows, could be tapped at a fraction—maybe even a tenth—of the cost of Brazilian forest gathering. Neither Rondon nor Roosevelt could have known this, but the price drop after 1911, as British plantation rubber undercut the price of Brazilian wild rubber, would be permanent.

Plantation rubber had just ruined the upper Amazon frontier. The Madeira-Mamoré Railroad would go bankrupt for lack of cargo. The river towns and trading posts where Roosevelt's party stopped on their way out of the Amazon would shrink for two or three generations, and the Manaus Opera House would stand empty. Only the Japanese occupation of British Malaysia and French Indochina during World War II briefly revived

Amazonian rubber tapping. Henry Ford tried to establish a gigantic rubber plantation, Fordlandia, but his elaborate company town complex went broke. People still tap natural latex along the rivers where Rondon and Roosevelt passed, but it is a precarious living.

The Indians who lived along the River of Doubt have remained. During their trip, Colonel Rondon and Colonel Roosevelt came prepared for "pacification." Rondon brought gifts for an encounter with strangers. He also brought along one of his soldiers, Antonio, the Paresi, whose language might be similar to the language of people whom they met. As the party paddled downriver, they saw little fish traps and footbridges built across streams. They heard hunting parties, and they entered a village whose inhabitants had just fled, leaving a fire burning. On one occasion, Cândido Rondon got too close to a Cinta Larga hunting band, with a sad result for his dog, Lobo. But it was rainy season, and during rainy season, game is scarce, trails are slippery, and the Cinta Larga men stay closer to the smoky fires inside their longhouses. In any case, the Cinta Larga elected to avoid contact and confrontation. Many years later, some Cinta Largas told another expedition that they had been warily shadowing the Roosevelt-Rondon party the whole time but in 1914 chose not to meet face to face.

Thanks to the collapse of the rubber boom, the

Cinta Larga's fate became relatively secure. Raids back and forth with their neighbors and epidemics were the bigger threats. But interlopers still crossed through this region, engaging in rubber tapping, lumbering fine woods, and doing small-scale gold panning. There were few of them, but some were murderously violent; in the early 1960s, Cinta Larga villages were massacred by a group of rubber tappers; this and other scandals led to an investigatory commission and the reorganization of Rondon's SPI into FUNAI (the Fundação Nacional Indígena, National Indian Foundation) in 1967.

Around the same time, Brazil's military government pushed to settle and develop the Amazon as a matter of national security and as a safety valve for overpopulation and landlessness among poor farmers in other regions. It cut a huge dirt highway, the Transamazonian, east-west through the Amazon, and bridged the Aripuanã River just downstream from the Roosevelt River. Fortunately for the Cinta Larga, the Transamazonian Highway was unfeasible to maintain for its light volume of truck traffic, and it quickly fell into disrepair. However, another highway and a homesteading program successfully settled the territory to the southwest of the Roosevelt River. The territory was named Rondônia, after Cândido Rondon, in 1956, and entered the union as a state in 1982.

Over time, in the 1980s and 1990s, Rondônia's

original settler homesteads were sold or grabbed to be consolidated into corporate cattle ranches. Seen today from an airplane, the state of Rondônia almost up to the west bank of the Roosevelt River is shaved bare of forest, like the state of Oregon. Now what protects the land of the Cinta Larga is a new Indian policy of creating "reserves." To the east of the Roosevelt River is still thick forest, a patchwork of federal wilderness areas, and Cinta Larga and Paresi Indian reserves.

This area today, like the whole Amazon, is well surveyed for gold and other minerals. The Cinta Larga have the good luck that only small gold deposits have been discovered; their bad luck is that they live among valuable tin deposits and a diamond field, possibly one of the ten largest in the world. In the 1980s and again in 2003, Cinta Larga leaders stood trial for fighting off diamond prospectors. They have been accused of renting access to the diamond fields to certain gangs. As they look for jobs and businesses of their own—Indians all over the Amazon want to earn enough to buy motorboats, hunting rifles, sewing machines, and soccer balls, and perhaps to send their children to high school in town—the Cinta Larga have joined coalitions of forest Indians trying to make a go of living in the reserves. They work with FUNAI, with Catholic social agencies, and with environmental and pro-Indian groups, but assassinations of chiefs suggest they are also engaged with diamond-mining crews.

Today the upper Roosevelt River has been traveled by adventure trekkers and whitewater kayakers. In 1927, the British aviator and explorer George Miller Dyott traveled the river and took film footage that was intercut with footage and photographs surviving from Roosevelt's expedition to make *The River of Doubt*, a 1928 documentary produced by the Roosevelt Film Library. In 1973, a commemorative expedition from the American Museum of Natural History, Roosevelt's original sponsor, including Theodore Roosevelt's grandson, Kermit Roosevelt Jr., retraced the expedition's route on its sixtieth anniversary. Brazilian outdoorsmen with light canoes and bright yellow whitewater kayaks have posted guides to the river, illustrated with photographs taken from their waterproof cameras, rating the rapids for difficulty. What for Roosevelt's expedition was a sharp bend in the river, the crunching groan of floodwater getting louder over rocks, a dismaying glimpse of the first teeth of rock through the brown and white water, and ominously narrowing walls of a canyon, today is a Class IV or a Class V, with Class VI the most difficult, considered extreme and exploratory. As well as the whitewater expedition camps, there is a truck stop on the Transamazonian Highway and a fly-fishing lodge whose customers fly in to a private airstrip.

The dangers in 1914 were not just rapids. At the advice of Anthony Fiala, their photographer and outfitter, they had laid on their own special order of concentrated, preserved food. Nonetheless, hunger affected them all. Living in the forest was never easy. On earlier expeditions while cutting the telegraph line, Rondon and his soldiers had learned to live off the land: they hunted, fished, and for a staple starch they gathered Brazil nuts to cook something like roasted chestnuts. When their pack mules and oxen died, they ate the meat and boiled the bones for soup. They were accustomed to living on short rations, and they were sometimes near the rivers where canoe peddlers sold flour, rice, and salt meat. The tough luck of the Rondon-Roosevelt expedition was that in 1913-14 the Brazil nut crop failed all over the Amazon. They had chosen to travel in the rainy season to avoid low-water snags and obstacles, but game is scarcer in the rainy season; fish are not trapped in slow pools. They were reduced to eating hearts of palm cut from the tops of trees. Hearts of palm are tasty but low in calories—good for a diet salad, not for soldiers hauling canoes. Even the Cinta Larga were sometimes hungry in the rainy season, as they relied more on root crops and stayed closer to their village. On earlier expeditions, some of Rondon's men and officers had died, swollen and delirious, "of beriberi," which we now know as a vitamin B1 deficiency disease, caused by a meager diet relying on too much polished rice or corn meal. On this trip, Rondon continued to cut his men's rations so that the Americans would have enough to eat, and hunger probably made them all more susceptible to fever.

The greatest danger was disease, however. Malaria was endemic in the Amazon. As Teddy Roosevelt, Kermit Roosevelt, and Father Zahm were planning their trip, they knew very well about the mosquito vector of yellow fever and malaria. Roosevelt had known about mosquitoes since the Spanish-American War campaign in Cuba, when doctors had figured out the connection with yellow fever. Strict mosquito control during the digging of the Panama Canal had saved the lives of thousands of workers. During the construction of the Madeira-Mamoré Railroad, strict mosquito control had been less successful, as almost the whole route crossed over marshes and swamps. It was the railroad that "cost a life for every tie laid down." On their expedition, the Americans brought special mosquito nets and bedding, and hats with net veils (which were most helpful against swarms of little stingless bees). Teddy, Kermit, Rondon, his officers, and probably all the soldiers had been exposed to malaria before, but their re-exposure was grueling. All of them took quinine regularly, and Dr. Cajazeira was giving some of them quinine injections for their fevers, but it was not enough.

Colonel Roosevelt lecturing about the expedition

Despite their awareness and all these precautions, everyone got sick. Early in the trip, Kermit was delirious with fever. In his narrative, Roosevelt downplayed his own illness, which was severe. Midway, he cut his leg hauling rope over slippery rock. The cut immediately became infected and turned into a spreading abscess. This, compounded with his malaria, laid him out with fevers close to 105 degrees. Alarmed at the spread of the infection, Dr. Cajazeira performed a painful field operation, which Roosevelt bore stoically, to drain the abscess on his leg. In two months Teddy Roosevelt lost fifty-five of his two-hundred-odd pounds. He didn't die then, and by the time they reached Manaus, he could face the press, but this trip certainly hastened his death in 1919, at age fifty-five. He had expected to run again for the Republican presidential nomination or to be drafted by his breakaway Bull Moose Party to run for governor of New York. His health after 1914 made it impossible.

The outcomes of the expedition were questioned in 1914 and remain debatable today. Roosevelt was accused quite unfairly of having taken a joy ride, of going on a guided safari down a river that was already charted. He stood up to his critics in lectures that worked from the draft map of the river, detailed the procedures of their expedition, and documented the collection of specimens for the Museum of Natural History. The truth could never shake off mockery, in cartoons and witty newspaper headlines, of the irresistible phrase "River of Doubt," but that is partly because all Roosevelt's life he had cultivated a bombastic persona in a traditional brash American style. His seriousness was always mixed with showmanship.

Rondon, on the other hand, was all reserve and stern solemnity, showmanship in another style. It got him what he wanted. After the expedition, he went back to his main business, finishing the telegraph line in 1915 and institutionalizing his nonviolent policy in the Service for the Protection of

Indians. Members of his commission continued their dangerous work. In 1917, Lieutenant Lyra, the cartographer of the expedition, drowned while surveying the Sepotuba River (now the Tenente Lira River) near where they had started their expedition. Amilcar[9] followed Rondon into the SPI. Rondon lived to be 92, a lifetime Positivist, the only peacetime field marshal in the Brazilian army, the stalwart—and sometimes self-critical—defender of policies of peaceful acculturation of Indians in Brazil.

Dain Borges
Associate Professor of History
University of Chicago
Chicago, Illinois
March 2016

NOTES

1. Joseph Conrad (1857-1924), Polish-born British novelist whose most famous work is *Heart of Darkness,* about a voyage up the Congo River into the heart of Africa.

2. Sir Ernest Henry Shackleton (1874-1922), Anglo-Irish explorer who led an expedition to the South Pole in 1914. Although his ship was destroyed, he and a small band sailed eight hundred miles to a whaling station and returned to rescue the entire crew.

3. The Mason-Dixon Line, upon request by heirs of William Penn and Lord Baltimore, was originally drawn by British surveyors Charles Mason and Jeremiah Dixon from 1763–67 and became the boundary between Pennsylvania and Maryland. Along with the Ohio River, it came to be regarded as the boundary between

the free and slave states and is still used as a figurative dividing line between North and South.

4. The Paraguayan War, 1864–70, also known as the War of the Triple Alliance, started when Paraguayan forces attacked Brazilian ships on the Paraguay River and invaded Brazilian towns in Mato Grosso. Brazil, allied with Argentina and Uruguay, defeated Paraguay in a series of bloody battles, many of them for the control of river fortresses. The male population of Paraguay was virtually annihilated, and Brazil secured its claims to Mato Grosso.

5. The French philosopher Auguste Comte (1789–1857) developed both a stage theory of history, predicting that it would culminate in a "positive" stage of peace and government by scientific elites, and a new-age Religion of Humanity.

6. Pedro II of Brazil (1825–91), the Brazilian-born heir to Portugal's Braganza dynasty, had ruled from 1841 to 1889. He was an amateur astronomer and a man of science himself—he spoke on Alexander Graham Bell's first telephone at the Philadelphia Exposition of 1876.

7. Floriano Peixoto (1839–95), second president of the Republic of Brazil, rose from the vice-presidency in a questionable constitutional maneuver and suspended civil rights for much of his presidency, ruling through ambitious young officers like Lauro Müller.

8. A political split in the far southern state of Rio Grande do Sul turned into an armed insurrection against Floriano Peixoto that captured much of the south of Brazil. Parts of the navy, including a restorationist monarchist admiral, rebelled in Rio de Janeiro and threatened bombardment of the capital.

9. In Brazil, both formally and informally, people are often referred to by the most common of their many names. Roosevelt was following local custom.

THROUGH THE
BRAZILIAN WILDERNESS

Colonel Roosevelt and Colonel Rondon aboard the river steamer Nyoac

PREFACE

This is an account of a zoogeographic reconnaissance through the Brazilian hinterland.

The official and proper title of the expedition is that given it by the Brazilian government: Expedição Científica Roosevelt-Rondon. When I started from the United States, it was to make an expedition, primarily concerned with mammalogy and ornithology, for the American Museum of Natural History of New York. This was undertaken under the auspices of Messrs. Osborn and Chapman, acting on behalf of the museum. In the body of this work I describe how the scope of the expedition was enlarged and how it was given a geographic as well as a zoological character, in consequence of the kind proposal of the Brazilian secretary of state for Foreign Affairs, General Lauro Müller. In its altered and enlarged form, the expedition was rendered possible only by the generous assistance of the Brazilian government. Throughout the body of the work will be found reference after reference to my colleagues and companions of the expedition, whose services to science I have endeavored to set forth, and for whom I shall always feel the most cordial friendship and regard.

THEODORE ROOSEVELT

SAGAMORE HILL,
    September 1, 1914

The Rapids of Navaïté

I. The Start

ONE DAY IN 1908, when my presidential term was coming to a close, Father [John Augustine] Zahm,[1] a priest whom I knew, came in to call on me. He had just returned from a trip across the Andes and down the Amazon and came in to propose that after I left the presidency he and I should go up the Paraguay into the interior of South America. At the time I wished to go to Africa, and so the subject was dropped; but from time to time afterward we talked it over. Five years later, in the spring of 1913, I accepted invitations conveyed through the governments of Argentina and Brazil to address certain learned bodies in these countries. Then it occurred to me that, instead of making the conventional tourist trip purely by sea round South America, after I had finished my lectures, I would come north through the middle of the continent into the valley of the Amazon; and I decided to write Father Zahm and tell him my intentions. Before doing so, however, I desired to see the authorities of the American Museum of Natural History,[2] in New York City, to find out whether they cared to have me take a couple of naturalists with me into Brazil and make a collecting trip for the museum.

Accordingly, I wrote to Frank Chapman, the curator of ornithology of the museum, and accepted his invitation to lunch at the museum one day early in June. At the lunch, in addition to various naturalists, to my astonishment I also found Father Zahm; and as soon as I saw him, I told him I was now intending to make the South American trip. It appeared that he had made up his mind that he would take it himself and had actually come on to see Mr. Chapman to find out if the latter could recommend a naturalist to go with him, and he at once said he would accompany me. Chapman was pleased when he found out that we intended to go up the Paraguay and across into the valley of the Amazon, because much of the ground over which we were to pass had not been covered by collectors. He saw Henry Fairfield Osborn, the president of the museum, who wrote me that the museum would be pleased to send under me a couple of naturalists, whom, with my approval, Chapman would choose.

The men whom Chapman recommended were Messrs. George K. Cherrie[3] and Leo E. Miller.[4] I gladly accepted both. The former was to attend chiefly to the ornithology and the latter to the mammalogy of the expedition, but each was to help out the other. No two better men for such a trip could have been found. Both were veterans of the tropical American forests. Miller was a young man, born in Indiana, an enthusiastic naturalist with good literary as well as scientific training. He was at the time in the Guiana forests, and joined us at Barbados.

6

Cherrie was an older man, born in Iowa, but now a farmer in Vermont. He had a wife and six children. Mrs. Cherrie had accompanied him during two or three years of their early married life in his collecting trips along the Orinoco. Their second child was born when they were in camp a couple of hundred miles from any white man or woman. One night a few weeks later, they were obliged to leave a camping place, where they had intended to spend the night, because the baby was fretful, and its cries attracted a jaguar, which prowled nearer and nearer in the twilight until they thought it safest once more to put out into the open river and seek a new resting place.

Cherrie had spent about twenty-two years collecting in the American tropics. Like most of the field naturalists I have met, he was an unusually efficient and fearless man; and willy-nilly he had been forced at times to vary his career by taking part in insurrections. Twice he had been behind the bars in consequence, on one occasion spending three months in a prison of a certain South American state, expecting each day to be taken out and shot. In another state he had, as an interlude to his ornithological pursuits, followed the career of a gunrunner, acting as such off and on for 2½ years. The particular revolutionary chief whose fortunes he was following finally came into power, and Cherrie immortalized his name by naming a new species of

7

The American members of the expedition: (left to right) Anthony Fiala, George K. Cherrie, Father John Augustus Zahm, Theodore Roosevelt, Kermit Roosevelt, Frank Harper, Leo E. Miller

ant-thrush after him—a delightful touch, in its practical combination of those not normally kindred pursuits, ornithology and gunrunning.

In Anthony Fiala,[5] a former arctic explorer, we found an excellent man for assembling equipment and taking charge of its handling and shipment. In addition to his four years in the arctic regions, Fiala had served in the New York Squadron in Puerto Rico during the Spanish War, and through his service in the squadron had been brought into contact with his little Tennessee wife. She came down with her four children to say goodbye to him when the steamer left. My secretary, Mr. Frank Harper, went with us. Jacob Sigg, who had served three years in the United States Army and was both a hospital nurse and a cook, as well as having a natural taste for adventure, went as the personal attendant of Father Zahm. In southern Brazil my son Kermit[6] joined me. He had been bridge building, and a couple of months previously, while on top of a long steel span, something went wrong with the derrick, he and the steel span coming down together on the rocky bed beneath. He escaped with two broken ribs, two teeth knocked out, and a knee partially dislocated but was practically all right again when he started with us.

For arms, the naturalists took 16-bore shotguns, one of Cherrie's having a rifle barrel underneath. The firearms for the rest of the party were supplied

*Anthony Fiala, The World's Greatest
Explorers cigarette card series*

by Kermit and myself, including my Springfield
rifle, Kermit's two Winchesters, a 405 and 30-40,
the Fox 12-gauge shotgun, and another 16-gauge
gun, and a couple of revolvers, a Colt and a Smith
& Wesson. We took from New York a couple of
canvas canoes, tents, mosquito bars [nets], plenty of
cheesecloth, including nets for the hats, and both
light cots and hammocks. We took ropes and pulleys, which proved invaluable on our canoe trip.

Each equipped himself with the clothing he fan-
cied. Mine consisted of khaki, such as I wore in
Africa, with a couple of United States Army flannel
shirts and a couple of silk shirts, one pair of hob-
nailed shoes with leggings, and one pair of laced
leather boots coming nearly to the knee. Both the

naturalists told me that it was well to have either the boots or leggings as a protection against snakebites, and I also had gauntlets because of the mosquitoes and sand flies. We intended where possible to live on what we could get from time to time in the country, but we took some United States Army emergency rations, and also ninety cans, each containing a day's provisions for five men, made up by Fiala.

The trip I proposed to take can be understood only if there is a slight knowledge of South American topography. The great mountain chain of the Andes extends down the entire length of the western coast, so close to the Pacific Ocean that no rivers of any importance enter it. The rivers of South America drain into the Atlantic. Southernmost South America, including over half of the territory of the Argentine Republic, consists chiefly of a cool, open plains country.

Northward of this country, and eastward of the Andes, lies the great bulk of the South American continent, which is included in the tropical and the subtropical regions. Most of this territory is Brazilian. Aside from certain relatively small stretches drained by coast rivers, this immense region of tropical and subtropical America east of the Andes is drained by the three great river systems of the Plate [Río de la Plata], the Amazon, and the Orinoco. At their headwaters the Amazon and the Orinoco systems are actually connected by a sluggish natural canal.

The headwaters of the northern affluents of the Paraguay and the southern affluents of the Amazon are sundered by a stretch of high land, which toward the east broadens out into the central plateau of Brazil. Geologically this is a very ancient region, having appeared above the waters before the dawning of the age of reptiles, or, indeed, of any true land vertebrates on the globe. This plateau is a region partly of healthy, rather dry and sandy, open prairie, partly of forest. The great and low-lying basin of the Paraguay, which borders it on the south, is one of the largest, and the still greater basin of the Amazon, which borders it on the north, is the very largest of all the river basins of the earth.

In these basins, but especially in the basin of the Amazon, and thence in most places northward to the Caribbean Sea, lie the most extensive stretches of tropical forest to be found anywhere. The forests of tropical West Africa, and of portions of the Farther-Indian region [Southeast Asia], are the only ones that can be compared with them. Much difficulty has been experienced in exploring these forests, because under the torrential rains and steaming heat, the rank growth of vegetation becomes almost impenetrable, and the streams difficult of navigation, while white men suffer much from the terrible insect scourges and the deadly diseases which modern science has discovered to be due very largely to insect bites. The fauna and flora, however, are of great interest. The American museum was particularly anxious to obtain collections from the divide between the headwaters of the Paraguay and the Amazon, and from the southern affluents of the Amazon. Our purpose was to ascend the Paraguay as nearly as possible to the head of navigation, thence cross to the sources of one of the affluents of the Amazon, and if possible descend it in canoes built on the spot. The Paraguay is regularly navigated as high as boats can go. The starting point for our trip was to be Asunción, in the state of Paraguay.

My exact plan of operations was necessarily a little indefinite, but on reaching Rio de Janeiro, the minister of foreign affairs, Mr. Lauro Müller,[7] who had been kind enough to take great personal interest in my trip, informed me that he had arranged that on the headwaters of the Paraguay, at the town of Cáceres, I would be met by a Brazilian Army colonel, himself chiefly Indian by blood, Colonel Rondon.[8] Colonel Rondon has been for a quarter of a century the foremost explorer of the Brazilian hinterland. He was at the time in Manaus, but his lieutenants were in Cáceres and had been notified that we were coming.

More important still, Mr. Lauro Müller—who is not only an efficient public servant but a man of wide cultivation, with a quality about him that reminded me of John Hay[9]—offered to help me make my trip of much more consequence than I had originally intended. He has taken a keen interest in the exploration and development of the interior of Brazil, and he believed that my expedition could be used as a means toward spreading abroad a more general knowledge of the country. He told me that he would cooperate with me in every way if I cared to undertake the leadership of a serious expedition into the unexplored portion of western Mato Grosso, and to attempt the descent of a river which flowed nobody knew whither, but which the best informed men believed would prove to be a very big river, utterly unknown to geographers.

I eagerly and gladly accepted, for I felt that with such help, the trip could be made of much scientific value and that a substantial addition could be made to the geographical knowledge of one of the least known parts of South America. Accordingly, it was arranged that Colonel Rondon and some assistants and scientists should meet me at or below Corumbá, and that we should attempt the descent of the river, of which they had already come across the headwaters.

I had to travel through Brazil, Uruguay, the Argentine, and Chile for six weeks to fulfill my speaking engagements. Fiala, Cherrie, Miller, and Sigg left me at Rio, continuing to Buenos Aires in the boat in which we had all come down from New

York. From Buenos Aires they went up the Paraguay to Corumbá, where they awaited me. The two naturalists went first, to do all the collecting that was possible; Fiala and Sigg traveled more leisurely, with the heavy baggage.

NOTES

1. John Augustine Zahm (1851–1921), Roman Catholic priest (Congregation of Holy Cross), educator, and author. Zahm's scholarship, interests, and accomplishments included teaching physics at the University of Notre Dame, lecturing on the relationship of science and religion, traveling extensively, and writing on the history of South America. His friendship with Theodore Roosevelt led to his inclusion in this expedition.

2. The American Museum of Natural History (New York) is a major center of research in the natural sciences. Theodore Roosevelt Sr. was among its founders, with its charter being signed in his home in 1869. His son, President Theodore Roosevelt, was a lifelong supporter. Its exhibits, including the Roosevelt Rotunda and the Theodore Roosevelt Memorial Hall, now draw more than five million visitors per year. Frank Michler Chapman (1864–1945), an ornithologist, was chairman of its Department of Birds; Henry Fairfield Osborn (1857–1935) was a paleontologist, Columbia University professor, and scientific administrator. He helped found the Bronx Zoo. In 1891, he joined the museum as a curator and was its president from 1908 to 1933.

3. George K. Cherrie (1865–1948), American ornithologist and expert on the birds of South America, to which he made more than forty collecting trips. He served as a curator of birds for the Field Museum (Chicago), the Brooklyn Museum, and the American Museum of Natural History.

4. Leo E. Miller (1887–1952), a field naturalist who collected specimens for AMNH from 1911 to 1914. After service in World War I, he retired and wrote fantasy novels about South America.

5. Anthony Fiala (1869–1950), explorer, soldier, artist, and writer.

He served in the Spanish American War, was the photographer for the Baldwin-Ziegler Polar Expedition (1901–02), and led the Ziegler Polar Expedition (1903-05). He subsequently wrote *Fighting the Polar Ice*. He retired to Connecticut to operate a sporting goods store.

6. Kermit Roosevelt (1889–1943), explorer, businessman, conservationist, and writer. Kermit was the second son of TR and Edith Kermit Carow Roosevelt. He accompanied his father on his African and Brazilian expeditions. After returning from Brazil, Kermit married Belle Willard, daughter of the U.S. ambassador to Spain. He served in WWI and WWII. Kermit, like his uncle, Elliott, suffered from alcoholism and depression. He committed suicide while stationed at Fort Richardson in Alaska.

7. Lauro Severiano Müller (1863–1929), Brazilian engineer, military officer, politician, and diplomat. Müller, the son of German settlers in Santa Catarina state, trained as an engineer at the military academy in Rio de Janeiro, rose in politics during the 1889 Republican revolution, was appointed interim governor of Santa Catarina, and elected congressman. In 1902, he was appointed cabinet minister of Public Works, and from 1912 to 1917, minister of Foreign Relations across two presidential administrations.

8. Cândido Mariano da Silva Rondon (1865–1958), Brazilian military officer and founding director of the Service for the Protection of Indians (1910). Rondon, who was himself of indigenous origin, trained as a military engineer and dedicated his career to securing Brazil's western borders and establishing nonviolent contact with remote Indians. His most dramatic accomplishment was to cut the telegraph line from the capital of Mato Grosso to the border town of Porto Antonio, from 1907–15. At Müller's orders, he interrupted his work to join Roosevelt's expedition.

9. John Milton Hay (1838–1905), American statesman, Republican Party kingmaker, and diplomat. He had served Abraham Lincoln as private secretary. He was William McKinley's secretary of state, and after McKinley's assassination in 1901, Hay eased Roosevelt's transition from vice president into the presidency by remaining as secretary of state and senior cabinet member. During Roosevelt's first presidency, Hay secured the 1903 treaties to establish the Panama Canal Zone and concessions to build the canal.

II. Up the Paraguay

O N THE AFTERNOON OF DECEMBER 9, we left the attractive and picturesque city of Asunción to ascend the Paraguay. With generous courtesy, the Paraguayan government had put at my disposal the gunboat-yacht of the president himself, a most comfortable river steamer, and so the opening days of our trip were pleasant in every way. The food was good, our quarters were clean, we slept well, below or on deck, usually without our mosquito nettings, and in daytime the deck was pleasant under the awnings. It was hot, of course, but we were dressed suitably in our exploring and hunting clothes and did not mind the heat. The river was low, for there had been dry weather for some weeks—judging from the vague and contradictory information I received, there is much elasticity to the terms "wet season" and "dry season" at this part of the Paraguay.

Under the brilliant sky, we steamed steadily up the mighty river; the sunset was glorious as we leaned on the port railing; and after nightfall, the moon, nearly full and hanging high in the heavens, turned the water to shimmering radiance. On the mud flats and sandbars, and among the green rushes of the bays and inlets, were stately waterfowl: crimson flamingos and rosy spoonbills, dark-colored ibis and white storks with black wings. Darters, with

17

The marketplace in Asunción

snakelike necks and pointed bills, perched in the trees on the brink of the river. Snowy egrets flapped across the marshes. Caimans were common, and differed from the crocodiles we had seen in Africa in two points: they were not alarmed by the report of a rifle when fired at, and they lay with the head raised instead of stretched along the sand.

For three days, as we steamed northward toward the Tropic of Capricorn, and then passed it, we were within the Republic of Paraguay. On our right, to the east, there was a fairly well settled country, where bananas and oranges were cultivated and other crops of hot countries raised. On the banks, we passed an occasional small town, or saw a ranch house close to the river's brink, or stopped for wood at some little settlement. Across the river to the west lay the level, swampy, fertile wastes known as the Chaco, still given over either to the wild Indians or to cattle ranching on a gigantic scale. The broad river ran in curves between mud banks, where terraces marked successive periods of flood. A belt of forest stood on each bank, but it was only a couple of hundred yards wide.

Back of it was the open country; on the Chaco side, this was a vast plain of grass, dotted with tall, graceful palms. In places, the belt of forest vanished and the palm-dotted prairie came to the river's edge. The Chaco is an ideal cattle country and not really unhealthy. It will be covered with ranches at a not distant day. But mosquitoes and many other winged-insect pests swarm over it. Nevertheless, for some as yet inscrutable reason, the river served as a barrier to certain insects which are menaces to the cattlemen.

With me on the gunboat was an old Western friend, Tex Rickard,[1] of the Panhandle and Alaska and various places in between. He now has a large tract of land and some thirty-five thousand head of cattle in the Chaco, opposite Concepción, at which city he was to stop. He told me that horses did not do well in the Chaco but that cattle throve and that while ticks swarmed on the east bank of the great river, they would not live on the west bank. Again and again he had crossed herds of cattle which were covered with the loathsome bloodsuckers; and in a couple of months every tick would be dead. The worst animal foes of man, indeed the only dangerous foes, are insects; and this is especially true in the tropics.

Late on the evening of the second day of our trip, just before midnight, we reached Concepción. On this day, when we stopped for wood or to get provisions—at picturesque places, where the women from rough mud-and-thatched cabins were washing clothes in the river, or where ragged horsemen stood gazing at us from the bank, or where dark, well-dressed ranchmen stood in front of red-roofed houses—we caught many fish. They belonged to one of the most formidable genera of fish in the world, the piranha, or cannibal fish, the fish that eats men when it can get the chance. Farther north there are species of small piranha that go in schools. At this point on the Paraguay, the piranha do not seem to go in regular schools, but they swarm in all the waters and attain a length of eighteen inches or over. They are the most ferocious fish in the world. Even the most formidable fish, the sharks or the barracudas, usually attack things smaller than themselves. But the piranhas habitually attack things much larger than themselves. They will snap a finger off a hand incautiously trailed in the water; they mutilate swimmers—in every river town in Paraguay there are men who have been thus mutilated; they will rend and devour alive any wounded man or beast; for blood in the water excites them to madness. They will tear wounded wild fowl to pieces and bite off the tails of big fish as they grow exhausted when fighting after being hooked. Miller, before I reached Asunción, had been badly bitten by one. Those that we caught sometimes bit through the hooks or the double strands of copper wire that served as leaders and got away. Those that we hauled on deck lived for many minutes.

Most predatory fish are long and slim, like the alligator-gar and pickerel. But the piranha is a short, deep-bodied fish, with a blunt face and a heavily undershot or projecting lower jaw which gapes widely. The razor-edged teeth are wedge-shaped like a shark's, and the jaw muscles possess great power. The rabid, furious snaps drive the teeth through flesh and bone. The head, with its short muzzle, staring malignant eyes, and gaping, cruelly armed jaws, is the embodiment of evil ferocity; and the actions of the fish exactly match its looks. I never witnessed an exhibition of such impotent, savage fury as was shown by the piranhas as they flapped on deck. When fresh from the water and thrown on the boards, they uttered an extraordinary squealing sound. As they flapped about, they bit with vicious eagerness at whatever presented itself. One of them flapped into a cloth and seized it with a bulldog grip. Another grasped one of its fellows; another snapped at a piece of wood and left the teeth marks deep therein. They are the pests of the waters, and it is necessary to be exceedingly cautious about either swimming or wading where they are found. Here on the Paraguay, the natives hold them in much respect, whereas the caimans are not feared at all. The only redeeming feature about them is that they are themselves fairly good to eat, although with too many bones

At daybreak of the third day, finding we were still moored off Concepción, we were rowed ashore and strolled off through the streets of the quaint, picturesque old town, a town which, like Asunción, was founded by the conquistadors three-quarters of a century before our own English and Dutch forefathers landed in what is now the United States. The Jesuits then took practically complete possession of what is now Paraguay, controlling and Christianizing the Indians and raising their flourishing missions to a pitch of prosperity they never elsewhere achieved. They were expelled by the civil authorities (backed by the other representatives of ecclesiastical authority) some fifty years before Spanish South America became independent.

We walked up the streets of Concepción, and interestedly looked at everything of interest: at the one-story houses, their windows covered with gratings of fretted ironwork and their occasional open doors giving us glimpses into cool inner courtyards, with trees and flowers; at the two-wheel carts, drawn by mules or oxen; at an occasional rider, with spurs on his bare feet, and his big toes thrust into the small stirrup rings; at the little stores and the warehouses for maté [herb tea leaves] and hides. Then we came to a pleasant little inn, kept by a Frenchman and his wife, of old Spanish style, with its patio, or inner court, but as neat as an inn in Normandy or Brittany. We were sitting at coffee, around a little table, when in came the colonel of the garrison—for Concepción is the second city in Paraguay. He told me that they had prepared a reception for me! I was in my rough hunting clothes, but there was nothing to do but to accompany my kind

23

Colonel Roosevelt, casually dressed, and officials at Concepcion

hosts and trust to their good nature to pardon my shortcomings in the matter of dress.

The colonel drove me about in a smart open carriage, with two good horses and a liveried driver. It was a much more fashionable turnout than would be seen in any of our cities save the largest, and even in them probably not in the service of a public official. In all the South American countries there is more pomp and ceremony in connection with public functions than with us, and at these functions the liveried servants, often with knee breeches and powdered hair, are like those seen at similar European functions; there is not the democratic simplicity which better suits our own habits of life and ways of thought. But the South Americans often surpass us, not merely in pomp and ceremony, but in what is of real importance, courtesy; in civility and courtesy we can well afford to take lessons from them.

We first visited the barracks, saw the troops in the setting-up exercises, and inspected the arms, the artillery, the equipment. There was a German lieutenant with the Paraguayan officers, one of several German officers who are now engaged in helping the Paraguayans with their army. The equipments and arms were in good condition; the enlisted men evidently offered fine material; and the officers were doing hard work. It is worthwhile for anti-militarists to ponder the fact that in every South American country where a really efficient army is developed, the increase in military efficiency goes hand in hand with a decrease in lawlessness and disorder, and a growing reluctance to settle internal disagreements by violence. They are introducing universal military service in Paraguay; the officers, many of whom have studied abroad, are growing to feel an increased esprit de corps, an increased pride in the army, and therefore a desire to see the army made the servant of the nation as a whole and not the tool of any faction or individual. If these feelings grow strong enough, they will be powerful factors in giving Paraguay what she most needs, freedom from revolutionary disturbance and therefore the chance to achieve the material prosperity without which as a basis there can be no advance in other and even more important matters.

Then I was driven to the city hall, accompanied by the *intendente*, or mayor, a German long settled in the country and one of the leading men of the city. There was a breakfast. When I had to speak, I impressed into my service as interpreter a young Paraguayan who was a graduate of the University of Pennsylvania. He was able to render into Spanish my ideas—on such subjects as orderly liberty and the far-reaching mischief done by the revolutionary habit—with clearness and vigor, because he thoroughly understood not only how I felt, but also the American way of looking at such things. My hosts were hospitality itself, and I enjoyed the unexpected greeting.

We steamed on up the river. Now and then we passed another boat—a steamer, or, to my surprise, perhaps a barkentine, or schooner. The Paraguay is a highway of traffic. Once we passed a big beef-canning factory. Ranches stood on either bank a few leagues apart, and we stopped at wood yards on the west bank. Indians worked around them. At one such yard the Indians were evidently part of the

Indians rolling logs at a wood station

regular force. Their squaws[2] were with them, cooking at queer open-air ovens. One small child had as
pets a parrot and a young coati—a kind of long-
nosed raccoon. Loading wood, the Indians stood in
a line, tossing the logs from one to the other. These
Indians wore clothes.

On this day we got into the tropics. Even in the
heat of the day, the deck was pleasant under the
awnings; the sun rose and set in crimson splendor;
and the nights, with the moon at the full, were
wonderful. At night Orion blazed overhead, and the
Southern Cross hung in the star-brilliant heavens
behind us. But after the moon rose, the constella-
tions paled; and clear in her light, the tree-clad
banks stood on either hand as we steamed steadily
against the swirling current of the great river.

At noon on the twelfth, we were at the Brazilian
boundary. On this day, we here and there came on
low, conical hills close to the river. In places the
palm groves broke through the belts of deciduous
trees and stretched for a mile or so right along the
river's bank. At times we passed cattle on the banks
or sandbars, followed by their herders; or a handsome ranch house, under a cluster of shady trees,
some bearing a wealth of red and some a wealth of
yellow blossoms; or we saw a horse corral among the
trees close to the brink, with the horses in it and a
barefooted man in shirt and trousers leaning against
the fence; or a herd of cattle among the palms; or a

big tannery or factory; or a little native hamlet came in sight.

We stopped at one tannery. The owner was a Spaniard, the manager an "Orientál," as he called himself, a Uruguayan, of German parentage. The peons, or workers, who lived in a long line of wooden cabins back of the main building, were mostly Paraguayans, with a few Brazilians, and a dozen German and Argentine foremen. There were also some wild Indians, who were camped in the usual squalid fashion of Indians who are hangers-on round the white man but have not yet adopted his ways. Most of the men were at work cutting wood for the tannery. The women and children were in camp. Some individuals of both sexes were naked to the waist. One little girl had a young ostrich as a pet.

Waterfowl were plentiful. We saw large flocks of wild Muscovy ducks. Our tame birds come from this wild species, and its absurd misnaming dates back to the period when the turkey and guinea pig were misnamed in similar fashion—our European forefathers taking a large and hazy view of geography, and including Turkey, Guinea, India, and Muscovy as places which, in their capacity of being outlandish, could be comprehensively used as including America. The Muscovy ducks were very good eating. Darters and cormorants swarmed. They waddled on the sandbars in big flocks and crowded the trees by the water's edge. Beautiful snow-white egrets also lit in the trees, often well back from the river. A full-foliaged tree of vivid green, its round surface crowded with these birds, as if it had suddenly blossomed with huge white flowers, is a sight worth seeing. Here and there on the sandbars we saw huge jabiru storks, and once a flock of white wood ibis among the trees on the bank.

On the Brazilian boundary, we met a shallow river steamer carrying Colonel Cândido Mariano da Silva Rondon and several other Brazilian members of the expedition. Colonel Rondon immediately showed that he was all, and more than all, that could be desired. It was evident that he knew his business thoroughly, and it was equally evident that he would be a pleasant companion. He was a class-mate of Mr. Lauro Müller at the Brazilian Military Academy. He is of almost pure Indian blood, and is a Positivist[3]—the Positivists are a really strong body in Brazil, as they are in France and indeed in Chile. The colonel's seven children have all been formally made members of the Positivist Church in Rio Janeiro. Brazil possesses the same complete liberty in matters religious, spiritual, and intellectual as we, for our great good fortune, do in the United States, and my Brazilian companions included Catholics and equally sincere men who described themselves as *libres penseurs* [free thinkers].

30

Colonel Rondon has spent the last twenty-four years in exploring the western highlands of Brazil, pioneering the way for telegraph lines and railroads. During that time he has traveled some fourteen thousand miles, on territory most of which had not previously been traversed by civilized man, and has built three thousand miles of telegraph. He has an exceptional knowledge of the Indian tribes and has always zealously endeavored to serve them and indeed to serve the cause of humanity wherever and whenever he was able. Thanks mainly to his efforts, four of the wild tribes of the region he has explored have begun to tread the road of civilization. They have taken the first steps toward becoming Christians. It may seem strange that among the first fruits of the efforts of a Positivist should be the conversion of those he seeks to benefit to Christianity. But in South America, Christianity is at least as much a status as a theology. It represents the indispensable first step upward from savagery. In the wilder and poorer districts, men are divided into the two great classes of "Christians" and "Indians." When an Indian becomes a Christian, he is accepted into and becomes wholly absorbed or partly assimilated by the crude and simple neighboring civilization, and then he moves up or down like any one else among his fellows.

Among Colonel Rondon's companions were Captain Amilcar de Magalhães, Lieutenant João

The Brazilian members of the expedition: (clockwise from top left) Col. Cândido Rondon, Capt. Amilcar de Magalhães, 1st Lt. João Salustiano Lyra, 2nd Lt. J.M. Vieira de Mello Filho, 1st Lt. Pirineus de Sousa, 2nd Lt. A. Lauriadó de Sant'Anna, Dr. José Antonio Cajazeira

Lyra, Lieutenant Joaquim de Mello Filho, and Doctor Euzébio de Oliveira, a geologist.[4]

The steamers halted; Colonel Rondon and several of his officers, spick and span in their white uniforms, came aboard; and in the afternoon I visited him on his steamer to talk over our plans.

During his trips, Colonel Rondon had met with various experiences with wild creatures. The Paraguayan caimans are not ordinarily dangerous to man, but they do sometimes become man-eaters and should be destroyed whenever the opportunity offers. The huge caimans and crocodiles of the Amazon are far more dangerous, and the colonel knew of repeated instances where men, women, and children had become their victims.

All such enemies, however, he regarded as utterly trivial compared to the real dangers of the wilderness—the torment and menace of attacks by the swarming insects, by mosquitoes and the even more intolerable tiny gnats, by the ticks, and by the vicious poisonous ants which occasionally cause villages and even whole districts to be deserted by human beings. These insects, and the fevers they cause, and dysentery and starvation and wearing hardship and accidents in rapids are what the pioneer explorers have to fear. The conversation was to me most interesting. The colonel spoke French about to the extent I did; but of course he and the others preferred Portuguese; and then Kermit was the interpreter.

In the evening, soon after moonrise, we stopped for wood at the little Brazilian town of Porto Murtinho. There are about twelve hundred inhabitants. Some of the buildings were of stone; a large private house with a castellated tower was of stone; there were shops, and a post office, stores, a restaurant and billiard hall, and warehouses for maté, of which much is grown in the region roundabout. Most of the houses were low, with overhanging, sloping eaves; and there were gardens with high walls, inside of which trees rose, many of them fragrant. We wandered through the wide, dusty streets and along the narrow sidewalks. It was a hot, still evening; the smell of the tropics was on the heavy December air. Through the open doors and windows we caught dim glimpses of the half-clad inmates of the poorer houses; women and young girls sat outside their thresholds in the moonlight.

All whom we met were most friendly: the captain of the little Brazilian garrison; the *intendente*; a local trader; another trader and ranchman, a Uruguayan, who had just received his newspaper containing my speech in Montevideo, and who, as I gathered from what I understood of his rather voluble Spanish, was much impressed by my views on democracy, honesty, liberty, and order (rather well-worn topics); and a Catalan who spoke French, and who was accompanied by his pretty daughter, a dear little girl of eight or ten, who said with much pride that she spoke three languages—Brazilian, Spanish, and Catalan! Her father expressed strongly his desire for a church and for a school in the little city.

When at last the wood was aboard, we resumed our journey. The river was like glass. In the white moonlight, the palms on the edge of the banks stood mirrored in the still water. We sat forward, and as we rounded the curves, the long silver reaches of the great stream stretched ahead of us, and the ghostly outlines of hills rose in the distance. Here and there prairie fires burned, and the red glow warred with the moon's radiance.

We took breakfast—the eleven-o'clock Brazilian breakfast—on Colonel Rondon's boat. Caimans were becoming more plentiful. The ugly brutes lay on the sand flats and mud banks like logs, always with the head raised, sometimes with the jaws open. We passed forests of palms that extended for leagues, and vast marshy meadows, where storks, herons, and ibis were gathered, with flocks of cormorants and darters on the sandbars, and stilts, skimmers, and clouds of beautiful swaying terns in the foreground. About noon we passed the highest point which the old Spanish conquistadors and explorers, [Domingo Martínez de] Irala and [Juan de] Ayolas, had reached in the course of their marvelous journeys in the first half of the sixteenth century— at a time when there was not a settlement in what is now the United States and when hardly a single

35

English sea captain had ventured so much as to cross the Atlantic.

By the following day, the country on the east bank had become a vast marshy plain dotted here and there by tree-clad patches of higher land. The morning was rainy, a contrast to the fine weather we had hitherto encountered. We passed wood yards and cattle ranches. At one of the latter, the owner, an Argentine of Irish parentage, who still spoke English with the accent of the land of his parents' nativity, remarked that this was the first time the American flag had been seen on the upper Paraguay, for our gunboat carried it at the masthead.

Early in the afternoon, having reached the part where both banks of the river were Brazilian territory, we came to the old colonial Portuguese fort of Coimbra. It stands where two steep hills rise, one on either side of the river, and it guards the water gorge between them. It was captured by the Paraguayans in the war of nearly half a century ago.[5] Some modern guns have been mounted, and there is a garrison of Brazilian troops. The white fort is perched on the hillside, where it clings and rises, terrace above terrace, with bastion and parapet and crenellated wall. At the foot of the hill, on the riverine plain, stretches the old-time village with its roofs of palm.

In the village dwell several hundred souls, almost entirely the officers and soldiers and their families.

There is one long street. The one-story daub-and-wattle houses have low eaves and steep sloping roofs of palm leaves or of split palm trunks. Under one or two old but small trees, there are rude benches; and for a part of the length of the street, there is a rough stone sidewalk. A little graveyard, some of the tombs very old, stands at one end. As we passed down the street, the wives and the swarming children of the garrison were at the doors and windows; there were women and girls with skins as fair as any in the northland, and others that were predominantly *negro* [black]. Most were of intervening shades. All this was paralleled among the men, and the fusion of the colors was going on steadily.

Around the village, black vultures were gathered. Not long before reaching it, we passed some rounded green trees, their tops covered with the showy wood ibis; at the same time we saw behind them, farther inland, other trees crowded with the more delicate forms of the shining white egrets.

On December 15, we reached Corumbá. For three or four miles before it is reached, the west bank, on which it stands, becomes high rocky ground, falling away into cliffs. The country roundabout was evidently well peopled. We saw gauchos, cattle herders—the equivalent of our own cowboys—riding along the bank. Women were washing clothes, and their naked children bathing, on the shore; we were told that caimans and pira-

The harbor at Corumbá

nhas rarely ventured near a place where so much was going on and that accidents generally occurred in ponds or lonely stretches of the river. Several steamers came out to meet us and accompanied us for a dozen miles, with bands playing and the passengers cheering, just as if we were nearing some town on the Hudson.

Corumbá is on a steep hillside, with wide, roughly paved streets, some of them lined with beautiful trees that bear scarlet flowers, and with well-built houses, most of them of one story, some of two or three stories. We were greeted with a reception by the municipal council and were given a state dinner. The hotel, kept by an Italian, was as comfortable as possible—stone floors, high ceilings, big windows and doors, a cool, open courtyard, and a shower bath. Of course Corumbá is still a frontier town. The vehicles are ox carts and mule carts; there are no carriages; and oxen as well as mules are used for riding. The water comes from a big central well; around it the water carts gather, and their contents are then peddled around at the different houses.

The families showed the mixture of races characteristic of Brazil; one mother, after the children had been photographed in their ordinary costume, begged that we return and take them in their Sunday clothes, which was accordingly done. In a year the railway from Rio will reach Corumbá; and then this city, and the country roundabout, will see much development.

At this point we rejoined the rest of the party, and very glad we were to see them. Cherrie and Miller had already collected some eight hundred specimens of mammals and birds.

NOTES

1. George Lewis (Tex) Rickard (1870/71–1929) was best known as a sports promoter and the operator of Madison Square Garden. He helped make professional sports, especially boxing, big business in the United States. Earlier in his checkered career, Rickard was a cowboy and town marshal in Texas, explored for gold in Alaska and diamonds in South Africa, and operated saloons in Alaska and Nevada, where he began promoting boxing matches. From 1910-15, he ran a cattle ranch in Paraguay.

2. This term for an Indian woman is now considered offensive.

3. Positivists: See Historical Introduction, p. lvi, n.5.

4. Amilcar Armando Botelho de Magalhães (1880–c. 1952), Brazilian military officer. He wrote memoirs on Rondon's work and studies on Brazilian Indians. He served for many years in the Service for the Protection of Indians. João Salustiano Lyra (1878–1917), Brazilian military engineer and surveyor who served under Rondon on several expeditions. Three years after the Rondon-Roosevelt expedition, he drowned while exploring a branch of the Sepotuba River. Joaquim Vieira de Mello Filho, Brazilian army officer who served with Rondon through 1918. Euzébio (or Eusébio) Paulo de Oliveira (1883–1939), Brazilian mining engineer and geologist. He served in Brazil's Geological and Mineralogical Service, 1907–39, and directed it, 1925–38. He was president of the Brazilian Academy of Sciences, 1931–33.

5. The Paraguayan War: See Historical Introduction, p. lvi, n. 4.

III. A Jaguar Hunt on the Taquari

THE MORNING AFTER OUR ARRIVAL AT Corumbá, I asked Colonel Rondon to inspect our outfit, for his experience of what is necessary in tropical traveling has been gained through a quarter of a century of arduous exploration in the wilderness. It was Fiala who had assembled our food tents, cooking utensils, and supplies of all kinds, and he and Sigg, during their stay in Corumbá, had been putting everything in shape for our start. Colonel Rondon at the end of his inspection said he had nothing whatever to suggest, that it was extraordinary that Fiala, without personal knowledge of the tropics, could have gathered the things most necessary, with the minimum of bulk and maximum of usefulness.

At Corumbá the weather was hot. In the patio of the comfortable little hotel, we heard the cicadas; but I did not hear the extraordinary screaming whistle of the locomotive cicada, which I had heard in the gardens of the house in which I stayed at Asunción. This was as remarkable a sound as any animal sound to which I have listened, except only the batrachian-like [frog- or toad-like] wailing of the tree hyrax in East Africa. The locomotive-whistle part of the utterance, however, resembles nothing so much as a small steam siren; when first heard, it seems impossible that it can be produced by an insect.

On December 17, Colonel Rondon and several members of our party started on a shallow river steamer for the ranch of Senhor de Barros, "Las Palmeiras," on the Rio Taquari. We went down the Paraguay for a few miles, and then up the Taquari. It was a beautiful trip. The shallow river—we were aground several times—wound through a vast, marshy plain, with occasional spots of higher land on which trees grew. There were many water birds. Darters swarmed. But the conspicuous and attractive bird was the stately jabiru stork. Flocks of these storks whitened the marshes and lined the riverbanks. They were not shy, for such big birds; before flying, they had to run a few paces and then launch themselves on the air. Once, at noon, a couple soared round overhead in wide rings, rising higher and higher. On another occasion, late in the day, a flock passed by, gleaming white with black points in the long afternoon lights, and with them were spoonbills, showing rosy amid their snowy companions. Caimans, always called *jacarés*, swarmed; and we killed scores of the noxious creatures.

In the late afternoon we secured a more interesting creature than the *jacarés*. Kermit had charge of two hounds, which we owed to the courtesy of one of our Argentine friends. They were biggish, nondescript animals, obviously good fighters, and they speedily developed the utmost affection for all the members of the expedition, but especially for Ker-

Caimans swarming in the river

mit, who took care of them. One we named "Shenzi." The other was called "Trigueiro." The chance now came to try them.

We were steaming between long stretches of coarse grass, about three feet high, when we spied from the deck a black object, very conspicuous against the vivid green. It was a giant anteater, or *tamanduá bandeira*, one of the most extraordinary creatures of the latter-day world. It is about the size of a rather small black bear. It has a very long, narrow, toothless snout, with a tongue it can project a couple of feet; it is covered with coarse, black hair, save for a couple of white stripes; it has a long, bushy tail and very powerful claws on its forefeet. It walks on the sides of its forefeet with these claws curved in under the foot. The claws are used in digging out anthills; but the beast has courage, and in a grapple is a rather unpleasant enemy, in spite of its toothless mouth, for it can strike a formidable blow with these claws. It sometimes hugs a foe, gripping him tight; but its ordinary method of defending itself is to strike with its long, stout, curved claws, which, driven by its muscular forearm, can rip open man or beast. Several of our companions had had dogs killed by these anteaters; and we came across one man with a very ugly scar down his back, where he had been hit by one, which charged him when he came up to kill it at close quarters.

As soon as we saw the giant *tamanduá,* we pushed

An anteater and a snake, by Charles Livingston Bull

off in a rowboat and landed only a couple of hundred yards distant from our clumsy quarry. The *tamanduá* throughout most of its habitat rarely leaves the forest, and it is a helpless animal in the open plain. The two dogs ran ahead, followed by Colonel Rondon and Kermit, with me behind carrying the rifle. In a minute or two, the hounds overtook the cantering, shuffling creature and promptly began a fight with it; the combatants were so mixed up that I had to wait another minute or so before I could fire without risk of hitting a dog. We carried our prize back to the bank and hoisted it aboard the steamer. The sun was just about to set, behind dim mountains, many miles distant across the marsh.

Soon afterward we reached one of the outstations of the huge ranch we were about to visit and hauled up alongside the bank for the night. There was a landing place, and sheds and corrals. Several of the peons [landless laborers], or gauchos [cowboys], had come to meet us. After dark they kindled fires and sat beside them singing songs in a strange minor key and strumming guitars. The red firelight flickered over their wild figures as they squatted away from the blaze, where the light and the shadow met. It was still and hot. There were mosquitoes, of course, and other insects of all kinds swarmed round every light; but the steamboat was comfortable, and we passed a pleasant night.

At sunrise we were off for the *fazenda*, the ranch

46

[Fazenda de Palmeiras] of M. de Barros. The baggage went in an ox cart—which had to make two trips, so that all of my belongings reached the ranch a day later than I did. We rode small, tough ranch horses. The distance was some twenty miles. The whole country was marsh, varied by stretches of higher ground; and, although these stretches rose only three or four feet above the marsh, they were covered with thick jungle, largely palmetto scrub, or else with open palm forest. For three or four miles we splashed through the marsh, now and then crossing boggy pools where the little horses labored hard not to mire down. Our dusky guide was clad in a shirt, trousers, and fringed leather apron and wore spurs on his bare feet; he had a rope for a bridle, and two or three toes of each foot were thrust into little iron stirrups

The pools in the marsh were drying. They were filled with fish, most of them dead or dying; and the birds had gathered to the banquet. The most notable dinner guests were the great jabiru storks; the stately creatures dotted the marsh. But ibis and herons abounded; the former uttered queer, querulous cries when they discovered our presence. The spurred lapwings were as noisy as they always are. The ibis and plover did not pay any heed to the fish; but the black carrion vultures feasted on them in the mud; and in the pools that were not dry, small alligators, the *jacaré-tinga*, were feasting also. In many places the stench from the dead fish was unpleasant.

Then for miles we rode through a beautiful open forest of tall, slender carandá palms, with other trees scattered among them. Green parakeets with black heads chattered as they flew; noisy green and red parrots climbed among the palms; and huge macaws, some entirely blue, others almost entirely red, screamed loudly as they perched in the trees or took wing at our approach. If one was wounded, its cries kept its companions circling around overhead. The naturalists found the bird fauna totally different from that which they had been collecting in the hill country near Corumbá, seventy or eighty miles distant; and birds swarmed, both species and individuals.

South America has the most extensive and most varied avifauna of all the continents. On the other hand, its mammalian fauna, although very interesting, is rather poor in number of species and individuals and in the size of the beasts. It possesses more mammals that are unique and distinctive in type than does any other continent save Australia, and they are of higher and much more varied types than in Australia. But there is nothing approaching the majesty, beauty, and swarming mass of the great mammalian life of Africa and, in a less degree, of tropical Asia; indeed, it does not even approach the similar mammalian life of North America and northern Eurasia, poor though this is compared

48

with the seething vitality of tropical life in the Old World.

During a geologically recent period, a period extending into that which saw man spread over the world in substantially the physical and cultural stage of many existing savages, South America possessed a varied and striking fauna of enormous beasts—saber-tooth tigers; huge lions; mastodons; horses of many kinds; camel-like pachyderms; giant ground sloths, mylodons the size of the rhinoceros; and many, many other strange and wonderful creatures. From some cause, concerning the nature of which we cannot at present even hazard a guess, this vast and giant fauna vanished completely, the tremendous catastrophe (the duration of which is unknown) not being consummated until within a few thousand or a few score thousand years. When the white man reached South America, he found the same weak and impoverished mammalian fauna that exists practically unchanged today. Elsewhere civilized man has been even more destructive than his very destructive uncivilized brothers of the magnificent mammalian life of the wilderness; for ages he has been rooting out the higher forms of beast life in Europe, Asia, and North Africa; and in our own day he has repeated the feat, on a very large scale, in the rest of Africa and in North America.

But in South America, although he is in places responsible for the wanton slaughter of the most interesting and the largest, or the most beautiful, birds, his advent has meant a positive enrichment of the wild mammalian fauna. None of the native grass-eating mammals, the graminivores, approach in size and beauty the herds of wild or half-wild cattle and horses, or so add to the interest of the landscape. There is every reason why the good people of South America should waken, as we of North America, very late in the day, are beginning to waken, and as the peoples of northern Europe—not southern Europe—have already partially wakened, to the duty of preserving from impoverishment and extinction the wild life which is an asset of such interest and value in our several lands; but the case against civilized man in this matter is gruesomely heavy anyhow, when the plain truth is told, and it is harmed by exaggeration.

After five or six hours' traveling through this country of marsh and of palm forest, we reached the ranch for which we were heading. In the neighborhood stood giant fig trees, singly or in groups, with dense, dark green foliage. Ponds, overgrown with water plants, lay about; wet meadow, and drier pastureland, open or dotted with palms and varied with tree jungle, stretched for many miles on every hand. There are some thirty thousand head of cattle on the ranch, besides herds of horses and droves of swine, and a few flocks of sheep and goats.

The home buildings of the ranch stood in a

quadrangle, surrounded by a fence or low stockade. One end of the quadrangle was formed by the ranch house itself, one story high, with whitewashed walls and red-tiled roof. Inside, the rooms were bare, with clean, whitewashed walls and palm-trunk rafters. There were solid wooden shutters on the unglazed windows. We slept in hammocks or on cots, and we feasted royally on delicious native Brazilian dishes. On another side of the quadrangle stood another long, low, white building with a red-tiled roof; this held the kitchen and the living rooms of the upper-grade peons, the headmen, the cook, and jaguar hunters, with their families: dark-skinned men, their wives showing varied strains of white, Indian, and Negro blood. The children tumbled merrily in the dust and were fondly tended by their mothers. Opposite the kitchen stood a row of buildings, some whitewashed daub and wattle, with tin roofs, others of erect palm logs with palm-leaf thatch. These were the saddle room, storehouse, chicken house, and stable. The chicken house was allotted to Kermit and Miller for the preparation of the specimens; and there they worked industriously. Nearby stood other buildings: sheds, and thatched huts of palm logs in which the ordinary peons lived, and big corrals.

In the quadrangle were flamboyant trees, with their masses of brilliant red flowers and delicately cut, vivid-green foliage. Noisy ovenbirds haunted these trees. In a high palm in the garden, a family of green parakeets had taken up their abode and were preparing to build nests. They chattered incessantly both when they flew and when they sat or crawled among the branches. Ibis and plover, crying and wailing, passed immediately overhead. Jacanas frequented the ponds nearby; the peons, with a familiarity which to us seems sacrilegious, but to them was entirely inoffensive and matter of course, called them "the Jesus Christ birds," because they walked on the water. There was a wealth of strange bird life in the neighborhood. There were large papyrus marshes, the papyrus not being a fifth, perhaps not a tenth, as high as in Africa. In these swamps were many blackbirds. Some uttered notes that reminded me of our own redwings. Others, with crimson heads and necks and thighs, fairly blazed; often a dozen sat together on a swaying papyrus stem, which their weight bent over. There were all kinds of extraordinary birds' nests in the trees.

There is still need for the work of the collector in South America. But I believe that already, so far as birds are concerned, there is infinitely more need for the work of the careful observer, who to the power of appreciation and observation adds the power of vivid, truthful, and interesting narration—which means, as scientists no less than historians should note, that training in the writing of good English is indispensable to any learned man who expects to make his learning count for what it ought to count in the effect on his fellow men. The outdoor naturalist, the faunal naturalist, who devotes himself primarily to a study of the habits and of the life histories of birds, beasts, fish, and reptiles, and who can portray truthfully and vividly what he has seen, could do work of more usefulness than any mere collector, in this upper Paraguay country. The work of the collector is indispensable, but it is only a small part of the work that ought to be done; and after collecting has reached a certain point, the work of the field observer with the gift for recording what he has seen becomes of far more importance.

The long days spent riding through the swamp, the *pantanal*, were pleasant and interesting. Several times we saw the *tamanduá bandeira*, the giant ant-bear. Kermit shot one, because the naturalists eagerly wished for a second specimen; afterward we were relieved of all necessity to molest the strange, out-of-date creatures. It was a surprise to us to find them habitually frequenting the open marsh. They were always on muddy ground, and in the papyrus swamp we found them in several inches of water. Out in the open marsh, the *tamanduá* could neither avoid observation, nor fight effectively, nor make good its escape by flight. It was curious to see one lumbering off at a rocking canter, the big bushy tail held aloft. One, while fighting the dogs, suddenly

The entire party returns to the ranch from a hunt

threw itself on its back, evidently hoping to grasp a dog with its paws; and it now and then reared, in order to strike at its assailants. In one patch of thick jungle, we saw a black howler monkey sitting motionless in a treetop. We also saw the swamp deer, about the size of our blacktail. It is a real swamp animal, for we found it often in the papyrus swamps and out in the open marsh, knee-deep in the water, among the aquatic plants.

The tough little horses bore us well through the marsh. Often in crossing bayous and ponds, the water rose almost to their backs; but they splashed and waded and if necessary swam through. The dogs were a wild-looking set. Some were of distinctly wolfish appearance. These, we were assured, were descended in part from the big red wolf of the neighborhood, a tall, lank animal, with much smaller teeth than a big northern wolf.

In the evenings after dinner we sat in the bare ranch dining room, or out under the trees in the hot darkness, and talked of many things: natural history with the naturalists and all kinds of other subjects both with them and with our Brazilian friends. Colonel Rondon is not simply "an officer and a gentleman" in the sense that is honorably true of the best army officers in every good military service. He is also a peculiarly hardy and competent explorer, a good field naturalist and scientific man, a student, and a philosopher. With him the conversation ranged from jaguar hunting and the perils of exploration in the Mato Grosso, the great wilderness, to Indian anthropology, to the dangers of a purely materialistic industrial civilization, and to Positivist morality. The colonel's Positivism was in very fact to him a religion of humanity, a creed which bade him be just and kindly and useful to his fellow men, to live his life bravely, and no less bravely to face death, without reference to what he believed, or did not believe, or to what the unknown hereafter might hold for him.

The native hunters who accompanied us were swarthy men of mixed blood. They were barefooted and scantily clad, and each carried a long, clumsy spear and a keen machete, in the use of which he was an expert. Now and then, in thick jungle, we had to cut out a path, and it was interesting to see one of them, although cumbered by his unwieldy spear, handling his half-broken little horse with complete ease while he hacked at limbs and branches. Of the two ordinarily with us, one was much the younger; and whenever we came to an unusually doubtful-looking ford or piece of boggy ground, the elder man always sent the younger one on and sat on the bank until he saw what befell the experimenter. Our guides were not only hunters but cattle herders. The coarse dead grass is burned to make room for the green young grass on which the cattle thrive. Every now and then one of the men, as he rode ahead of us, without leaving the saddle, would drop a lighted match into a tussock of tall dead blades; and even as we who were behind rode by, tongues of hot flame would be shooting up and a local prairie fire would have started.

In the afternoon of this same day one of the jaguar hunters—merely ranch hands, who knew something of the chase of the jaguar—who had been searching for tracks, rode in with the information that he had found fresh sign at a spot in the swamp about nine miles distant. Next morning we rose at two and had started on our jaguar hunt at three. Colonel Rondon, Kermit, and I, with the two trailers, or jaguar hunters, made up the party, each on a weedy, undersized marsh pony, accustomed to traversing the vast stretches of morass; and we were accompanied by a brown boy, with saddlebags holding our lunch, who rode a long-horned trotting steer, which he managed by a string through its nostril and lip. The two trailers carried each a long, clumsy spear. We had a rather poor pack. Besides our own two dogs, neither of which was used to jaguar hunting, there were the ranch dogs, which were well-nigh worthless, and then two jaguar hounds borrowed for the occasion from a ranch six or eight leagues distant.

As our shabby little horses shuffled away from the ranch house, the stars were brilliant and the Southern Cross hung well up in the heavens, tilted

Colonel Roosevelt with a lad riding a long-horned steer

to the right. The landscape was spectral in the light of the waning moon. At the first shallow ford, as horses and dogs splashed across, an alligator, the *jacaré-tinga*, some five feet long, floated unconcernedly among the splashing hoofs and paws; evidently at night it did not fear us. Hour after hour we slogged along. Then the night grew ghostly with the first dim gray of the dawn. The sky had become overcast. The sun rose red and angry through broken clouds; his disk flamed behind the tall, slender columns of the palms and lit the waste fields of papyrus. The black monkeys howled mournfully. The birds awoke. Macaws, parrots, parakeets screamed at us and chattered at us as we rode by. Ibis called with wailing voices, and the plovers shrieked as they wheeled in the air. We waded across bayous and ponds, where white lilies floated on the water and thronging lilac flowers splashed the green marsh with color.

At last, on the edge of a patch of jungle, in wet ground, we came on fresh jaguar tracks. Both the jaguar hounds challenged the sign. They were unleashed and galloped along the trail, while the other dogs noisily accompanied them. The hunt led right through the marsh. Evidently the jaguar had not the least distaste for water. Probably it had been hunting for capybaras [the largest known rodent, an aquatic guinea pig, the size of a small sheep] or tapirs, and it had gone straight through ponds and long, winding, narrow ditches or bayous, where it must now and then have had to swim for a stroke or two. It had also wandered through the island-like stretches of tree-covered land, the trees at this point being mostly palms and tarumans; the taruman is almost as big as a live oak, with glossy foliage and a fruit like an olive. The pace quickened, the motley pack burst into yelling and howling, and then a sudden quickening of the note showed that the game had either climbed a tree or turned to bay in a thicket. The former proved to be the case. The dogs

Parrots of the Amazon

had entered a patch of tall tree jungle, and as we cantered up through the marsh, we saw the jaguar high among the forked limbs of a taruman tree. It was a beautiful picture—the spotted coat of the big, lithe, formidable cat fairly shone as it snarled defiance at the pack below. I did not trust the pack; the dogs were not staunch, and if the jaguar came down and started, I feared we might lose it. So I fired at once, from a distance of seventy yards. I was using my favorite rifle, the little Springfield with which I have killed most kinds of African game, from the lion and elephant down; the bullets were the sharp, pointed kind, with the end of naked lead. At the shot, the jaguar fell like a sack of sand through the branches, and although it staggered to its feet, it went but a score of yards before it sank down, and when I came up, it was dead under the palms, with three or four of the bolder dogs riving [tearing] at it.

The jaguar is the king of South American game, ranking on an equality with the noblest beasts of the chase of North America, and behind only the huge and fierce creatures which stand at the head of the big game of Africa and Asia. This one was an adult female. It was heavier and more powerful than a full-grown male cougar, or African panther or leopard. It was a big, powerfully built creature, giving the same effect of strength that a tiger or lion does, and that the lithe leopards and pumas do not. Its flesh, by the way, proved good eating, when we had it for supper, although it was not cooked in the way it ought to have been.

We frequently came across ponds tenanted by numbers of capybaras. They are said to be shy elsewhere. Here they were tame. The water was their home and refuge. They usually went ashore to feed on the grass, and made well-beaten trails in the marsh immediately around the water; but they must have traveled these at night, for we never saw them more than a few feet away from the water in the daytime. Even at midday we often came on them standing beside a bayou or pond. The dogs would rush wildly at such a standing beast, which would wait until they were only a few yards off and then dash into and under the water. The dogs would also run full tilt into the water, and it was then really funny to see their surprise and disappointment at the sudden and complete disappearance of their quarry. Often a capybara would stand or sit on its haunches in the water, with only its blunt, short-eared head above the surface, quite heedless of our presence. But if alarmed, it would dive, for capybaras swim with equal facility on or below the surface; and if they wish to hide, they rise gently among the rushes or water-lily leaves with only their nostrils exposed. In these waters the capybaras and small caimans paid no attention to one another, swimming and resting in close proximity. They both had the same enemy, the jaguar. The capybara is a game

A jaguar killing a tapir

animal only in the sense that a hare or rabbit is. The flesh is good to eat, and its amphibious habits and queer nature and surroundings make it interesting. In some of the ponds, the water had about gone, and the capybaras had become for the time being beasts of the marsh and the mud, although they could always find little slimy pools, under a mass of water lilies, in which to lie and hide.

Our whole stay on this ranch was delightful. On the long rides we always saw something of interest, and often it was something entirely new to us. Early one morning we came across two armadillos—the big, nine-banded armadillo. We were riding with the pack through a dry, sandy pasture country, dotted with clumps of palms, round the trunks of which grew a dense jungle of thorns and Spanish bayonets. The armadillos were feeding in an open space between two of these jungle clumps, which were about a hundred yards apart. One was on all fours; the other was in a squatting position, with its forelegs off the ground. Their long ears were very prominent. The dogs raced at them. I had always supposed that armadillos merely shuffled along and curled up for protection when menaced; and I was almost as surprised as if I had seen a turtle gallop when these two armadillos bounded off at a run, going as fast as rabbits. One headed back for the nearest patch of jungle, which it reached. The other ran at full speed—and ran really fast, too—until it nearly reached the other patch, a hundred yards distant, the dogs in full cry immediately behind it. Then it suddenly changed its mind, wheeled in its tracks, and came back like a bullet right through the pack. Dog after dog tried to seize it or stop it and turned to pursue it; but its wedge-shaped snout and armored body, joined to the speed at which it was galloping, enabled it to drive straight ahead through its pursuers, not one of which could halt it or grasp it, and it reached in safety its thorny haven of refuge. It had run at speed about 150 yards. I was much impressed by this unexpected exhibition; evidently this species of armadillo only curls up as a last resort and ordinarily trusts to its speed, and to the protection its build and its armor give it while running, in order to reach its burrow or other place of safety. Twice, while laying railway tracks near São Paulo, Kermit had accidentally dug up armadillos with a steam shovel.

There were big anthills, some of them of huge dimensions, scattered through the country. Sometimes they were built against the stems of trees. We did not here come across any of the poisonous or biting ants which, when sufficiently numerous, render certain districts uninhabitable. They are ordinarily not very numerous. Those of them that march in large bodies kill nestling birds and at once destroy any big animal unable to get out of their way. It has been suggested that nestlings in their nests are in some way immune from the attack of

*Mammals of the Amazon: Top: nine-banded armadillo;
middle: capybaras; bottom: collared peccary*

these ants. The experiments of our naturalists tended to show that this was not the case. They plundered any nest they came across and could get at.

Once we saw a small herd of peccaries [piglike mammals], one a sow followed by three little pigs—they are said to have only two young, but we saw three, although of course it is possible one belonged to another sow. The herd galloped into a mass of thorny cover the hounds could not penetrate; and when they were in safety, we heard them utter, from the depths of the jungle, a curious moaning sound.

The water birds were always a delight. We shot merely the two or three specimens the naturalists needed for the museum. I killed a wood ibis on the wing with the handy little Springfield, and then lost all the credit I had thus gained by a series of inexcusable misses, at long range, before I finally killed a jabiru. Kermit shot a jabiru with the Luger automatic. The great, splendid birds, standing about as tall as a man, show fight when wounded and advance against their assailants, clattering their formidable bills.

One day we found the nest of a jabiru in a mighty fig tree, on the edge of a patch of jungle. It was a big platform of sticks, placed on a horizontal branch. There were four half-grown young standing on it. We passed it in the morning, when both parents were also perched alongside; the sky was then

*Peccaries and cattleya in a forest, by
Charles Livingston Bull*

overcast, and it was not possible to photograph it with the small camera. In the early afternoon when we again passed it, the sun was out, and we tried to get photographs. Only one parent bird was present at this time. It showed no fear. I noticed that, as it stood on a branch near the nest, its bill was slightly open. It was very hot, and I suppose it had opened its bill just as a hen opens her bill in hot weather. As we rode away, the old bird and the four young birds were standing motionless, and with gliding flight, the other old bird was returning to the nest. It is hard to give an adequate idea of the wealth of bird life in these marshes. A naturalist could with the utmost advantage spend six months on such a ranch as that we visited. He would have to do some collecting, but only a little. Exhaustive observation in the field is what is now most needed. Most of this wonderful and harmless bird life should be protected by law, and the mammals should receive reasonable protection. The books now most needed are those dealing with the life histories of wild creatures.

One afternoon, several score cattle were driven into a big square corral near the house, in order to brand the calves and a number of unbranded yearlings and two-year-olds. A special element of excitement was added by the presence of a dozen big bulls which were to be turned into draft oxen. The agility, nerve, and prowess of the ranch workmen, the herders, or gauchos, were noteworthy. The dark-skinned men were obviously mainly of Indian and Negro descent, although some of them also showed a strong strain of white blood. They wore the usual shirt, trousers, and fringed leather apron, and hats. Their bare feet must have been literally as tough as horn; for when one of them roped a big bull, he would brace himself, bending back until he was almost sitting down and digging his heels into the ground,

Roping bulls at Las Palmeiras ranch

and the galloping beast would be stopped short and whirled completely round when the rope tautened. The maddened bulls, and an occasional steer or cow, charged again and again with furious wrath; but two or three ropes would settle on the doomed beast, and down it would go; and when it was released and rose and charged once more, with greater fury than ever, the men, shouting with laughter, would leap up the sides of the heavy stockade.

We stayed at the ranch until a couple of days before Christmas. Hitherto the weather had been lovely. The night before we left, there was a torrential tropic downpour. It was not unexpected, for we had been told that the rainy season was overdue. The following forenoon, the baggage started, in a couple of two-wheeled ox carts, for the landing where the steamboat awaited us. Each cart was drawn by eight oxen. The huge wheels were over seven-feet high. Early in the afternoon, we followed on horseback and overtook the carts as darkness fell, just before we reached the landing on the river's bank. The last few miles, after the final reaches of higher, tree-clad ground had been passed, were across a level plain of low ground on which the water stood, sometimes only up to the ankles of a man on foot, sometimes as high as his waist. Directly in front of us, many leagues distant, rose the bold mountains that lie west of Corumbá. Behind them the sun was setting and kindled the overcast heavens with lurid splendor. Then the last rose tints faded from the sky; the horses plodded wearily through the water; on every side stretched the marsh, vast, lonely, desolate in the gray of the half-light. We overtook the ox carts. The cattle strained in the yokes; the drivers wading alongside cracked their whips and uttered strange cries; the carts rocked and swayed as the huge wheels churned through the mud and water. As the last light faded, we reached the small patches of dry land at the landing, where the flat-bottomed side-wheel steamboat was moored to the bank.

Next morning, with real regret, we waved good-bye to our dusky attendants, as they stood on the bank, grouped around a little fire, beside the big, empty ox carts. A dozen miles downstream a row-boat fitted for a spritsail [three- or four-sided sail] put off from the bank. The owner, a countryman from a small ranch, asked for a tow to Corumbá, which we gave. He had with him in the boat his comely brown wife—who was smoking a very large cigar—their two children, a young man, and a couple of trunks and various other belongings. On Christmas Eve we reached Corumbá and rejoined the other members of the expedition.

IV. The Headwaters of the Paraguay

At corumbá our entire party, and all their belongings, came aboard our good little river-boat, the *Nyoac*. Christmas Day saw us making our way steadily upstream against the strong current and between the green and beautiful banks of the upper Paraguay. The shallow little steamer was jammed with men, dogs, rifles, partially cured skins, boxes of provisions, ammunition, tools, and photographic supplies, bags containing tents, cots, bedding, and clothes, saddles, hammocks, and the other necessaries for a trip through the "great wilderness," the Mato Grosso of western Brazil.

It was a brilliantly clear day, and, although of course in that latitude and at that season the heat was intense later on, it was cool and pleasant in the early morning. We sat on the forward deck, admiring the trees on the brink of the sheer riverbanks, the lush, rank grass of the marshes, and the many water birds. The two pilots, one black and one white, stood at the wheel. Colonel Rondon read Thomas à Kempis. Kermit, Cherrie, and Miller squatted outside the railing on the deck over one paddle wheel and put the final touches on the jaguar skins. Fiala satisfied himself that the boxes and bags were in place. It was probable that hardship lay in the future; but the day was our own, and the day was pleasant. In the evening the afterdeck, open all

The Nyoac

around, where we dined, was decorated with green boughs and rushes, and we drank the health of the president of the United States and of the president of Brazil.

Now and then we passed little ranches on the river's edge. This is a fertile land, pleasant to live in, and any settler who is willing to work can earn his living. There are mines; there is water power; there is abundance of rich soil. The country will soon be opened by rail. It offers a fine field for immigration and for agricultural, mining, and business development; and it has a great future.

Cherrie and Miller had secured a little owl a month before in the Chaco, and it was traveling with them in a basket. It was a dear little bird, very tame and affectionate. It liked to be handled and petted; and when Miller, its especial protector, came

74

into the cabin, it would make queer little noises as a signal that it wished to be taken up and perched on his hand.

We saw on the banks, screamers—big, crested waders of archaic type, with spurred wings, rather short bills, and no especial affinities with other modern birds. In one meadow by a pond, we saw three marsh deer, a buck and two does. They stared at us, with their thickly haired tails raised on end. These tails are black underneath, instead of white as in our whitetail deer.

The scientists preparing specimens on the Nyoac

Next day we spent ascending the São Lourenço. It was narrower than the Paraguay, naturally, and the swirling brown current was, if anything, more rapid. The strange tropical trees, standing densely on the banks, were matted together by long bush ropes— lianas, or vines, some very slender and very long. Sometimes we saw brilliant red or blue flowers, or masses of scarlet berries on a queer palm-like tree, or an array of great white blossoms on a much larger tree. In a lagoon bordered by the taquara bamboo, a school of big otters were playing; when they came to the surface, they opened their mouths like seals and made a loud hissing noise. The crested scream-ers, dark gray and as large as turkeys, perched on the very topmost branches of the tallest trees. Hyacinth macaws screamed harshly as they flew across the river. Among the trees was the guan, another pecu-liar bird as big as a big grouse, and with certain hab-its of the wood grouse, but not akin to any northern game bird. The windpipe of the male is very long, extending down to the end of the breastbone, and the bird utters queer guttural screams. A dead caiman floated downstream, with a black vulture devouring it. Capybaras stood or squatted on the banks; sometimes they stared stupidly at us; some-times they plunged into the river at our approach.

At long intervals we passed little clearings. In each stood a house of palm logs, with steeply pitched roof of palm thatch; and nearby were patches of corn and manioc [cassava]. The dusky owner, and perhaps his family, came out on the bank to watch us as we passed. It was a hot day—the thermometer on the deck in the shade stood at nearly 100 degrees Fahrenheit. Biting flies came aboard even when we were in midstream.

Next day we were ascending the Cuiabá River. It had begun raining in the night, and the heavy downpour continued throughout the forenoon. In the morning we halted at a big cattle ranch to get fresh milk and beef. There were various houses, sheds, and corrals near the river's edge, and fifty or sixty milk cows were gathered in one corral. Spurred plover, or lapwings, strolled familiarly among the hens. Parakeets and red-headed tanagers lit in the trees over our heads. A kind of primitive houseboat was moored at the bank. A woman was cooking breakfast over a little stove at one end. The crew were ashore. The boat was one of those which are really stores and which travel up and down these rivers, laden with what the natives most need and stopping wherever there is a ranch. They are the only stores which many of the country dwellers see from year's end to year's end. They float downstream, and upstream are poled by their crew, or now and then get a tow from a steamer. This one had a house with a tin roof; others bear houses with thatched roofs, or with roofs made of hides. The river wound through vast marshes broken by belts of woodland.

The American flag is hoisted at the São João ranch as Colonel Roosevelt steps ashore

On the morning of the 28th, we reached the home buildings of the great São João *fazenda,* the ranch of Senhor João da Costa Marques. Our host himself, and his son, Dom João the younger, who was state secretary of agriculture, and the latter's charming wife, and the president of Mato Grosso, and several other ladies and gentlemen, had come down the river to greet us, from the city of Cuiabá, several hundred miles farther upstream. As usual, we were treated with whole-hearted and generous hospitality. Some miles below the ranch house the party met us, on a stern-wheel steamboat and a launch, both decked with many flags.

The handsome white ranch house stood only a few rods back from the river's brink, in a grassy opening dotted with those noble trees, the royal palms. Other trees, buildings of all kinds, flower gardens, vegetable gardens, fields, corrals, and enclosures with high white walls stood near the house. A detachment of soldiers or state police, with a band, were in front of the house, and two flagpoles, one with the Brazilian flag already hoisted. The American flag was run up on the other as I stepped ashore, while the band played the national anthems of the two countries.

The house held much comfort; and the comfort was all the more appreciated because even indoors the thermometer stood at 97°F. In the late afternoon, heavy rain fell and cooled the air. We were riding at the time. Around the house, the birds were tame: the parrots and parakeets crowded and chattered in the tree tops; jacanas played in the wet ground just back of the garden; ibises and screamers called loudly in the swamps a little distance off.

Until we came actually in sight of this great ranch house, we had been passing through a hot, fertile, pleasant wilderness, where the few small palm-roofed houses, each in its little patch of sugar cane, corn, and manioc stood very many miles apart. One of these little houses stood on an old Indian mound, exactly like the mounds which form the only hillocks along the lower Mississippi and

79

An Indian fishing village on the edge of the river

which are also of Indian origin. These occasional Indian mounds, made ages ago, are the highest bits of ground in the immense swamps of the upper Paraguay region. There are still Indian tribes in this neighborhood.

We passed an Indian fishing village on the edge of the river, with huts, scaffoldings for drying the fish, hammocks, and rude tables. They cultivated patches of bananas and sugar cane. Out in a shallow place in the river was a scaffolding on which the Indians stood to spear fish. The Indians were friendly, peaceable souls, for the most part dressed like the poorer classes among the Brazilians.

Next morning, there was to have been a great rodeo, or roundup, and we determined to have a hunt first, as there were still several kinds of beasts of the chase, notably tapirs and peccaries, of which the naturalists desired specimens. Dom João, our host, and his son accompanied us. Theirs is a noteworthy family. Born in Mato Grosso, in the tropics, our host had the look of a northerner and, although a grandfather, he possessed an abounding vigor and energy such as very few men of any climate or surroundings do possess. All of his sons are doing well. The son who was with us was a stalwart, powerful man, a pleasant companion, an able public servant, a finished horseman, and a skilled hunter. He carried a sharp spear, not a rifle, for in Mato Grosso it is the custom in hunting the jaguar for riflemen and spearmen to go in at him together when he turns at bay, the spearman holding him off if the first shot fails to stop him, so that another shot can be put in. Altogether, our host and his son reminded one of the best type of American ranchmen and planters, of those planters and ranchmen who are adepts in bold and manly field sports, who are capital men of business, and who also often supply to the state skilled and faithful public servants. The hospitality the father and son extended to us was patriarchal: neither, for instance, would sit at table with their guests at the beginning of the formal meals; instead they exercised a close personal supervision over the feast. Our charming hostess, however, sat at the head of the table.

At six in the morning we started, all of us on fine horses. The day was lowering and overcast. A dozen dogs were with us, but only one or two were worth anything. Three or four ordinary countrymen, the ranch hands, or *vaqueiros*, accompanied us; they were mainly of Indian blood and would have been called peons, or *caboclos*,[1] in other parts of Brazil, but were always spoken to and of as *camaradas*. They were, of course, chosen from among the men who were hunters, and each carried his long, rather heavy and clumsy jaguar spear. In front rode our vigorous host and his strapping son, the latter also carrying a jaguar spear. The bridles and saddles of the big ranchmen and of the gentlefolk generally were handsome and were elaborately ornamented with silver. The stirrups, for instance, were not only of silver, but contained so much extra metal in ornamented bars and rings that they would have been awkward for less practiced riders. Indeed, as it was, they were adapted only for the tips of boots with long, pointed toes, and were impossible for our feet; our hosts' stirrups were long, narrow silver slippers. The *camaradas*, on the other hand, had saddles and bridles, and rusty little iron stirrups into which they thrust their naked toes. But all, gentry and commonalty alike, rode equally well and with the same skill and fearlessness.

To see our hosts gallop at headlong speed over any kind of country toward the sound of the dogs with their quarry at bay, or to see them handle their horses in a morass, was a pleasure. It was equally a pleasure to see a *camarada* carrying his heavy spear, leading a hound in a leash, and using his machete to cut his way through the tangled vine ropes of a jungle, all at the same time and all without the slightest reference to the plunges, and the odd and exceedingly jerky behavior, of his wild, half-broken horse—for on such a ranch most of the horses are apt to come in the categories of half-broken or else of broken-down. One dusky tatterdemalion wore a pair of boots from which he had removed the soles, his bare, spur-clad feet projecting from beneath the uppers. He was on a little devil of a stallion, which he rode blindfold for a couple of miles, and there was a regular circus when he removed the bandage; but evidently it never occurred to him that the animal was hardly a comfortable riding horse for a man going out hunting and encumbered with a spear, a machete, and other belongings.

The eight hours that we were out we spent chiefly in splashing across the marshes, with excursions now and then into vine-tangled belts and clumps of timber. Some of the bayous we had to cross were uncomfortably boggy. We had to lead the horses through one, wading ahead of them; and even so, two of them mired down, and their saddles had to be taken off before they could be gotten out. Among the marsh plants were fields and strips of the great caeté rush. These caeté flags towered above the other and lesser marsh plants. They were higher than the heads of the horsemen. Their two or three huge banana-like leaves stood straight up on end. The large brilliant flowers—orange, red, and yellow—were joined into a singularly shaped and solid string or cluster. Hummingbirds buzzed round these flowers; one species, the sickle-billed hummer, has its bill especially adapted for use in these queerly shaped blossoms and gets its food only from them, never appearing around any other plant.

The birds were tame, even those striking and beautiful birds which under man's persecution are so apt to become scarce and shy. The huge jabiru

84

storks, stalking through the water with stately dignity, sometimes refused to fly until we were only a hundred yards off; one of them flew over our heads at a distance of thirty or forty yards. The screamers, crying "curu-curu," and the ibises, wailing dolefully, came even closer. The wonderful hyacinth macaws, in twos and threes, accompanied us at times for several hundred yards, hovering over our heads and uttering their rasping screams.

In one wood, we came on the black howler monkey. The place smelled almost like a menagerie. Not watching with sufficient care, I brushed against a sapling on which the venomous fire ants swarmed. They burnt the skin like red-hot cinders and left little sores. More than once in the drier parts of the marsh we met small caimans making their way from one pool to another. My horse stepped over one before I saw it. The dead carcasses of others showed that on their wanderings they had encountered jaguars or human foes.

We had been out about three hours, when one of the dogs gave tongue [barked or bayed upon seeing game] in a large belt of woodland and jungle to the left of our line of march through the marsh. The other dogs ran to the sound, and after a while the long barking told that the thing, whatever it was, was at bay or else in some refuge. We made our way toward the place on foot. The dogs were baying excitedly at the mouth of a huge hollow log, and very short examination showed us that there were two peccaries within, doubtless a boar and sow. However, just at this moment the peccaries bolted from an unsuspected opening at the other end of the log, dove into the tangle, and instantly disappeared with the hounds in full cry after them. It was twenty minutes later before we again heard the pack baying. With much difficulty, and by the incessant swinging of the machetes, we opened a trail through the network of vines and branches. This time there was only one peccary, the boar. He was at bay in a half-hollow stump. The dogs were about his head, raving with excitement, and it was not possible to use the rifle; so I borrowed the spear of Dom João the younger and killed the fierce little boar therewith.

This was an animal akin to our collared peccary, smaller and less fierce than its white-jawed kinsfolk. It is a valiant and truculent little beast, nevertheless, and if given the chance will bite a piece the size of a teacup out of either man or dog. It is found singly or in small parties, feeds on roots, fruits, grass, and delights to make its home in hollow logs. If taken young, it makes an affectionate and entertaining pet. When the two were in the hollow log, we heard them utter a kind of moaning, or menacing, grunt, long drawn.

An hour or two afterward, we unexpectedly struck the fresh tracks of two jaguars and at once loosed the dogs, who tore off yelling, on the line of the scent. Unfortunately, just at this moment, the clouds burst and a deluge of rain drove in our faces. So heavy was the downpour that the dogs lost the trail and we lost the dogs. We found them again only owing to one of our *caboclos*; an Indian with a queer Mongolian face, and no brain at all that I could discover, apart from his special dealings with wild creatures, cattle, and horses. He rode in a huddle of rags; but nothing escaped his eyes, and he rode anything anywhere. The downpour continued so heavily that we knew the rodeo had been abandoned, and we turned our faces for the long, dripping, splashing ride homeward. Through the gusts of driving rain we could hardly see the way. Once the rain lightened, and half a mile away, the sunshine gleamed through a rift in the leaden cloud mass. Suddenly in this rift of shimmering brightness, there appeared a flock of beautiful white egrets. With strong, graceful wing beats the birds urged their flight, their plumage flashing in the sun. They then crossed the rift and were swallowed in the gray gloom of the day.

On the marsh, the dogs several times roused capybaras. Where there were no ponds of sufficient size, the capybaras sought refuge in flight through the tangled marsh. They ran well. Kermit and Fiala went after one on foot, full speed, for a mile and a half, with two hounds, which then bayed it—literally bayed it [with escape cut off], for the capybara

87

*The cover of the book about palm trees
presented to Colonel Roosevelt*

fought with the courage of a gigantic woodchuck. If the pack overtook a capybara, they of course speedily finished it; but a single dog of our not-very-valorous outfit was not able to overmatch its shrill-squeaking opponent.

Near the ranch house, about forty feet up in a big tree, was a jabiru's nest containing young jabirus. The young birds exercised themselves by walking solemnly round the edge of the nest and opening and shutting their wings. Their heads and necks were down-covered, instead of being naked like those of their parents. Fiala wished to take a moving picture of them while thus engaged, and so, after arranging his machine, he asked Harper to rouse the young birds by throwing a stick up to the nest. He did so, whereupon one young jabiru hastily opened its wings in the desired fashion, at the same time seizing the stick in its bill! It dropped it at once, with an air of comic disappointment, when it found that the stick was not edible.

Next morning, the sky was leaden, and a drenching rain fell as we began our descent of the river. The rainy season had fairly begun. For our good fortune, we were still where we had the cabins aboard the boat, and the ranch house, in which to dry our clothes and soggy shoes; but in the intensely humid atmosphere, hot and steaming, they stayed wet a long time and were still moist when we put them on again. Before we left the house where we had been treated with such courteous hospitality— the finest ranch house in Mato Grosso, on a huge ranch where there are some sixty thousand head of horned cattle—the son of our host, Dom João the younger, the jaguar hunter, presented me with two magnificent volumes on the palms of Brazil, the work of Doctor J. Barbosa Rodrigues, one-time director of the Botanical Gardens at Rio de Janeiro. The two folios were in a box of native cedar. No gift more appropriate, none that I would in the future value more as a reminder of my stay in Mato Grosso, could have been given me.

All that afternoon the rain continued. It was still pouring in torrents when we left the Cuiabá for the São Lourenço and steamed up the latter a few miles before anchoring; Dom João the younger had accompanied us in his launch. The little river steamer was of very open build, as is necessary in such a hot climate; and to keep things dry necessitated also keeping the atmosphere stifling.

[Several days later], we descended the São Lourenço to its junction with the Paraguay, and once more began the ascent of the latter. At one cattle ranch where we stopped, the troupials, or big black and yellow orioles, had built a large colony of their nests on a dead tree near the primitive little ranch house. The birds were breeding; the old ones were feeding the young. In this neighborhood the naturalists found many birds that were new to them, including a tiny woodpecker no bigger than a ruby-crowned kinglet. They had collected two night monkeys—nocturnal monkeys, not as agile as the ordinary monkey; these two were found at dawn, having stayed out too late

The junction of the São Lourenço and the Paraguay is a day's journey above Corumbá. From Corumbá, there is a regular service by shallow steamers to Cuiabá, at the head of one fork, and to São Luis de Cáceres, at the head of the other. The steamers are not powerful, and the voyage to each little city takes a week. There are other forks that are navigable. Above Cuiabá and Cáceres launches go upstream for several days' journey, except during the driest parts of the season. North of this marshy plain lies the highland, the Planalto, where the nights are cool and the climate healthy. But I wish emphatically to record my view that these marshy plains, although hot, are also healthy; and, moreover, the mosquitoes, in most places, are not in sufficient numbers to be a serious pest, although of course there must be nets for protection against them at night. The country is excellently suited for settlement and offers a remarkable field for cattle growing.

Moreover, it is a paradise for water birds and for many other kinds of birds, and for many mammals. It is literally an ideal place in which a field naturalist could spend six months or a year. It is readily accessible, it offers an almost virgin field for work, and the life would be healthy as well as delightfully attractive. The man should have a steam launch. In it he could with comfort cover all parts of the country from south of Coimbra to north of Cuiabá and Cáceres. There would have to be a good deal of collecting (although nothing in the nature of butchery should be tolerated), for the region has only been superficially worked, especially as regards mammals. But if the man were only a collector, he would leave undone the part of the work best worth doing. The region offers extraordinary opportunities for the study of the life histories of birds which, because of their size, their beauty, or their habits, are of exceptional interest.

There was so much of interest all along the banks that we were continually longing to stop and spend days where we were. Mixed flocks of scores of cormorants and darters covered certain trees, both at sunset and after sunrise. Although there was no deep forest, merely belts or fringes of trees along the river, or in patches back of it, we frequently saw monkeys in this riverine tree fringe—active common monkeys and black howlers of more leisurely gait. We saw caimans and capybaras sitting socially near one another on the sandbanks. At night we heard the calling of large flights of tree ducks. These were now the most common of all the ducks, although there were many Muscovy ducks also. The evenings were pleasant and not hot, as we sat on the forward deck; there was a waxing moon. The screamers were among the most noticeable birds. They were noisy; they perched on the very tops of the trees, not down among the branches; and they were not shy. They should be carefully protected by law, for they readily become tame, and then come familiarly round the houses. From the steamer we now and then saw beautiful orchids in the trees on the riverbank.

One afternoon we stopped at the home buildings, or headquarters, of one of the great outlying ranches [Fazenda do Descalvados] of the Brazil Land and Cattle Company, the Farquhar syndicate, under the management of Murdo Mackenzie[2]— than whom we have in the United States no better citizen or more competent cattleman. On this ranch there are some seventy thousand head of stock. We were warmly greeted by McLean, the head of the ranch, and his assistant Ramsey, an old Texan friend. Among the other assistants, all equally cordial, were several Belgians and Frenchmen. The hands were Paraguayans and Brazilians, and a few Indians—a hard-bit set, each of whom always goes armed and knows how to use his arms, for there are constant collisions with cattle thieves from across the Bolivian border, and the ranch has to protect itself. These cowhands, *vaqueiros*, were of the type with which we were now familiar: dark-skinned, lean, hard-faced men, in slouch hats, worn shirts and trousers, and fringed leather aprons, with heavy spurs on their bare feet. They are wonderful riders and ropers, and fear neither man nor beast. I noticed one Indian *vaqueiro* standing in exactly the attitude of a

93

Vaqueiros standing before the ranch house of the Brazil Land and Cattle Company

Shilluk of the White Nile, with the sole of one foot against the other leg, above the knee. This is a region with extraordinary possibilities of cattle raising.

At this ranch, there was a tannery; a slaughter house; a cannery; a church; buildings of various kinds and all degrees of comfort for the thirty or forty families who made the place their headquarters; and the handsome, white, two-story big house, standing among lemon trees; and flamboyants [flame trees] on the river brink. There were all kinds of pets around the house. The most fascinating was a wee, spotted fawn which loved being petted. Half a dozen curassows [dark, crested birds] of different species strolled through the rooms; there were also parrots of several different species, and immediately outside the house, four or five herons, with unclipped wings, which would let us come within a few feet and then fly gracefully off, shortly afterward returning to the same spot. They included big and little white egrets and also the mauve and pearl-colored heron, with a partially black head and many-colored bill, which flies with quick, repeated wing flappings, instead of the usual slow heron wing beats.

By the morning of January 5, we had left the marsh region. There were low hills here and there, and the land was covered with dense forest. From time to time we passed little clearings with palm-thatched houses. We were approaching Cáceres, where the easiest part of our trip would end. We had lived in much comfort on the little steamer. The food was plentiful and the cooking good. At night we slept on deck in cots or hammocks. The mosquitoes were rarely troublesome, although in the daytime we were sometimes bothered by numbers of biting horse flies. The bird life was wonderful. One of the characteristic sights we were always seeing was that of a number of heads and necks of cormorants and snake birds, without any bodies, projecting above water, and disappearing as the steamer approached. Skimmers and thick-billed tern were plentiful here right in the heart of the continent. In addition to the spurred lapwing, characteristic and most interesting resident of most of South America, we found tiny red-legged plover, which also breed and are at home in the tropics.

In the late afternoon of the 5th, we reached the quaint, old-fashioned little town of São Luis de Cáceres, on the outermost fringe of the settled region of the state of Mato Grosso, the last town we should see before reaching the villages of the Amazon. As we approached, we passed half-clad black washerwomen on the river's edge. The men, with the local band, were gathered at the steeply sloping foot of the main street, where the steamer came to her moorings. Groups of women and girls, white and brown, watched us from the low bluff; their skirts and bodices were red, blue, green, of all colors.

Arrival at São Luis de Cáceres

Sigg had gone ahead with much of the baggage; he met us in an improvised motorboat, consisting of a dugout, to the side of which he had clamped our Evinrude motor; he was giving several of the local citizens of prominence a ride, to their huge enjoyment. The streets of the little town were unpaved, with narrow brick sidewalks. The one-story houses were white or blue, with roofs of red tiles and window shutters of latticed woodwork, come down from colonial days and tracing back through Christian and Moorish Portugal to a remote Arab ancestry. Pretty faces, some dark, some light, looked out from these windows; their mothers' mothers, for generations past, must thus have looked out of similar windows in the vanished colonial days. But now, even here in Cáceres, the spirit of the new Brazil is moving; a fine new government school has been started, and we met its principal, an earnest man doing excellent work, one of the many teachers who, during the last few years, have been brought to Mato Grosso from São Paulo, a center of the new educational movement which will do so much for Brazil.

Father Zahm went to spend the night with some French Franciscan friars, capital fellows. I spent the night at the comfortable house of Lieutenant Lyra, a hot-weather house with thick walls, big doors, and an open patio bordered by a gallery. Lieutenant Lyra was to accompany us; he was an old companion of Colonel Rondon's explorations. We visited one or two of the stores to make some final purchases, and in the evening strolled through the dusky streets and under the trees of the plaza; the women and girls sat in groups in the doorways or at the windows, and here and there a stringed instrument tinkled in the darkness.

From Cáceres onward we were entering the scene of Colonel Rondon's explorations. For some eighteen years he was occupied in exploring and in opening telegraph lines through the eastern or north-middle part of the great forest state, the wilderness state of the Mato Grosso —the "great wilderness," or, as Australians would call it, "the bush." Then, in 1907, he began to penetrate the unknown region lying to the north and west. He was the head of the exploring expeditions sent out by the Brazilian government to traverse for the first time this unknown land; to map for the first time the courses of the rivers which from the same divide run into the upper portions of the Tapajós and the Madeira, two of the mighty affluents of the Amazon; and to build telegraph lines across to the Madeira, where a line of Brazilian settlements, connected by steamboat lines and a railroad, again occurs. Three times he penetrated into this absolutely unknown, Indian-haunted wilderness, being absent for a year or two at a time and suffering every imaginable hardship, before he made his way through to the Madeira and completed the telegraph line across.

The officers and men of the Brazilian Army and the civilian scientists who followed him shared the toil and the credit of the task. Some of his men died of beriberi [disease caused by lack of vitamin B]; some were killed or wounded by the Indians; he himself almost died of fever; again and again his whole party was reduced almost to the last extremity by starvation, disease, hardship, and the over-exhaustion due to wearing fatigues. In dealing with the wild, naked savages, he showed a combination

99

of fearlessness, wariness, good judgment, and resolute patience and kindliness. The result was that they ultimately became his firm friends, guarded the telegraph lines, and helped the few soldiers left at the isolated, widely separated little posts.

He and his assistants explored, and mapped for the first time, the Juruena and the Ji-Paraná, two important affluents of the Tapajós and the Madeira, respectively. The Tapajós and the Madeira, like the Orinoco and Rio Negro, have been highways of travel for a couple of centuries. The Madeira (as later the Tapajós) was the chief means of ingress, a century and a half ago, to the little Portuguese settlements of this far interior region of Brazil; one of these little towns, named Mato Grosso, being the original capital of the province. It has long been abandoned by the government, and practically so by its inhabitants, the ruins of palace, fortress, and church now rising amid the rank tropical luxuriance of the wild forest.

The mouths of the main affluents of these highway rivers were as a rule well known. But in many cases, nothing but the mouth was known. The river itself was not known, and it was placed on the map by guesswork. Colonel Rondon found, for example, that the course of the Ji-Paraná was put down on the map two degrees out of its proper place. He, with his party, was the first to find out its sources, the first to traverse its upper course, the first to map its length. He and his assistants performed a similar service for the Juruena, discovering the sources, discovering and descending some of the branches, and for the first time making a trustworthy map of the main river itself, until its junction with the Tapajós. Near the watershed between the Juruena and the Ji-Paraná, he established his farthest station to the westward, named José Bonifácio, after one of the chief republican patriots of Brazil.[3]

A couple of days' march northwestward from this station, he in 1909 came across a part of the stream of a river running northward between the Ji-Paraná and the Juruena; he could only guess where it debouched, believing it to be into the Madeira, although it was possible that it entered the Ji-Paraná or Tapajós. The region through which it flows was unknown, no civilized man having ever penetrated it; and as all conjecture as to what the river was, as to its length, and as to its place of entering into some highway river, was mere guesswork, he had entered it on his sketch maps as the Rio da Dúvida, the River of Doubt.

Among the officers of the Brazilian Army and the scientific civilians who have accompanied him, there have been not only expert cartographers, photographers, and telegraphists, but astronomers, geologists, botanists, and zoologists. Their reports, published in excellent shape by the Brazilian government, make an invaluable series of volumes, reflecting the highest credit on the explorers, and on the government itself. Colonel Rondon's own accounts of his explorations, of the Indian tribes he has visited, and of the beautiful and wonderful things he has seen, possess a peculiar interest.

NOTES

1. *Caboclos*: people of mixed Brazilian Indian and European or African ancestry.

2. Murdo Mackenzie (1850–1939) was a Scottish-born cattleman who emigrated in 1885 to operate the various British cattle operations in the American West. He was recognized nationally through his leadership of cattle industry associations. He became a friend of Roosevelt, who appointed him to the National Conservation Commission in 1908. In 1912, Mackenzie moved to São Paulo to manage the Brazil Land, Cattle, and Packing Company, which owned 2.5 million acres, large cattle herds, packing houses, and its own extensive railroad. He returned to Denver in 1918 and subsequently was a director of the Federal Reserve of Denver.

3. José Bonifácio de Andrada e Silva (1763–1838), Brazilian statesman who played a key role in Brazil's attainment of independence from Portugal.

V. Up the River of Tapirs

AFTER LEAVING CÁCERES, we went up the Sepotuba, which in the local Indian dialect means River of Tapirs. This river is only navigable for boats of size when the water is high. It is a swift, fairly clear stream, rushing down from the Planalto, the high uplands, through the tropical lowland forest. On the right hand, or western bank, and here and there on the left bank, the forest is broken by natural pastures and meadows, and at one of these places, known as Porto do Campo, sixty or seventy miles above the mouth, there is a good-sized cattle ranch. Here we halted, because the launch, and the two *pranchas*—native trading boats with houses on their decks—which it towed, could not carry our entire party and outfit. Accordingly most of the baggage and some of the party were sent ahead to where we were to meet our pack train, at Tapirapuá.

Meanwhile the rest of us made our first camp under tents at Porto do Campo, to wait the return of the boats. The tents were placed in a line, with the tent of Colonel Rondon and the tent in which Kermit and I slept, in the middle, beside one another. In front of these two, on tall poles, stood the Brazilian and American flags; and at sunrise and sunset, the flags were hoisted and hauled down while the trumpet sounded and all of us stood at attention. Camp was pitched beside the ranch buildings. In the trees near the tents grew wonderful violet orchids.

Many birds were around us; I saw some of them, and Cherrie and Miller many, many more. They ranged from party-colored macaws, green parrots, and big gregarious cuckoos down to a brilliant green-and-chestnut kingfisher, 5¼ inches long, and a tiny orange-and-green manakin, smaller than any bird I have ever seen except a hummer. We also saw a bird that really was protectively colored, a kind of whippoorwill, which even the sharp-eyed naturalists could only make out because it moved its head. We saw orange-bellied squirrels with showy orange tails. Lizards were common. We killed our first poisonous snake (the second we had seen), an evil lance-headed jararaca that was swimming the river. We also saw a black-and-orange harmless snake, nearly eight feet long, which we were told was akin to the mussurana; and various other snakes.

One day while paddling in a canoe on the river, hoping that the dogs might drive a tapir to us, they drove into the water a couple of small bush deer instead. There was no point in shooting them; we caught them with ropes thrown over their heads, for the naturalists needed them as specimens, and all of us needed the meat. One of the men was stung by a single big red marabunta wasp. For twenty-four hours he was in great pain and incapacitated for work. In a lagoon, two of the dogs had the tips of their tails bitten off by piranhas as they swam, and the ranch hands told us that in this lagoon one of their hounds had been torn to pieces and completely devoured by the ravenous fish. It was a further illustration of the uncertainty of temper and behavior of these ferocious little monsters. In other lagoons, they had again and again left us and our dogs unmolested. They vary locally in aggressiveness just as sharks and crocodiles in different seas and rivers vary.

On the morning of January 9th, we started out for a tapir hunt. Tapirs are hunted with canoes, as they dwell in thick jungle and take to the water when hounds follow them. In this region, there were extensive papyrus swamps and big lagoons, back from the river, and often the tapirs fled to these for refuge, throwing off the hounds. In these places, it was exceedingly difficult to get them; our best chance was to keep to the river in canoes and paddle toward the spot in the direction of which the hounds, by the noise, seemed to be heading. We started in four canoes. Three of them were Indian dugouts, very low in the water. The fourth was our Canadian canoe, a beauty, light, safe, roomy, made of thin slats of wood and cement-covered canvas. Colonel Rondon, Fiala with his camera, and I went in this canoe, together with two paddlers. The paddlers were natives of the poorer class.

The hounds were at first carried in two of the

Colonel Roosevelt and Colonel Rondon returning from a hunt

dugouts and then let loose on the banks. We went upstream for a couple of hours against the swift current, the paddlers making good headway with their pointed paddles—the broad blade of each paddle was tipped with a long point so that it could be thrust into the mud to keep the low dugout against the bank. The tropical forest came down almost like a wall, the tall trees laced together with vines, and the spaces between their trunks filled with a low, dense jungle. In most places it could only be penetrated by a man with a machete. With few exceptions, the trees were unknown to me, and their native names told me nothing. On most of them the foliage was thick; among the exceptions were the cecropias, growing by preference on new-formed alluvial soil bare of other trees, whose rather scanty leaf bunches were, as I was informed, the favorite food of sloths. We saw one or two squirrels among the trees and a family of monkeys. There were few sandbanks in the river and no waterfowl save an occasional cormorant. But as we pushed along near the shore, where the branches overhung and dipped in the swirling water, we continually roused little flocks of bats. They were hanging from the boughs right over the river, and when our approach roused them, they zigzagged rapidly in front of us for a few rods and then again dove in among the branches.

At last we landed at a point of ground where there was little jungle and where the forest was com-

A tangled forest

posed of palms and was fairly open. It was a lovely bit of forest. The colonel strolled off in one direction, returning an hour later with a squirrel for the naturalists. Meanwhile Fiala and I went through the palm wood to a papyrus swamp. Many trails led through the woods and especially along the borders of the swamp; and, although their principal makers had evidently been cattle, yet there were in them footprints of both tapir and deer. The tapir makes a footprint much like that of a small rhinoceros, being one of the odd-toed ungulates. We could hear the dogs now and then, evidently scattered and running on various trails. They were a worthless lot of cur hounds. They would chase tapir or deer or anything else that ran away from them as long as the trail was easy to follow; but they were not staunch, even after animals that fled, and they would have nothing whatever to do with animals that were formidable.

The colonel returned, and not long afterward, one of the paddlers who had been watching the river called out to us that there was a tapir in the water, a good distance upstream and that two of the other boats were after it. We jumped into the canoe, and the two paddlers dug their blades in the water as they drove her against the strong current, edging over for the opposite bank. The tapir was coming downstream at a great rate, only its queer head above water, while the dugouts were closing rapidly on it, the paddlers uttering loud cries. As the tapir turned slightly to one side or the other, the long, slightly upturned snout and the strongly pronounced arch of the crest along the head and upper neck gave it a marked and unusual aspect. I could not shoot, for it was directly in line with one of the pursuing dugouts. Suddenly it dived, the snout being slightly curved downward as it did so. There was no trace of it; we gazed eagerly in all directions; the dugout in front came alongside our canoe and the paddlers rested, their paddles ready. Then we made out the tapir clambering up the bank. It had dived at right angles to the course it was following and swum underwater to the very edge of the shore, rising under the overhanging tree branches at a point where a drinking trail for game led down a break in the bank. The branches partially hid it, and it was in deep shadow, so that it did not offer a very good shot. My bullet went into its body too far back, and the tapir disappeared in the forest at a gallop as if unhurt, although the bullet really secured it, by making it unwilling to trust to its speed and leave the neighborhood of the water.

Three or four of the hounds were by this time swimming the river, leaving the others yelling on the opposite side; and as soon as the swimmers reached the shore, they were put on the tapir's trail and galloped after it, giving tongue. In a couple of minutes, we saw the tapir take to the water far upstream, and after it we went as fast as the paddles could urge us through the water. We were not in time to head it, but fortunately some of the dogs had come down to the river's edge at the very point where the tapir was about to land and turned it back. Two or three of the dogs were swimming. We were more than half the breadth of the river away from the tapir and somewhat downstream, when it dived. It made an astonishingly long swim beneath the water this time, almost as if it had been a hippopotamus, for it passed completely under our canoe and rose between us and the hither bank. I shot it, the bullet going into its brain, while it was thirty or forty yards from shore. It sank at once.

There was now nothing to do but wait until the body floated. I feared that the strong current would roll it downstream over the riverbed, but my companions assured me that this was not so and that the body would remain where it was until it rose, which would be in an hour or two. They were right, except as to the time. For over a couple of hours we paddled, or anchored ourselves by clutching branches close to the spot, or else drifted down a mile and paddled up again near the shore, to see if the body had caught anywhere. Then we crossed the river and had lunch at the lovely natural picnic ground. We had very nearly given up the tapir, when it suddenly floated only a few rods from where it had sunk. With no little difficulty, the big, round, black body was hoisted into the canoe, and we all turned our prows downstream. The skies had been lowering for some time, and now—too late to interfere with the hunt or cause us any annoyance—a heavy downpour of rain came on and beat upon us. Little we cared, as the canoe raced forward, with the tapir the lying in the bottom, and a dry, comfortable camp ahead of us.

When we reached camp and Father Zahm saw the tapir, he reminded me of something I had completely forgotten. When, some six years previously, he had spoken to me in the White House about taking this South American trip, I had answered that I could not, as I intended to go to Africa, but added that I hoped some day to go to South America and that if I did so, I should try to shoot both a jaguar and a tapir, as they were the characteristic big-game animals of the country. "Well," said Father Zahm, "now you've shot them both!"

The storm continued heavy until after sunset. Then the rain stopped and the full moon broke through the cloud rack. Father Zahm and I walked up and down in the moonlight, talking of many things, from Dante and our own plans for the future, to the deeds and the wanderings of the old-time Spanish conquistadors in their search for the Gilded King, and of the Portuguese adventurers who then divided with them the mastery of the oceans and of the unknown continents beyond.

This was an attractive and interesting camp in

more ways than one. The *vaqueiros* with their wives and families were housed on the two sides of the field in which our tents were pitched. On one side was a big, whitewashed, tile-roofed house in which the foreman dwelt—an olive-skinned, slightly built, wiry man, with an olive-skinned wife and eight as pretty, fair-haired children as one could wish to see. He usually went barefoot, and his manners were not merely good but distinguished. Corrals and outbuildings were near this big house. On the opposite side of the field stood the row of steep-roofed, palm-thatched huts in which the ordinary cowhands lived with their dusky helpmeets and children.

Each night from these palm-thatched quarters we heard the faint sounds of a music that went far back of civilization to a savage ancestry nearby in point of time and otherwise immeasurably remote; for through the still, hot air, under the brilliant moonlight, we heard the monotonous throbbing of a tom-tom drum and the twanging of some old stringed instrument. The small black turkey buzzards, here always called crows, were as tame as chickens near the big house, walking on the ground or perched in the trees beside the corral, waiting for the offal of the slaughtered cattle. Two palm trees near our tent were crowded with the long, hanging nests of one of the cacique orioles. We lived well, with plenty of tapir beef, which was good, and venison of the bush deer, which was excellent; and as much ordinary beef as we wished, and fresh milk, too—a rarity in this country. There were very few mosquitoes, and everything was as comfortable as possible.

The tapir I killed was a big one. I did not wish to kill another, unless, of course, it became advisable to do so for food; whereas I did wish to get some specimens of the big, white-lipped peccary, the *queixada* (pronounced "cashada") of the Brazilians, which would make our collection of the big mammals of the Brazilian forests almost complete.

I spent a couple of days of hard work in getting the big, white-lipped peccaries—white-lipped being rather a misnomer, as the entire under jaw and lower cheek are white. They were said to be found on the other side of, and some distance back from, the river. Colonel Rondon had sent out one of our attendants, an old follower of his, a full-blood Paresi Indian, to look for tracks. This was an excellent man, who dressed and behaved just like the other good men we had, and was called Antonio Paresi. He found the tracks of a herd of thirty or forty *queixadas,* and the following morning we started after them.

On the first day we killed nothing. We were rather too large a party, for one or two of the visiting *fazendeiros* [Brazilian ranchers] came along with their dogs. I doubt whether these men very much wished to overtake our game, for the big peccary is a murderous foe of dogs (and is sometimes dangerous to men). One of their number frankly refused to come or to let his dogs come, explaining that the fierce wild swine were "very badly brought up" (a literal translation of his words) and that respectable dogs and men ought not to go near them. The other *fazendeiros* merely feared for their dogs, a groundless fear, I believe, as I do not think that the dogs could by any exertion have been dragged into dangerous proximity with such foes. The ranch foreman, Benedetto, came with us, and two or three other *camaradas*, including Antonio, the Paresi Indian. The horses were swum across the river, each being led beside a dugout. Then we crossed with the dogs; our horses were saddled; and we started.

It was a picturesque cavalcade. The native hunters, of every shade from white to dark copper, all wore leather leggings that left the soles of their feet bare, and on their bare heels wore spurs with wheels four inches across. They went in single file, for no other mode of travel was possible; and the two or three leading men kept their machetes out and had to cut every yard of our way while we were in the forest. The hunters rode little stallions, and their hounds were gelded.

In one grove the fig trees were killing the palms, just as in Africa they kill the sandalwood trees. In the gloom of this grove, there were no flowers, no bushes; the air was heavy; the ground was brown with moldering leaves. Almost every palm was serving as a prop for a fig tree. The fig trees were in every stage of growth. The youngest ones merely ran up the palms as vines. In the next stage, the vine had thickened and was sending out shoots, wrapping the palm stem in a deadly hold. Some of the shoots were thrown round the stem like the tentacles of an immense cuttlefish. Others looked like claws, which were hooked into every crevice and round every projection. In the stage beyond this, the palm had been killed, and its dead carcass appeared between the big, winding vine trunks; and later the palm had disappeared and the vines had united into a great fig tree. Water stood in black pools at the foot of the murdered trees, and of the trees that had murdered them. There was something sinister and evil in the dark stillness of the grove; it seemed as if sentient beings had writhed themselves round and were strangling other sentient beings.

Now and then we were bitten and stung by the venomous fire ants, and ticks crawled upon us. Once we were assailed by more serious foes, in the shape of a nest of marabunta wasps, not the biggest kind, but about the size of our hornets. We were at the time passing through dense jungle, under tall trees, in a spot where the down timber, holes, tangled creepers, and thorns made the going difficult. The leading men were not assailed, although they were now and then cutting the trail. Colonel Rondon and I were in the middle of the column, and the swarm attacked us; both of us were badly stung on the face, neck, and hands, the colonel even more severely than I was. He wheeled and rode to the rear and I to the front; our horses were stung too; and we went at a rate that a moment previously I would have deemed impossible over such ground.

In these forests the multitude of insects that bite, sting, devour, and prey upon other creatures, often with accompaniments of atrocious suffering, passes belief. The very pathetic myth of "beneficent nature" could not deceive even the least wise being if he once saw for himself the iron cruelty of life in the tropics. Of course "nature"—in common parlance a wholly inaccurate term, by the way, especially when used as if to express a single entity—is entirely ruthless, no less so as regards types than as regards individuals, and entirely indifferent to good or evil, and works out her ends or no ends with utter disregard of pain and woe.

The following morning at sunrise we started again. This time only Colonel. Rondon and I went with Benedetto and Antonio the Indian. We brought along four dogs, which it was fondly hoped might chase the *queixadas*. Two of them disappeared on the track of a tapir, and we saw them no more; one of the others promptly fled when we came across the tracks of our game and would not even venture after them in our company; the remaining

117

one did not actually run away and occasionally gave tongue, but could not be persuaded to advance unless there was a man ahead of him. However, Colonel Rondon, Benedetto, and Antonio formed a trio of hunters who could do fairly well without dogs.

After four hours of riding, Benedetto, who was in the lead, suddenly stopped and pointed downward. We were riding along a grassy intervale between masses of forest, and he had found the fresh track of a herd of big peccaries crossing from left to right. There were apparently thirty or forty in the herd. The small peccaries go singly or in small parties and when chased take refuge in holes or hollow logs, where they show valiant fight; but the big peccaries go in herds of considerable size and are so truculent that they are reluctant to run and prefer either to move slowly off chattering their tusks and grunting, or else actually to charge. Where much persecuted, the survivors gradually grow more willing to run, but their instinct is not to run but to trust to their truculence and their mass action for safety. They inflict a fearful bite and frequently kill dogs.

They often charge the hunters, and I have heard of men being badly wounded by them, while almost every man who hunts them often is occasionally forced to scramble up a tree to avoid a charge. But I have never heard of a man being killed by them. They sometimes surround the tree in which the man has taken refuge and keep him up it. Cherrie, on one occasion in Costa Rica, was thus kept up a tree for several hours by a great herd of three or four hundred of these peccaries; and this although he killed several of them. Ordinarily, however, after making their charge, they do not turn but pass on out of sight. Their great foe is the jaguar, but unless he exercises much caution, they will turn the tables on him. Cherrie, also in Costa Rica, came on the body of a jaguar which had evidently been killed by a herd of peccaries some twenty-four hours previously. The ground was trampled up by their hoofs, and the carcass was rent and slit into pieces.

Benedetto, as soon as we discovered the tracks, slipped off his horse, changed his leggings for sandals, threw his rifle over his arm, and took the trail of the herd, followed by the only dog which would accompany him. The peccaries had gone into a broad belt of forest, with a marsh on the farther side. At first Antonio led the colonel and me, all of us on horseback, at a canter round this belt to the marsh side, thinking the peccaries had gone almost through it. But we could hear nothing. The dog only occasionally barked, and then not loudly. Finally we heard a shot. Benedetto had found the herd, which showed no fear of him; he had backed out and fired a signal shot. We all three went into the forest on foot toward where the shot had been fired. It was dense jungle and stiflingly hot. We could not see clearly for more than a few feet, or move easily without free use of the machetes. Soon we heard the ominous groaning of the herd, in front of us, and almost on each side. Then Benedetto joined us, and the dog appeared in the rear.

We moved slowly forward, toward the sound of the fierce moaning grunts which were varied at times by a castanet chattering of the tusks. Then we dimly made out the dark forms of the peccaries moving very slowly to the left. My companions each chose a tree to climb at need and pointed out one for me. I fired at the half-seen form of a hog, through the vines, leaves, and branches; the colonel fired; I fired three more shots at other hogs; and the Indian also fired. The peccaries did not charge; walking and trotting, with bristles erect, groaning and clacking their tusks, they disappeared into the jungle. We could not see one of them clearly; and not one was left dead. But a few paces on, we came across one of my wounded ones, standing at bay by a palm trunk; and I killed it forthwith.

The dog would not even trail the wounded ones, but here Antonio came to the front. With eyes almost as quick and sure as those of a wild beast, he had watched after every shot and was able to tell the results in each case. He said that in addition to the one I had just killed, I had wounded two others so seriously that he did not think they would go far and that Colonel Rondon and he himself had each badly wounded one; and, moreover, he showed the trails each wounded animal had taken. The event justified him. In a few minutes, we found my second one dead. Then we found Antonio's. Then we found my third one alive and at bay, and I killed it with another bullet. Finally, we found the colonel's. I told him I should ask the authorities of the American museum to mount his and one or two of mine in a group, to commemorate our hunting together.

On the ride home, we saw a buck of the small species of bush deer. It was only a patch of red in the bush, a good distance off, but I was lucky enough to hit it. In spite of its small size, it was a full-grown male, of a species we had not yet obtained. The antlers had recently been shed, and the new antler growth had just begun. A great jabiru stork let us ride by him 150 yards off without thinking it worthwhile to take flight. This day we saw many of the beautiful violet orchids; and in the swamps were multitudes of flowers, red, yellow, lilac, of which I did not know the names.

The country along this river is a fine natural cattle country, and some day it will surely see a great development. It was opened to development by Colonel Rondon only five or six years ago. Already an occasional cattle ranch is to be found along the banks. When railroads are built into these interior portions of Mato Grosso, the whole region will grow and thrive amazingly—and so will the rail-

Colonel Rondon and Colonel Roosevelt make a noontime halt

roads. The growth will not be merely material. An immense amount will be done in education, using the word *education* in its broadest and most accurate sense, as applying to both mind and spirit, to both the child and the man.

Colonel Rondon is not merely an explorer. He has been and is now a leader in the movement for the vital betterment of his people, the people of Mato Grosso. The poorer people of the backcountry everywhere suffer because of the harsh and improper laws of debt. In practice, these laws have resulted in establishing a system of peonage, such as has grown up here and there in our own nation. A radical change is needed in this matter; and the colonel is fighting for the change. In school matters, the colonel has precisely the ideas of our wisest and most advanced men and women in the United States. Cherrie—who is not only an exceedingly efficient naturalist and explorer in the tropics, but is also a thoroughly good citizen at home—is the chairman of the school board of the town of Newfane, in Vermont. He and the colonel, and Kermit and I, talked over school matters at length and were in hearty accord as to the vital educational needs of both Brazil and the United States: the need of combining industrial with purely mental training, and the need of having the widespread popular education, which is and must be supported and paid for by the government, made a purely governmental

Colonel Rondon

and absolutely nonsectarian function, administered by the state alone, without interference with, nor furtherance of, the beliefs of any reputable church.

The colonel is also head of the Indian service of Brazil, being what corresponds roughly with our commissioner of Indian affairs. Here, also, he is taking the exact view that is taken in the United States by the staunchest and wisest friends of the Indians. The Indians must be treated with intelligent and sympathetic understanding, no less than with justice and firmness; and until they become citizens, absorbed into the general body politic, they must be the wards of the nation, and not of any private association, lay or clerical, no matter how well-meaning.

The Sepotuba River was scientifically explored and mapped for the first time by Colonel Rondon in 1908, as head of the Brazilian Telegraphic Commission. This was during the second year of his exploration and opening of the unknown northwestern wilderness of Mato Grosso. Most of this wilderness had never previously been trodden by the foot of a civilized man. Not only were careful maps made and much other scientific work accomplished, but posts were established and telegraph lines constructed.

When Colonel Rondon began the work, he was a major. He was given two promotions, to lieutenant colonel and colonel, while absent in the wilderness. His longest and most important exploring trip, and the one fraught with most danger and hardship, was begun by him in 1909, on May 3rd, the anniversary of the discovery of Brazil. He left Tapirapuá that day, and he reached the Madeira River on Christmas, December 25, of the same year, having descended the Ji-Paraná. The mouth of this river had long been known, but its upper course for half its length was absolutely unknown when Rondon descended it. Among those who took part under him in this piece of exploration were the present Captain Amilcar and Lieutenant Lyra, and two better or more efficient men for such wilderness work it would be impossible to find. They acted as his two chief assistants on our trip. In 1909, the party exhausted all their food, including even the salt, by August. For the last four months they lived exclusively on the game they killed, on fruits, and on wild honey. Their equipage was what the men could carry on their backs. By the time the party reached the Madeira, they were worn out by fatigue, exposure, and semi-starvation; and their enfeebled bodies were racked by fever.

The work of exploration accomplished by Colonel Rondon and his associates during these years was as remarkable as, and in its results even more important than, any similar work undertaken elsewhere on the globe at or about the same time. Its value was recognized in Brazil. It received no recognition by the geographical societies of Europe or the United States.

The work done by the original explorers of such a wilderness necessitates the undergoing of untold hardship and danger. Their successors, even their immediate successors, have a relatively easy time. Soon the road becomes so well beaten that it can be traversed without hardship by any man who does not venture from it—although if he goes off into the wilderness for even a day, hunting or collecting, he will have a slight taste of what his predecessors endured. The wilderness explored by Colonel Rondon is not yet wholly subdued and still holds menace to human life. At Cáceres, he received notice of the death of one of his gallant subordinates, Captain Cardoso. He died from beriberi, far out in the wilderness along our proposed line of march. Colonel Rondon also received news that a boat ascending the Ji-Paraná, to carry provisions to meet those of our party who were to descend that stream, had been upset, the provisions lost, and three men drowned.

The risk and hardship are such that the ordinary men, the *camaradas*, do not like to go into the wilderness. The men who go with the Telegraphic Commission on the rougher and wilder work are paid seven times as much as they earn in civilization. On this trip of ours, Colonel Rondon met with much difficulty in securing someone who could cook. He asked the cook on the little steamer *Nyoac* to go with us; but the cook with unaffected horror responded: "Senhor, I have never done anything to deserve punishment!"

Five days after leaving us, the launch, with one of the native trading boats lashed alongside, returned. On the 13th, we broke camp, loaded ourselves and all our belongings on the launch and the houseboat, and started upstream for Tapirapuã. All told, there were about thirty men, with five dogs and tents, bedding and provisions; fresh beef, growing rapidly less fresh; skins—all and everything jammed together.

It rained most of the first day and part of the first night. After that, the weather was generally overcast and pleasant for traveling; but sometimes rain and torrid sunshine alternated. The cooking—and it was good cooking—was done at a funny little open-air fireplace, with two or three cooking pots placed at the stern of the houseboat.

The fireplace was a platform of earth, taken from anthills, and heaped and spread on the boards of the boat. Around it, the dusky cook worked with philosophic solemnity in rain and shine. Our attendants, friendly souls with skins of every shade and hue, slept most of the time, curled up among boxes, bundles, and slabs of beef. An enormous land turtle was tethered toward the bow of the houseboat. When the men slept too near it, it made futile efforts to scramble over them; and in return, now and then, one of them gravely used it for a seat.

Slowly, the throbbing engine drove the launch and its unwieldy side partner against the swift current. The river had risen. We made about a mile and a half an hour. Ahead of us the brown water street stretched in curves between endless walls of dense tropical forest. It was like passing through a gigantic greenhouse. Uauássú and buriti palms, cecropias, huge figs, feathery bamboos, strange yellow-stemmed trees, low trees with enormous leaves, tall trees with foliage as delicate as lace, trees with buttressed trunks, trees with boles rising smooth and straight to lofty heights, all woven together by a tangle of vines, crowded down to the edge of the river. Their drooping branches hung down to the water, forming a screen through which it was impossible to see the bank and exceedingly difficult to penetrate to the bank. Rarely one of them showed flowers—large white blossoms, or small red or yellow blossoms. More often the lilac flowers of the begonia vine made large patches of color. Innumerable epiphytes [air plants] covered the limbs and even grew on the roughened trunks. We saw little bird life—a darter now and then, and kingfishers flitting from perch to perch.

At long intervals we passed a ranch. At one, the large, red-tiled, whitewashed house stood on a grassy slope behind mango trees. The wooden shutters were thrown back from the unglazed windows, and the big rooms were utterly bare—not a book, not an ornament. A palm, loaded with scores of the pendulous nests of the troupials, stood near the door. Behind were orange trees and coffee plants, and nearby fields of bananas, rice, and tobacco. The sallow foreman was courteous and hospitable. His dark-skinned womenfolk kept in the furtive background. Like most of the ranches, it was owned by a company with headquarters at Cáceres.

The trip was pleasant and interesting, although there was not much to do on the boat. It was too crowded to move around, save with a definite purpose. We enjoyed the scenery; we talked—in English, Portuguese, bad French, and broken German. Some of us wrote. Fiala made sketches of improved tents, hammocks, and other field equipment, suggested by what he had already seen. Some of us read books. Colonel Rondon, neat, trim, alert, and soldierly, studied a standard work on applied geographical astronomy. Father Zahm read a novel by Fogazzaro. Kermit read Camoens [sic][1] and a couple of Brazilian novels, *O Guarani* and *Innocencia*. My own reading varied from *Quentin Durward* and Gibbon to the *Chanson de Roland*. Miller took out his little pet owl Moses, from the basket in which Moses dwelt, and gave him food and water. Moses crooned and chuckled gratefully when he was stroked and tickled.

Late the first evening, we moored to the bank by a little *fazenda* of the poorer type. The houses were of palm leaves. Even the walls were made of the huge fronds or leafy branches of the uauássú palm, stuck upright in the ground and the blades plaited together. Some of us went ashore. Some stayed on the boats. There were no mosquitoes, the weather was not oppressively hot, and we slept well. By five o'clock next morning, we had each drunk a cup of delicious Brazilian coffee, and the boats were underway.

All day we steamed slowly upstream. We passed two or three *fazendas*. At one, where we halted to get milk, the trees were overgrown with pretty little yellow orchids. At dark, we moored at a spot where there were no branches to prevent our placing the boats directly alongside the bank. There were hardly any mosquitoes. Most of the party took their hammocks ashore, and the camp was pitched amid singularly beautiful surroundings. The trees were uauássú palms, some with the fronds cresting very tall trunks, some with the fronds—seemingly longer—rising almost from the ground. The fronds were of great length; some could not have been less than fifty feet long. Bushes and tall grass, dew-drenched and glittering with the green of emeralds, grew in the open spaces between.

We left at sunrise the following morning. One of the sailors had strayed inland. He got turned round and could not find the river, and we started before discovering his absence. We stopped at once, and with much difficulty, he forced his way through the vine-laced and thorn-guarded jungle toward the sound of the launch's engines and of the bugle which was blown. In this dense jungle, when the sun is behind clouds, a man without a compass who strays a hundred yards from the river may readily become hopelessly lost.

As we ascended the river the uauássú palms became constantly more numerous. At this point, for many miles, they gave their own character to the forest on the riverbanks. Everywhere their long, curving fronds rose among the other trees, and in places, their lofty trunks made them hold their heads higher than the other trees. But they were never as tall as the giants among the ordinary trees. On one towering palm we noticed a mass of beautiful violet orchids growing from the side of the trunk, halfway to the top. On another big tree, not a palm, which stood in a little opening, there hung well over a hundred troupials' nests. Besides two or three small ranches, we this day passed a large ranch. The various houses and sheds, all palm-thatched, stood by the river in a big space of cleared ground, dotted with uauássú palms. A native houseboat was moored by the bank. Women and children looked from the unglazed windows of the houses; men stood in front of them. The biggest house was enclosed by a stockade of palm logs, thrust end-on into the ground. Cows and oxen grazed round about; and carts with solid wheels, each wheel made of a single disk of wood, were tilted on their poles.

We made our noonday halt on an island where very tall trees grew, bearing fruits that were pleasant to the taste. Other trees on the island were covered with rich red and yellow blossoms, and masses of delicate blue flowers and of star-shaped white flowers grew underfoot. Hither and thither across the surface of the river flew swallows, with so much white in their plumage that as they flashed in the sun, they seemed to have snow-white bodies, borne by dark wings. The current of the river grew swifter; there were stretches of broken water that were almost rapids; the laboring engine strained and sobbed as with increasing difficulty it urged forward the launch and her clumsy consort. At nightfall we moored beside the bank, where the forest was open enough to permit a comfortable camp. That night the ants ate large holes in Miller's mosquito netting and almost devoured his socks and shoelaces.

At sunrise we again started. There were occasional stretches of swift, broken water, almost rapids, in the river; everywhere the current was swift, and our progress was slow. The *prancha* was towed at the end of a hawser, and her crew poled. Even thus we only just made the riffle in more than one case. Two or three times cormorants and snake birds, perched on snags in the river or on trees alongside it, permitted the boat to come within a

Toucan

few yards. In one piece of high forest we saw a party of toucans, conspicuous even among the treetops because of their huge bills and the leisurely expertness with which they crawled, climbed, and hopped among the branches. We went by several *fazendas.*

Shortly before noon—January 16—we reached Tapirapuã, the headquarters of the Telegraphic Commission. It was an attractive place, on the riverfront, and it was gaily bedecked with flags, not only those of Brazil and the United States, but of all the other American republics, in our honor. There was a large, green square, with trees standing in the middle of it. On one side of this square were the buildings of the Telegraphic Commission; on the other, those of a big ranch, of which this is the headquarters. In addition, there were stables, sheds, outhouses, and corrals; and there were cultivated fields nearby. Milk cows, beef cattle, oxen, and mules wandered almost at will. There were two or three wagons and carts, and a traction automobile, used in the construction of the telegraph line, but not available in the rainy season, at the time of our trip.

Here we were to begin our trip overland, on pack mules and pack oxen, scores of which had been gathered to meet us. Several days were needed to apportion the loads and arrange for the several divisions in which it was necessary that so large a party should attempt the long wilderness march, through a country where there was not much food for man or beast, and where it was always possible to run into a district in which fatal cattle or horse diseases were prevalent.

Fiala, with his usual efficiency, took charge of handling the outfit of the American portion of the expedition, with Sigg as an active and useful assistant. Harper, who like the others worked with whole-hearted zeal and cheerfulness, also helped him, except when he was engaged in helping the naturalists. The two latter, Cherrie and Miller, had so far done the hardest and the best work of the expedition. They had collected about a thousand birds and 250 mammals. It was not probable that they would do as well during the remainder of our trip, for we intended thenceforth to halt as little, and march as steadily, as the country, the weather, and the condition of our means of transportation permitted.

Assembling the pack train for the journey

I kept continually wishing that they had more time in which to study the absorbingly interesting life histories of the beautiful and wonderful beasts and birds we were all the time seeing. Every first-rate museum must still employ competent collectors; but I think that a museum could now confer most lasting benefit, and could do work of most permanent good, by sending out into the immense wildernesses, where wild nature is at her best, trained observers with the gift of recording what they have observed. Such men should be collectors, for collecting is still necessary; but they should also, and indeed primarily, be able themselves to see, and to set vividly before the eyes of others, the full life histories of the creatures that dwell in the waste spaces of the world.

At this camp the heat was great—from 91 to 104 Fahrenheit—and the air very heavy, being saturated with moisture; and there were many rainstorms. But there were no mosquitoes, and we were very comfortable. Thanks to the neighborhood of the ranch, we fared sumptuously, with plenty of beef, chickens, and fresh milk. Two of the Brazilian dishes were delicious: *canja*, a thick soup of chicken and rice, the best soup a hungry man ever tasted; and beef chopped in rather small pieces and served with a well-flavored but simple gravy. The mule allotted me as a riding beast was a powerful animal, with easy gaits. The Brazilian government had waiting for me a very handsome silver-mounted saddle and bridle; I was much pleased with both. However, my exceedingly rough and shabby clothing made an incongruous contrast.

At Tapirapuá we broke up our baggage—as well as our party. We sent forward the Canadian canoe—which, with the motor engine and some kerosene, went in a cart drawn by six oxen—and a hundred sealed tin cases of provisions, each containing rations for a day for six men. They had been put up in New York under the special direction of Fiala, for use when we got where we wished to take good and varied food in small compass. All the skins, skulls, and alcoholic specimens, and all the baggage not absolutely necessary, were sent back down the Paraguay and to New York, in charge of Harper. The separate baggage trains, under the charge of Captain Amilcar, were organized to go in one detachment. The main body of the expedition, consisting of the American members and of Colonel Rondon, Lieutenant Lyra, and Doctor [José Antonio] Cajazeira, with their baggage and provisions, formed another detachment.

NOTES

1. Luís Vaz de Camões (1524/25–80), Portugal's great national poet.

VI. Through the Highland Wilderness of Western Brazil

FROM TAPIRAPUÁ our course lay northward up to and across the Planalto, the highland wilderness of Brazil. From the edges of this highland country, which is geologically very ancient, the affluents of the Amazon to the north, and of the Plate to the south, flow, with immense and devious loops and windings.

Two days before we ourselves started with our mule train, a train of pack oxen left, loaded with provisions, tools, and other things, which we would not need until, after a month or six weeks, we began our descent into the valley of the Amazon. There were about seventy oxen. Most of them were well broken, but there were about a score which were either not broken at all or else very badly broken. These were loaded with much difficulty and bucked like wild broncos. Again and again they scattered their loads over the corral and over the first part of the road. The pack men, however—copper-colored, black, and dusky-white—were not only masters of their art, but possessed tempers that could not be ruffled; when they showed severity, it was because severity was needed and not because they were angry. They finally got all their long-horned beasts loaded and started on the trail with them.

On January 21, we ourselves started, with the mule train. Of course, as always in such a journey, there was some confusion before the men and the animals of the train settled down to the routine performance of duty. In addition to the pack animals we all had riding mules. The first day we journeyed about twelve miles, then crossing the Sepotuba and camping beside it, below a series of falls, or rather rapids. The country was level. It was a great natural pasture, covered with a very open forest of low, twisted trees, bearing a superficial likeness to the Cross Timbers [region] of Texas and Oklahoma. It is as well fitted for stock raising as Oklahoma; and there is also much fine agricultural land, while the river will ultimately yield electric power. It is a fine country for settlement. The heat is great at noon, but the nights are not uncomfortable.

We were supposed to be in the middle of the rainy season, but hitherto most of the days had been fine, varied with showers. The astonishing thing was the absence of mosquitoes. Insect pests that work by day can be stood, and especially by settlers, because they are far less serious foes in the clearings than in the woods. The mosquitoes and other night foes offer the really serious and unpleasant problem, because they break one's rest. Hitherto, during our travels up the Paraguay and its tributaries, in this level, marshy tropical region of western Brazil, we had practically not been bothered by mosquitoes at all in our home camps. Out in the woods, they were at times a serious nuisance, and Cherrie and Miller had been subjected to real torment by them during some of their special expeditions; but there were practically none on the ranches and in our camps in the open fields by the river, even when marshes were close by. I was puzzled—and delighted—by their absence. Settlers need not be deterred from coming to this region by the fear of insect foes.

This does not mean that there are not such foes. Outside of the clearings, and off the beaten tracks of travel, they teem. There are ticks, poisonous ants, wasps—of which some species are really serious menaces—biting flies, and gnats. I merely mean that, unlike so many other tropical regions, this particular region is, from the standpoint of the settler and the ordinary traveler, relatively free from insect pests and a pleasant place of residence. The original explorer, and to an only less degree the hardworking field naturalist or big-game hunter, have to face these pests, just as they have to face countless risks, hardships, and difficulties. This is inherent in their several professions or avocations. Many regions in the United States where life is now absolutely comfortable and easygoing offered most formidable problems to the first explorers a century or two ago. We must not fall into the foolish error of thinking that the first explorers need not suffer terrible hardships, merely because the ordinary travelers, and even the settlers who come after them, do not have to endure such danger, privation, and wearing fatigue—although the first among the genuine settlers also have to undergo exceedingly trying experiences. The early explorers and adventurers make fairly well-beaten trails at heavy cost to themselves. Ordinary travelers, with little discomfort and no danger, can then traverse these trails; but it is incumbent on them neither to boast of their own experiences nor to misjudge the efforts of the pioneers because, thanks to these very efforts, their own lines fall in pleasant places.

The ordinary traveler, who never goes off the beaten route and who on this beaten route is carried by others, without himself doing anything or risking anything, does not need to show much more initiative and intelligence than an express package. He does nothing; others do all the work, show all the forethought, take all the risk—and are entitled to all the credit. He and his valise are carried in practically the same fashion, and for each the achievement stands about on the same plane.

If this kind of traveler is a writer, he can of course do admirable work, work of the highest value; but the value comes because he is a writer and observer, not because of any particular credit that attaches to him as a traveler. When a man travels across Arizona in a Pullman car, we do not think of him as having performed a feat bearing even the most remote resemblance to the feats of the first explorers of those waterless wastes; whatever admiration we feel in connection with his trip is reserved for the traffic superintendent, engineer, fireman, and brakeman. But as regards the less-known continents, such as South America, we sometimes fail to remember these obvious truths.

There yet remains plenty of exploring work to be done in South America, as hard, as dangerous, and almost as important as any that has already been done, work such as has recently been done, or is now being done, by men and women such as [John D.] Haseman, [William Curtis] Farrabee, and Miss [Maria Emilie] Snethlage.[1] The collecting naturalists who go into the wilds and do first-class work encounter every kind of risk and undergo every kind of hardship and exertion. Explorers and naturalists of the right type have open to them in South America a field of extraordinary attraction and difficulty. But to excavate ruins that have already long been known, to visit out-of-the-way towns that date from colonial days, to traverse old, even if uncomfortable, routes of travel, or to ascend or descend highway rivers like the Amazon, the Paraguay, and the lower Orinoco—all of these exploits are well worth performing, but they in no sense represent exploration or adventure, and they do not entitle the performer, no matter how well he writes and no matter how much of real value he contributes to human knowledge, to compare himself in any way with the real wilderness wanderer, or to criticize the latter. Such a performance entails no hardship or difficulty worth heeding. Its value depends purely on observation, not on action. The man *does* little; he merely records what he sees. He is only the man of the beaten routes. The true wilderness wanderer, on the contrary, must be a man of action as well as of observation. He must have the heart and the body to do and to endure, no less than the eye to see and the brain to note and record.

Let me make it clear that I am not depreciating the excellent work of so many of the men who have not gone off the beaten trails. I merely wish to make it plain that this excellent work must not be put in the class with that of the wilderness explorer. It is excellent work, nevertheless, and has its place, just as the work of the true explorer has its place. Both stand in sharpest contrast with the actions of those alleged explorers, among whom Mr. [Arnold Henry] Savage Landor[2] stands in unpleasant prominence.

From the Sepotuba rapids, our course at the outset lay westward. The first day's march away from the river lay through dense tropical forest. Away from the broad, beaten route, every step of a man's progress represented slashing a trail with the machete through the tangle of bushes, low trees, thorny scrub, and interlaced creepers. There were palms of new kinds, very tall, slender, straight, and graceful, with rather short and few fronds. The wild plantains, or *pacovas*, thronged the spaces among the trunks of the tall trees; their boles were short, and their broad, erect leaves gigantic; they bore brilliant red-and-orange flowers. There were trees whose trunks bellied into huge swellings. There were towering trees with buttressed trunks, whose leaves made a fretwork against the sky far overhead. Gorgeous red-and-green trogons [birds], with long tails, perched motionless on the lower branches and uttered a loud, thrice-repeated whistle. We heard the calling of the false bellbird, which is gray instead of white like the true bellbirds; it keeps among the very topmost branches. Heavy rain fell shortly after we reached our camping place.

Next morning at sunrise, we climbed a steep slope to the edge of the Paresi plateau, at a level of about two thousand feet above the sea. We were on the Planalto, the high central plain of Brazil, the healthy land of dry air, of cool nights, of clear, running brooks. The sun was directly behind us when we topped the rise. Reining in, we looked back over the vast Paraguayan marshes, shimmering in the long morning lights. Then, turning again, we rode forward, casting shadows far before us. It was twenty miles to the next water, and in hot weather, the journey across this waterless, shadeless, sandy stretch of country is hard on the mules and oxen. But on this day the sky speedily grew overcast, and a cool wind blew in our faces as we traveled at a quick, running walk over the immense rolling plain. The ground was sandy; it was covered with grass and with a sparse growth of stunted, twisted trees, never more than a few feet high. There were rheas—ostriches—and small pampas deer on this plain; the coloration of the rheas made it difficult to see them at a distance, whereas the bright red coats of the little deer, and their uplifted flags as they ran, advertised them afar off. We also saw the footprints of cougars and of the small-toothed, big, red wolf. Cougars are the most inveterate enemies of these small South American deer, both those of the open grassy plain and those of the forest.

It is not nearly as easy to get lost on these open plains as in the dense forest; and where there is a long, reasonably straight road or river to come back to, a man even without a compass is safe. But in these thick South American forests, especially on cloudy days, a compass is an absolute necessity. We were struck by the fact that the native hunters and ranchmen on such days continually lost themselves and, if permitted, traveled for miles through the forest either in circles or in exactly the wrong direction. They had no such sense of direction as the forest-dwelling Ndorobo hunters in Africa had, or as the true forest-dwelling Indians of South America are said to have. On certainly half a dozen occasions, our guides went completely astray, and we had to take command, to disregard their assertions, and to lead the way aright by sole reliance on our compasses.

On this cool day we traveled well. The air was wonderful; the vast open spaces gave a sense of abounding vigor and freedom. Early in the afternoon we reached a station made by Colonel Rondon in the course of his first explorations. There were several houses with whitewashed walls, stone floors, and tiled or thatched roofs. They stood in a wide, gently sloping valley. Through it ran a rapid brook of cool water, in which we enjoyed delightful baths. The heavy, intensely humid atmosphere of the low, marshy plains had gone; the air was clear and fresh; the sky was brilliant; far and wide we looked over a landscape that seemed limitless; the breeze that blew in our faces might have come from our own northern plains. The midday sun was very hot, but it was hard to realize that we were in the Torrid Zone. There were no mosquitoes, so that we never put up our nets when we went to bed but wrapped ourselves in our blankets and slept soundly through the cool, pleasant nights. Surely in the future this region will be the home of a healthy, highly civilized population. It is good for cattle raising, and the valleys are fitted for agriculture. From June to September the nights are often really cold. Any sound northern race could live here; and in such a land, with such a climate, there would be much joy of living.

The big motor vans filled with baggage

On these plains the Telegraphic Commission uses motor trucks; and these now served to relieve the mules and oxen, for some of them, especially among the oxen, already showed the effects of the strain. Traveling in a wild country with a pack train is not easy on the pack animals. It was strange to see these big motor vans out in the wilderness where there was not a settler, not a civilized man except the employees of the Telegraphic Commission. They were handled by Lieutenant [Alcides] Lauriadó [de Sant'Anna], who, with Lieutenant [Joaquim Vieira de] Mello [Filho], had taken special charge of our transport service; both were exceptionally good and competent men.

148

The following day we again rode on across the Planalto. In the early afternoon, in the midst of a downpour of rain, we crossed the divide between the basins of the Paraguay and the Amazon. That evening we camped on a brook whose waters ultimately ran into the Tapajós. The rain fell throughout the afternoon, now lightly, now heavily, and the mule train did not get up until dark. But enough tents and flies [tents without walls] were pitched to shelter all of us. Fires were lit, and—after a fourteen hours' fast—we feasted royally on beans and rice and pork and beef, seated around ox skins spread upon the ground. The sky cleared; the stars blazed down through the cool night; and wrapped in our blankets, we slept soundly, warm and comfortable.

Next morning the trail had turned, and our course led northward and at times east of north. We traversed the same high, rolling plains of coarse grass and stunted trees. Kermit, riding a big, iron-mouthed, bull-headed white mule, rode off to one side on a hunt and rejoined the line of march carrying two bucks of the little pampas deer, or field deer, behind his saddle. These deer are very pretty and graceful, with a tail like that of the Colombian blacktail. Standing motionless facing one, in the sparse scrub, they are hard to make out; if seen sideways, the reddish of their coats, contrasted with the greens and grays of the landscape, betrays them; and when they bound off, the upraised white tail is very conspicuous. They carefully avoid the woods in which their cousins, the little bush deer, are found and go singly or in couples. Their odor can be made out at quite a distance, but it is not rank. They still carried their antlers. Their venison was delicious.

At this camp the auto vans again joined us. They were to go direct to the first telegraph station, at the great falls of the Utiariti, on the Rio Papagaio. Of course they traveled faster than the mule train. Father Zahm, attended by Sigg, started for the falls in them. Cherrie and Miller also went in them, because they had found that it was very difficult to collect birds, and especially mammals, when we were moving every day, packing up early each morning, and the mule train arriving late in the afternoon or not until nightfall. Moreover, there was much rain, which made it difficult to work except under the tents. Accordingly, the two naturalists desired to get to a place where they could spend several days and collect steadily, thereby doing more effective work. The rest of us continued with the mule train, as was necessary.

It was always a picturesque sight when camp was broken, and again at nightfall when the laden mules came stringing in and their burdens were thrown down, while the tents were pitched and the fires lit. We breakfasted before leaving camp, the aluminum cups and plates being placed on ox hides, round which we sat, on the ground or on campstools. We fared well, on rice, beans, and crackers, with canned corned beef and salmon or any game that had been shot, and coffee, tea, and maté. I then usually sat down somewhere to write, and when the mules were nearly ready, I popped my writing materials into my duffel bag—war-sack, as we would have called it in the old days on the plains. I found that the mules usually arrived so late in the afternoon or evening that I could not depend upon being able to write at that time. Of course, if we made a very early start, I could not write at all. At night, there were no mosquitoes. In the daytime, gnats and sand flies and horseflies sometimes bothered us a little, but not much. Small stingless bees lit on us in numbers and crawled over the skin, making a slight tickling; but we did not mind them until they became very numerous. There was a good deal of rain, but not enough to cause any serious annoyance.

Colonel Rondon and Lieutenant Lyra held many discussions as to whither the Rio da Dúvida flowed, and where its mouth might be. Its provisional name—"River of Doubt"—was given it precisely because of this ignorance concerning it; an ignorance which it was one of the purposes of our trip to dispel. It might go into the Ji-Paraná, in which case its course must be very short; it might flow into the Madeira low down, in which case its course would be very long; or, which was unlikely, it might flow into the Tapajós. There was another river, of which Colonel Rondon had come across the head-waters, whose course was equally doubtful, although in its case there was rather more probability of its flowing into the Juruena, by which name the Tapajós is known for its upper half. To this unknown river Colonel Rondon had given the name Ananás, because when he came across it, he found a deserted Indian field with pineapples, which the hungry explorers ate greedily. Among the things the colonel and I hoped to accomplish on the trip was to do a little work in clearing up one or the other of these two doubtful geographical points, and thereby to push a little forward the knowledge of this region.

Originally, as described in the first chapter, my trip was undertaken primarily in the interest of the American Museum of Natural History of New York, to add to our knowledge of the birds and mammals of the far interior of the western Brazilian wilderness; and the labels of our baggage and scientific equipment, printed by the museum, were entitled "Colonel Roosevelt's South American Expedition for the American Museum of Natural History." But, as I have already mentioned, at Rio, the Brazilian government, through the secretary of foreign affairs, Doctor Lauro Müller, suggested that I should combine the expedition with one by Colonel Rondon, which they contemplated making, and thereby make both expeditions of broader scientific interest. I accepted the proposal with much pleasure; and we found, when we joined Colonel Rondon and his associates, that their baggage and equipment had been labeled by the Brazilian government "Expedição Científica Roosevelt-Rondon." This thenceforth became the proper and official title of the expedition.

Cherrie and Miller did the chief zoological work. The geological work was done by a Brazilian member of the expedition, Euzébio de Oliveira. The astronomical work necessary for obtaining the exact geographical location of the rivers and points of note was to be done by Lieutenant Lyra, under the supervision of Colonel Rondon; and at the telegraph stations this astronomical work would be checked by wire communications with one of Colonel Rondon's assistants at Cuiabá, Lieutenant Caetano, thereby securing a minutely accurate comparison of time. The sketch maps and surveying and cartographical work generally were to be made under the supervision of Colonel Rondon by Lyra, with assistance from Fiala and Kermit. Captain Amilcar handled the worst problem—transportation; the medical member was Doctor Cajazeira.

At night around the campfire my Brazilian companions often spoke of the first explorers of this vast wilderness of western Brazil—men whose very names are now hardly known, but who did each his part in opening the country which will some day see such growth and development. Among the most notable of them was a Portuguese, Ricardo Franco [de Almeida Serra],[3] who spent forty years at the work, during the last quarter of the eighteenth and the opening years of the nineteenth centuries. He ascended for long distances the Xingu and the Tapajós, and went up the Madeira and Guaporé, crossing to the headwaters of the Paraguay and partially exploring there also. He worked among and with the Indians, much as Mungo Park[4] worked with the natives of West Africa, having none of the aids, instruments, and comforts with which even the hardiest of modern explorers are provided. He was one of the men who established the beginnings of the province of Mato Grosso.

For many years the sole method of communication between this remote interior province and civilization was by the long, difficult, and perilous route which led up the Amazon and Madeira; and its then capital, the town of Mato Grosso, the seat of the captain general, with its palace, cathedral, and fortress, was accordingly placed far to the west, near the Guaporé. When less circuitous lines of communication were established farther eastward, the old capital was abandoned, and the tropic wilderness surged over the lonely little town. The tomb of the old colonial explorer still stands in the ruined cathedral, where the forest has once more come to its own. But civilization is again advancing to reclaim the lost town and to revive the memory of the wilderness wanderer who helped to found it. Colonel Rondon has named a river after Franco; a range of mountains has also been named after him; and the colonel, acting for the Brazilian government, has established a telegraph station in what was once the palace of the captain general.

Our northward trail led along the high ground a league or two to the east of the northward-flowing Rio Sacre. Each night we camped on one of the small tributary brooks that fed it. Fiala, Kermit, and I occupied one tent. In the daytime the pium flies, vicious little sand flies, became bad enough to make us finally use gloves and head nets. There were many heavy rains, which made the traveling hard for the mules. The soil was more often clay than sand, and it was slippery when wet. The weather was overcast, and there was usually no oppressive heat even at noon. At intervals along the trail we came on the staring skull and bleached skeleton of a mule or ox. Day after day we rode forward across endless flats of grass and of low, open, scrubby forest, the trees standing far apart and in most places being but little higher than the head of a horseman. Some of them carried blossoms, white, orange, yellow, pink; and there were many flowers, the most beautiful being the morning glories. Among the trees were bastard rubber trees and dwarf palmetto; if the latter grew more than a few feet high, their tops were torn and disheveled by the wind.

Anthills were frequently taller than a man

There was very little bird or mammal life; there were few long vistas, for in most places it was not possible to see far among the gray, gnarled trunks of the wind-beaten little trees. Yet the desolate landscape had a certain charm of its own, although not a charm that would be felt by any man who does not take pleasure in mere space and freedom and wildness, and in plains standing empty to the sun, the wind, and the rain.

One feature in common with the African landscape was the abundance of anthills, some as high as a man. They were red in the clay country, gray where it was sandy; and the dirt houses were also in trees, while their raised tunnels traversed trees and ground alike. At some of the camping places, we had to be on our watch against the swarms of leaf-carrying ants. These are so called in the books— the Brazilians call them *carregadores*, or porters— because they are always carrying bits of leaves and blades of grass to their underground homes. They are inveterate burden bearers, and they industriously cut into pieces and carry off any garment they can get at; and we had to guard our shoes and clothes from them, just as we had often had to guard all our belongings against the termites. These ants did not bite us; but we encountered huge black ants, an inch and a quarter long, which were very vicious, and their bite was not only painful but quite poisonous.

Praying mantes were common, and one evening at supper, one had a comical encounter with a young dog, a jovial near-puppy, of Colonel Rondon's, named Cartucho. Cartucho was lying with his head on the oxhide that served as table, waiting with poorly dissembled impatience for his share of the banquet. The mantis flew down on the oxhide and proceeded to crawl over it, taking little flights from one corner to another; and whenever it thought itself menaced, it assumed an attitude of seeming devotion and real defiance. Soon it lit in front of Cartucho's nose. Cartucho cocked his big ears forward, stretched his neck, and cautiously sniffed at the new arrival, not with any hostile design, but merely to find out whether it would prove to be a playmate. The mantis promptly assumed an attitude of prayer. This struck Cartucho as both novel and interesting, and he thrust his sniffing black nose still nearer. The mantis dexterously thrust forward first one and then the other armed foreleg, touching the intrusive nose, which was instantly jerked back and again slowly and inquiringly brought forward. Then the mantis suddenly flew in Cartucho's face, whereupon Cartucho, with a smothered yelp of dismay, almost turned a back somersault; and the triumphant mantis flew back to the middle of the oxhide, among the plates, where it reared erect and defied the laughing and applauding company.

Colonel Rondon and Colonel Roosevelt ride beneath the telegraph line

On the morning of the 29th, we were rather late in starting because the rain had continued through the night into the morning, drenching everything. After nightfall, there had been some mosquitoes, and the piums were a pest during daylight; where one bites, it leaves a tiny black spot on the skin which lasts for several weeks. In the slippery mud one of the pack mules fell and injured itself so that it had to be abandoned. Soon after starting, we came on the telegraph line which runs from Cayubá; this was the first time we had seen it. Two Paresi Indians joined us, leading a pack bullock. These two Indians were in the employ of the Telegraphic Commission and had been patrolling the telegraph line. The bullock carried their personal belongings and the tools with which they could repair a break. The commission pays the ordinary Indian worker 66 cents a day; a very good worker gets $1, and the chief $1.66. No man gets anything unless he works. Colonel Rondon, by just, kindly, and understanding treatment of these Indians, who previously had often been exploited and maltreated by rubber gatherers, has made them the loyal friends of the government. He has gathered them at the telegraph stations, where they cultivate fields of manioc, beans, potatoes, maize, and other vegetables, and where he is introducing them to stock raising; and the entire work of guarding and patrolling the line is theirs.

After six hours' march, we came to the crossing of the Rio Sacre at the beautiful waterfall appropriately called the Salto Belo [beautiful leap]. This is the end of the automobile road. Here there is a small Paresi village. The men of the village work the ferry by which everything is taken across the deep and rapid river. The ferryboat is made of planking placed on three dugout canoes, and runs on a trolley. Before crossing, we enjoyed a good swim in the swift, clear, cool water. The Indian village, where we camped, is placed on a jutting tongue of land round which the river sweeps just before it leaps from the overhanging precipice. The falls themselves are very lovely. Just above them is a wooded island, but the river joins again before it races forward for the final plunge. There is a sheer drop of forty or fifty yards, with a breadth two or three times as great; and the volume of water is large.

On the left or hither bank, a cliff extends for several hundred yards below the falls. Green vines have flung themselves down over its face, and they are met by other vines thrusting upward from the mass of vegetation at its foot, glistening in the perpetual mist from the cataract and clothing even the rock surfaces in vivid green. The river, after throwing itself over the rock wall, rushes off in long curves at the bottom of a thickly wooded ravine, the white water churning among the black boulders. There is a perpetual rainbow at the foot of the falls. The

Breakfast at Salto Belo Falls

masses of green water that are hurling themselves over the brink dissolve into shifting, foaming columns of snowy lace. On the edge of the cliff below the falls, Colonel Rondon had placed benches, giving a curious touch of rather conventional tourist civilization to this cataract far out in the lonely wilderness. It is well worth visiting for its beauty. It is also of extreme interest because of the promise it holds for the future. Lieutenant Lyra informed me that they had calculated that this fall would furnish thirty-six thousand horsepower.

Eight miles off we were to see another fall of much greater height and power. There are many rivers in this region which would furnish almost unlimited motive force [power source] to populous manufacturing communities. The country round about is healthy. It is an upland region of good climate; we were visiting it in the rainy season, the season when the nights are far less cool than in the dry season, and yet we found it delightful. There is much fertile soil in the neighborhood of the streams, and the teeming lowlands of the Amazon and the Paraguay could readily—and with immense advantage to both sides—be made tributary to an industrial civilization seated on these highlands. A telegraph line has been built to and across them. A railroad should follow. Such a line could be easily built, for there are no serious natural obstacles. In advance of its construction a trolley line could be

Paresi children

run from Cuiabá to the falls, using the power furnished by the latter. Once this is done, the land will offer extraordinary opportunities to settlers of the right kind: to home makers and to enterprising business men of foresight, coolness, and sagacity who are willing to work with the settlers, the immigrants, the home makers, for an advantage which shall be mutual.

The Paresi Indians, whom we met here, were exceedingly interesting. They were to all appearance an unusually cheerful, good-humored, pleasant-natured people. Their teeth were bad; otherwise, they appeared strong and vigorous, and there were plenty of children. The colonel was received as a valued friend and as a leader who was to be followed and obeyed. He is raising them by degrees—the only way by which to make the rise permanent. In this village he has got them to substitute for the flimsy Indian cabins houses of the type usual among the poorer field laborers and backcountry dwellers in Brazil. These houses have roofs of palm thatch, steeply pitched. They are usually open at the sides, consisting merely of a framework of timbers, with a wall at the back; but some have the ordinary four walls, of erect palm logs. The hammocks are slung in the houses, and the cooking is also done in them, with pots placed on small open fires, or occasionally in a kind of clay oven. The big gourds for water, and the wicker baskets, are placed on the ground or hung on the poles.

The men had adopted, and were wearing, shirts and trousers, but the women had made little change in their clothing. A few wore print dresses, but obviously only for ornament. Most of them, especially the girls and young married women, wore nothing but a loincloth in addition to bead necklaces and bracelets. The nursing mothers—and almost all the mothers were nursing—sometimes carried the child slung against their side of hip, seated in a cloth belt, or sling, which went over the opposite shoulder of the mother. The women seemed to be well treated, although polygamy is practiced. The children were

Top: Paresi woman weaving a hammock; bottom: Paresi mothers carrying their children

loved by everyone; they were petted by both men and women, and they behaved well to one another, the boys not seeming to bully the girls or the smaller boys. Most of the children were naked, but the girls early wore the loincloth; and some, both of the little boys and the little girls, wore colored print garments, to the evident pride of themselves and their parents.

In each house, there were several families, and life went on with no privacy but with good humor, consideration, and fundamentally good manners. The man or woman who had nothing to do lay in a hammock or squatted on the ground leaning against a post or wall. The children played together, or lay in little hammocks, or tagged round after their mothers; and when called, they came trustfully up to us to be petted or given some small trinket; they were friendly little souls and accustomed to good treatment. One woman was weaving a cloth; another was making a hammock; others made ready melons and other vegetables and cooked them over tiny fires. The men, who had come in from work at the ferry or along the telegraph lines, did some work themselves or played with the children; one cut a small boy's hair and then had his own hair cut by a friend. But the absorbing amusement of the men was an extraordinary game of ball.

These Paresi Indians enthusiastically play football with their heads.[5] The game is not only native to

The game of headball played by Paresi Indians

them, but I have never heard or read of its being played by any other tribe or people. They use a light, hollow rubber ball of their own manufacture. It is circular and about eight inches in diameter. The players are divided into two sides and stationed much as in association football, and the ball is placed on the ground to be put in play as in football. Then a player runs forward, throws himself flat on the ground, and butts the ball toward the opposite side. This first butt, when the ball is on the ground, never lifts it much, and it rolls and bounds toward the opponents. One or two of the latter run toward it; one throws himself flat on his face and butts the ball back. Usually this butt lifts it, and it flies back in a curve well up in the air; and an opposite player, rushing toward it, catches it on his head with such a swing of his brawny neck, and such precision and address, that the ball bounds back through the air as a football soars after a drop kick. If the ball flies off to one side or the other, it is brought back and again put in play. Often it will be sent to and fro a dozen times, from head to head, until finally it rises with such a sweep that it passes far over the heads of the opposite players and descends behind them. Then shrill, rolling cries of good-humored triumph arise from the victors, and the game instantly begins again with fresh zest.

There are, of course, no such rules as in a specialized ballgame of civilization; and I saw no disputes. There may be eight or ten, or many more, players on each side. The ball is never touched with the hands or feet, or with anything except the top of the head. It is hard to decide whether to wonder most at the dexterity and strength with which it is hit or butted with the head, as it comes down through the air, or at the reckless speed and skill with which the players throw themselves headlong on the ground to return the ball if it comes low down. Why they do not grind off their noses I cannot imagine. Some of the players hardly ever failed to catch and return the ball if it came in their neighborhood, and with such a vigorous toss of the head that it often flew in a great curve for a really astonishing distance.

That night a pack ox got into the tent in which Kermit and I were sleeping, entering first at one end and then at the other. It is extraordinary that he did not waken us; but we slept undisturbed while the ox deliberately ate our shirts, socks, and under-clothes! It chewed them into rags. One of my socks escaped, and my undershirt, although chewed full of holes, was still good for some weeks' wear; but the other things were in fragments.

In the morning Colonel Rondon arranged for us to have breakfast over on the benches under the trees by the waterfall, whose roar, lulled to a thun-derous murmur, had been in our ears before we slept and when we waked. There could have been no more picturesque place for the breakfast of such a party as ours. All travelers who really care to see what is most beautiful and most characteristic of the far interior of South America should in their journey visit this region and see the two great waterfalls. They are even now easy of access; and as soon as the traffic warrants it, they will be made still more so; then, from São Luis de Cáceres, they will be speedily reached by light steamboat up the Sepotuba and by a day or two's automobile ride, with a couple of days on horseback in between.

The colonel held a very serious council with the Paresi Indians over an incident which caused him grave concern. One of the commission's employees, a Negro, had killed a wild Nhambiquara Indian; but it appeared that he had really been urged on and aided by the Paresis, as the members of the tribe to which the dead Indian belonged were much given to carrying off the Paresi women and in other ways making themselves bad neighbors. The colonel tried hard to get at the truth of the matter; he went to the biggest Indian house, where he sat in a hammock—an Indian child cuddling solemnly up to him, by the way—while the Indians sat in other hammocks and stood round about, but it was impossible to get an absolutely frank statement.

It appeared, however, that the Nhambiquaras had made a descent on the Paresi village in the momentary absence of the men of the village; but the latter, notified by the screaming of the women, had returned in time to rescue them. The Negro was with them, and, having a good rifle, he killed one of the aggressors. The Paresis were, of course, in the right, but the colonel could not afford to have his men take sides in a tribal quarrel.

It was only a two hours' march across to the Papagaio at the Falls of Utiariti, so named by their discoverer, Colonel Rondon, after the sacred falcon of the Paresis. On the way, we passed our Indian friends, themselves bound thither; both the men and the women bore burdens—the burdens of some of the women, poor things, were heavy—and even the small naked children carried the live hens. At Utiariti there is a big Paresi settlement and a telegraph station kept by one of the employees of the commission. His pretty brown wife is acting as schoolmistress to a group of little Paresi girls. The Paresi chief has been made a major and wears a uniform accordingly. The commission has erected good buildings for its own employees and has superintended the erection of good houses for the Indians. Most of the latter still prefer the simplicity of the loincloth, in their ordinary lives, but they proudly wore their civilized clothes in our honor. When in the late afternoon the men began to play a regular match game of headball, with a scorer or umpire to keep count, they soon discarded most of their clothes, coming down to nothing but trousers or a

Utiariti Falls

loincloth. Two or three of them had their faces stained with red ochre. Among the women and children looking on were a couple of little girls who paraded about on stilts.

The great waterfall was half a mile below us. Lovely though we had found Salto Belo, these falls were far superior in beauty and majesty. They are twice as high and twice as broad; and the lay of the land is such that the various landscapes in which the waterfall is a feature are more striking. A few hundred yards above the falls the river turns at an angle and widens. The broad, rapid shallows are crested with whitecaps. Beyond this wide expanse of flecked and hurrying water rise the mist columns of the cataract; and as these columns are swayed and broken by the wind, the forest appears through and between them.

From below, the view is one of singular grandeur. The fall is over a shelving ledge of rock which goes in a nearly straight line across the river's course. But at the left there is a salient in the cliff line, and here, accordingly, a great cataract of foaming water comes down almost as a separate body, in advance of the line of the main fall. I doubt whether, excepting, of course, Niagara, there is a waterfall in North America which outranks this if both volume and beauty are considered. Above the fall, the river flows through a wide valley with gently sloping sides. Below, it slips along, a torrent of whity-green water, at the bottom of a deep gorge; and the sides of the gorge are clothed with a towering growth of tropical forest.

Next morning the cacique [chief] of these Indians, in his major's uniform, came to breakfast, and bore himself with entire propriety. It was raining heavily—it rained most of the time—and a few minutes previously I had noticed the cacique's two wives, with three or four other young women, going out to the manioc fields. It was a picturesque group. The women were all mothers, and each carried a nursing child. They wore loincloths or short skirts. Each carried on her back a wickerwork basket supported by a head strap which went around her forehead. Each carried a belt slung diagonally across her body, over her right shoulder; in this the child was carried, against and perhaps astride of her left hip. They were comely women, who did not look jaded or cowed; and they laughed cheerfully and nodded to us as they passed through the rain on their way to the fields. But the contrast between them and the chief in his soldier's uniform seated at breakfast was rather too striking; and, incidentally, it etched in bold lines the folly of those who idealize the life of even exceptionally good and pleasant-natured savages.

Although it was the rainy season, the trip up to this point had not been difficult, and from May to October, when the climate is dry and at its best, there would be practically no hardship at all for travelers and visitors. This is a healthy plateau. But, of course, the men who do the first pioneering, even in country like this, encounter dangers and run risks; and they make payment with their bodies. At more than one halting place, we had come across the forlorn grave of some soldier or laborer of the commission. The grave mound lay within a rude stockade; and an uninscribed wooden cross, gray and weather-beaten, marked the last resting place of the unknown and forgotten man beneath, the man who had paid with his humble life the cost of pushing the frontier of civilization into the wild savagery of the wilderness. Farther west, the conditions become less healthy. At this station, Colonel Rondon received news of sickness and of some deaths among the employees of the commission in the country to the westward, which we were soon to enter. Beriberi and malignant malarial fever were the diseases which claimed the major number of the victims.

Surely these are "the men who [merely] do the work for which they draw the wage."[6] Kermit had with him the same copy of Kipling's poems which he had carried through Africa. At these falls, there was one sunset of angry splendor; and we contrasted this going down of the sun, through broken rain clouds and over leagues of wet tropical forest, with the desert sunsets we had seen in Arizona and Sonora, and along the Guaso Nyiro north and west of Mount Kenya, when the barren mountains were changed into flaming "ramparts of slaughter and peril" standing above "the wine-dark flats below."[7]

It rained during most of the day after our arrival at Utiariti. Whenever there was any letup, the men promptly came forth from their houses and played headball with the utmost vigor; and we would listen to their shrill, undulating cries of applause and triumph until we also grew interested and strolled over to look on. They are more infatuated with the game than an American boy is with baseball or football. It is an extraordinary thing that this strange and exciting game should be played by, and only by, one little tribe of Indians in what is almost the very center of South America. If any traveler or ethnologist knows of a tribe elsewhere that plays a similar game, I wish he would let me know. To play it demands great activity, vigor, skill, and endurance. Looking at the strong, supple bodies of the players, and at the number of children roundabout, it seemed as if the tribe must be in vigorous health; yet the Paresis have decreased in numbers, for measles and small-pox have been fatal to them.

By the evening, the rain was coming down more heavily than ever. It was not possible to keep the moisture out of our belongings; everything became moldy except what became rusty. It rained all that night, and daylight saw the downpour continuing with no prospect of cessation. The pack mules could not have gone on with the march; they were already

Anthony Fiala making a motion picture of the Paresi

rather done up by their previous ten days' labor through rain and mud, and it seemed advisable to wait until the weather became better before attempting to go forward. Moreover, there had been no chance to take the desired astronomical observations. There was very little grass for the mules; but there was abundance of a small-leaved plant eight or ten inches high—unfortunately, not very nourishing—on which they fed greedily. In such weather and over such muddy trails, oxen travel better than mules.

In spite of the weather, Cherrie and Miller, whom, together with Father Zahm and Sigg, we had found awaiting us, made good collections of birds and mammals. Among the latter were opossums and mice that were new to them. The birds included various forms so unlike our home birds that the enumeration of their names would mean nothing. One of the most interesting was a large black-and-white woodpecker, the white predominating in the plumage. Several of these woodpeckers were usually found together. They were showy, noisy, and restless, and perched on twigs, in ordinary bird fashion, at least as often as they clung to the trunks in orthodox woodpecker style. The prettiest bird was a tiny manakin, coal-black, with a red-and-orange head.

On February 2, the rain let up, although the sky remained overcast and there were occasional show-

The Paresis' dance

ers. I walked off with my rifle for a couple of leagues; at that distance, from a slight hillock, the mist columns of the falls were conspicuous in the landscape. The only mammal I saw on the walk was a rather hairy armadillo, with a flexible tail, which I picked up and brought back to Miller—it showed none of the speed of the nine-banded armadillos we met on our jaguar hunt. Judging by its actions, as it trotted about before it saw me, it must be diurnal in habits. It was new to the collection.

I spent much of the afternoon by the waterfall. Under the overcast sky, the great cataract lost the deep green and fleecy white of the sunlit falling waters. Instead it showed opaline hues and tints of topaz and amethyst. At all times, and under all lights, it was majestic and beautiful.

Colonel Rondon had given the Indians various presents, those for the women including calico prints, and, what they especially prized, bottles of scented oil, from Paris, for their hair. The men held a dance in the late afternoon. For this occasion, most, but not all, of them cast aside their civilized clothing and appeared as doubtless they would all have appeared had none but themselves been present. They were absolutely naked except for a beaded string round the waist. Most of them were spotted and dashed with red paint, and on one leg wore anklets which rattled. A number carried pipes through which they blew a kind of deep stifled whistle in time to the dancing. One of them had his pipe leading into a huge gourd, which gave out a hollow, moaning boom. Many wore two red or green or yellow macaw feathers in their hair, and one had a macaw feather stuck transversely through the septum of his nose.

They circled slowly round and round, chanting and stamping their feet, while the anklet rattles clattered and the pipes droned. They advanced to the wall of one of the houses, again and again chanting and bowing before it; I was told this was a demand for drink. They entered one house and danced in a ring around the cooking fire in the middle of the earth floor; I was told that they were then reciting the deeds of mighty hunters and describing how they brought in the game. They drank freely from gourds and pannikins [cups] of a fermented drink made from manioc which were brought out to them. During the first part of the dance, the women remained in the houses and all the doors and windows were shut and blankets hung to prevent the possibility of seeing out. But during the second part, all the women and girls came out and looked on. They were themselves to have danced when the men had finished but were overcome with shyness at the thought of dancing with so many strangers looking on. The children played about with unconcern throughout the ceremony, one of them throwing high in the air, and again catching in his hands, a loaded feather, a kind of shuttlecock.

In the evening, the growing moon shone through the cloud rack. Anything approaching fair weather always put our men in good spirits; and the mule-teers squatted in a circle by a fire near a pile of packs and listened to a long, monotonously and rather mournfully chanted song about a dance and a love affair. We ourselves worked busily with our photographs and our writing. There was so much humidity in the air that everything grew damp and stayed damp, and mold gathered quickly. At this season, it is a country in which writing, taking photographs, and preparing specimens are all works of difficulty, at least so far as concerns preserving and sending home the results of the labor; and a man's clothing is never really dry. From here Father Zahm returned to Tapirapuá, accompanied by Sigg.

NOTES

1. John D. Haseman (?–1969), American ichthyologist who did extensive field work in South America. From 1908–10, he worked in Brazil under the auspices of the Carnegie Museum of Natural History. William Curtis Farrabee (1865–1925), American ethnographic explorer and anthropologist who specialized in Amazonian societies. Maria Emilie Snethlage (1868–1929), German-born Brazilian ornithologist. She conducted many field trips throughout Brazil and was director of Museu Paraense Emílio Goeldi in Belém, 1914–22.

2. Arnold Henry Savage Landor (1865–1924), English artist and

travel writer. His book *Across Unknown South America* was published in 1913.

3. Ricardo Franco de Almeida Serra (1748–1809), Portuguese military engineer. He occupied the zone of Mato Grosso, establishing Portuguese claims against Spain.

4. Mungo Park (1771–1806), Scottish explorer. Park was known as the first European to explore the interior of West Africa along the Niger River.

5. The game, called zikunariti or xikunahiti, is considered unique to certain indigenous groups in Mato Grosso, such as the Paresis.

6. From "The Wage-Slaves" by Rudyard Kipling (1865–1936), English poet.

7. From Kipling's *Bridge-Guard in the Karroo.*

VII. With a Mule Train Across Nhambiquara Land

FROM THIS POINT we were to enter a still wilder region, the land of the naked Nhambiquaras. On February 3, the weather cleared and we started with the mule train and two ox carts. Fiala and Lieutenant Lauriadó stayed at Utiariti to take canoes and go down the Papagaio, which had not been descended by any scientific party, and perhaps by no one. They were then to descend the Juruena and Tapajós, thereby performing a necessary part of the work of the expedition. Our remaining party consisted of Colonel Rondon, Lieutenant Lyra, the doctor, Oliveira, Cherrie, Miller, Kermit, and myself. On the Juruena we expected to meet the pack-ox train with Captain Amilcar and Lieutenant Mello; the other Brazilian members of the party had returned. We had now begun the difficult part of the expedition. The pium flies were becoming a pest. There was much fever and beriberi in the country we were entering. The feed for the animals was poor; the rains had made the trails slippery and difficult; and many, both of the mules and the oxen, were already weak, and some had to be abandoned. We left the canoe, the motor, and the gasoline; we had hoped to try them on the Amazonian rivers, but we were obliged to cut down everything that was not absolutely indispensable.

Before leaving, we prepared for shipment back to the museum some of the bigger skins and also some of the weapons and utensils of the Indians, which Kermit had collected. These included woven fillets, and fillets made of macaw feathers, for use in the dances; woven belts; a gourd in which the sacred drink is offered to the god Enoerey;[1] wickerwork baskets; flutes or pipes; anklet rattles; hammocks; a belt of the kind used by the women in carrying the babies, with the weaving frame. All these were Paresi articles.

He also secured from the Nhambiquaras wickerwork baskets of a different type and bows and arrows. The bows were seven feet long and the arrows five feet. There were blunt-headed arrows for birds; arrows with long, sharp wooden blades for tapir, deer, and other mammals; and the poisoned war arrows, with sharp barbs, poison-coated and bound on by fine thongs, and with a long, hollow wooden guard to slip over the entire point and protect it until the time came to use it. When people talk glibly of "idle" savages, they ignore the immense labor entailed by many of their industries and the really extraordinary amount of work they accomplish by the skillful use of their primitive and ineffective tools.

It was not until early in the afternoon that we started into the *sertão*, as Brazilians call the wilderness. We drove with us a herd of oxen for food. After going about fifteen miles, we camped beside the swampy headwaters of a little brook. It was at the spot where nearly seven years previously Rondon and Lyra had camped on the trip when they discovered Utiariti Falls and penetrated to the Juruena. When they reached this place, they had been thirty-six hours without food. They killed a bush deer—a small deer—and ate literally every particle. The dogs devoured the entire skin. For much of the time on this trip, they lived on wild fruit, and the two dogs that remained alive would wait eagerly under the trees and eat the fruit that was shaken down.

Next day the weather was still fair. Our march lay through country like that which we had been traversing for ten days. Skeletons of mules and oxen were more frequent; and once or twice by the wayside we passed the graves of officers or men who had died on the road. Barbed wire encircled the desolate little mounds. We camped on the west bank of the Buriti River. Here there is a *balsa*, or ferry, run by two Paresi Indians, as employees of the Telegraphic Commission, under the colonel. Each had a thatched house, and each had two wives—all these Indians are pagans. All were dressed much like the poorer peasants of the Brazilian backcountry, and all were pleasant and well-behaved. The women ran the ferry about as well as the men. They had no cultivated fields, and for weeks they had been living only on game and honey; and they hailed with joy our advent and the quantities of beans and rice which, together with some beef, the colonel left with them. They feasted most of the night. Their houses contained their hammocks, baskets, and other belongings, and they owned some poultry. In one house was a tiny parakeet, very much at home, and familiar, but by no means friendly, with strangers.

There are wild Nhambiquaras in the neighborhood, and recently several of these had menaced the two ferrymen with an attack, even shooting arrows at them. The ferrymen had driven them off by firing their rifles in the air; and they expected and received the colonel's praise for their self-restraint, for the colonel is doing all he can to persuade the Indians to stop their blood feuds.

The night we reached the Buriti it rained heavily, and next day the rain continued. In the morning, the mules were ferried over, while the oxen were swum across. Half a dozen of our men—whites, Indians, and Negroes, all stark naked and uttering wild cries, drove the oxen into the river and then, with powerful overhand strokes, swam behind and alongside them as they crossed, half breasting the swift current. It was a fine sight to see the big, long-horned, staring beasts swimming strongly, while the sinewy naked men urged them forward, utterly at ease in the rushing water. We made only a short day's journey, for, owing to the lack of grass, the mules had to be driven off nearly three miles from our line of march, in order to get them feed. We camped at the headwaters of a little brook called Huatsui, which is Paresi for "monkey."

Accompanying us on this march was a soldier bound for one of the remoter posts. With him trudged his wife. They made the whole journey on foot. There were two children. One was so young that it had to be carried alternately by the father and mother. The other, a small boy of eight, and much the best of the party, was already a competent wilderness worker. He bore his share of the belongings on the march, and when camp was reached, sometimes himself put up the family shelter. They were mainly of Negro blood. Struck by the woman's uncomplaining endurance of fatigue, we offered to take her and the baby in the automobile, while it accompanied us. But, alas! this proved to be one of those melancholy cases where the effort to relieve hardship well endured results only in showing that those who endure the adversity cannot stand even a slight prosperity. The woman proved a querulous traveler in the auto, complaining that she was not made as comfortable as, apparently, she had expected; and after one day, the husband declared he was not willing to have her go unless he went too; and the family resumed their walk.

In this neighborhood, there were multitudes of the big, gregarious, crepuscular or nocturnal spiders. On arriving in camp, at about four in the afternoon, I ran into a number of remains of their webs and saw a very few of the spiders themselves sitting in the webs midway between trees. I then strolled a couple of miles up the road ahead of us under the line of telegraph poles. It was still bright sunlight and no spiders were out; in fact, I did not suspect their presence along the line of telegraph poles, although I ought to have done so, for I continually ran into long strings of tough, fine web, which got across my face or hands or rifle barrel. I returned just at sunset, and the spiders were out in force. I saw dozens of colonies, each of scores or hundreds of individuals. Many were among the small trees alongside the broad, cleared trail. But most were dependent from the wire itself. Their webs had all been made or repaired since I had passed. Each was sitting in the middle of his own wheel, and all the wheels were joined to one another; and the whole pendent fabric hung by fine ropes from the wire above and was in some cases steadied by guy ropes, thrown thirty feet off to little trees alongside. I watched them until nightfall, and evidently, to them, after their day's rest, their day's work had just begun.

Here we had to cut down our baggage and rearrange the loads for the mule train. Cherrie and Miller had a most workmanlike equipment, including a very light tent and two light flies. One fly they gave for the kitchen use, one fly was allotted to Ker-

mit and me, and they kept only the tent for themselves. Colonel Rondon and Lyra went in one tent;
the doctor and Oliveira in another. Each of us got
rid of everything above the sheer necessities. This
was necessary because of the condition of the baggage animals. The oxen were so weak that the effort
to bring on the carts had to be abandoned. Nine of
the pack mules had already been left on the road
during the three days' march from Utiariti. In the
first expeditions into this country, all the baggage
animals had died; and even in our case the loss was
becoming very heavy.

This state of affairs is due to the scarcity of forage
and the type of country. Good grass is scanty, and
the endless leagues of sparse, scrubby forest render
it exceedingly difficult to find the animals when
they wander. They must be turned absolutely loose
to roam about and pick up their scanty subsistence
and must be given as long a time as possible to feed
and rest; even under these conditions, most of them
grow weak when, as in our case, it is impossible to
carry corn. They cannot be found again until after
daylight, and then hours must be spent in gathering
them; and this means that the march must be made
chiefly during the heat of the day, the most trying
time. Often some of the animals would not be
brought in until so late that it was well on in the
forenoon, perhaps midday, before the bulk of the
pack train started; and they reached the camping

The Jurnena River

place as often after nightfall as before it. Under such conditions, many of the mules and oxen grew constantly weaker and ultimately gave out; and it was imperative to load them as lightly as possible and discard all luxuries, especially heavy or bulky luxuries.

Our march continued through the same type of high, nearly level upland, covered with scanty, scrubby forest. It is the kind of country known to the Brazilians as *chapadão*—pronounced almost as if it were a French word and spelled *shapadón*.

The Juruena is the name by which the Tapajós goes along its upper course. Where we crossed, it was a deep, rapid stream, flowing in a heavily wooded valley with rather steep sides. We were ferried across on the usual balsa, a platform on three dugouts, running by the force of the current on a wire trolley. There was a clearing on each side with a few palms, and on the farther bank were the buildings of the telegraph station. This is a wild country, and the station was guarded by a few soldiers under the command of Lieutenant Marino, a native of Rio Grande do Sul, a blond man who looked like an Englishman—an agreeable companion, and a good and resolute officer, as all must be who do their work in this wilderness.

There were several houses on the rise of the farther bank, all with thatched roofs, some of them with walls of upright tree trunks, some of them daub and wattle. Into one of the latter, with two rooms, we took our belongings. The sand flies were bothersome at night, coming through the interstices in the ordinary mosquito nets. The first night they did this, I got no sleep until morning, when it was cool enough for me to roll myself in my blanket and put on a head net. Afterward, we used fine nets of a kind of cheesecloth. They were hot, but they kept out all, or almost all, of the sand flies and other small tormentors.

Here we overtook the rearmost division of Captain Amilcar's bullock train. Our own route had diverged, in order to pass the great falls. Captain Amilcar had come direct, overtaking the pack oxen, which had left Tapirapuá before we did, laden with material for the Dúvida trip. He had brought the oxen through in fine shape, losing only three beasts with their loads and had himself left the Juruena the morning of the day we reached there. His weakest animals left that evening, to make the march by moonlight; and as it was desirable to give them thirty-six hours' start, we halted for a day on the banks of the river. It was not a wasted day. In addition to bathing and washing our clothes, the naturalists made some valuable additions to the collection—including a boldly marked black, blue, and white jay—and our photographs were developed and our writing brought abreast of the date. Traveling through a tropical wilderness in the rainy season, when the amount of baggage that can be taken is strictly limited, entails not only a good deal of work, but also the exercise of considerable ingenuity if the writing and photographing, and especially the preservation, of the specimens are to be done in satisfactory shape.

At the telegraph office, we received news that the voyage of Lauriadó and Fiala down the Papagaio had opened with a misadventure. In some bad rapids, not many miles below the falls, two of the canoes had been upset, half of their provisions and all of Fiala's baggage lost, and Fiala himself nearly drowned.

At the Juruena, we met a party of Nhambiquaras, very friendly and sociable, and very glad to see Colonel Rondon. They were originally exceedingly hostile and suspicious, but the colonel's unwearied thoughtfulness and good temper, joined with his indomitable resolution, enabled him to avoid war and to secure their friendship and even their aid. He never killed one. Many of them are known to him personally. He is on remarkably good terms with them, and they are very fond of him—although this does not prevent them from now and then yielding to temptation, even at his expense, and stealing a dog or something else which strikes them as offering an irresistible attraction. They cannot be employed at steady work, but they do occasional odd jobs and are excellent at hunting up strayed mules or oxen;

The party meets the Nhambiquaras at the Juruena River

and a few of the men have begun to wear clothes, purely for ornament. Their confidence and bold friendliness showed how well they had been treated. Probably half of our visitors were men; several were small boys; one was a woman with a baby; the others were young married women and girls.

Both sexes were well-made and rather good-looking, with fairly good teeth, although some of them seemed to have skin diseases. They were a laughing, easy-tempered crew, and the women were as well fed as the men and were obviously well treated, from the savage standpoint. Among these Nhambiquaras, the women were more completely naked than the men, although the difference was not essential. The men wore a string around the waist. Most of them wore nothing else, but a few had loosely hanging from this string in front a scanty tuft of dried grass or a small piece of cloth, which, however, was of purely symbolic use so far as either protection or modesty was concerned. The women did not wear a stitch of any kind anywhere on their bodies. They did not have on so much as a string, or a bead, or even an ornament in their hair.

All of them—men, women, and children, laughing and talking—crowded around us, whether we were on horseback or on foot. They flocked into the house, and when I sat down to write, surrounded me so closely that I had to push them gently away. The women and girls often stood holding one an-

A Nhambiquara man

other's hands, or with their arms over one another's shoulders or around one another's waists, offering an attractive picture. The men had holes pierced through the septum of the nose and through the upper lip, and wore a straw through each hole. The women were not marked or mutilated. It seems like a contradiction in terms, but it is nevertheless a fact that the behavior of these completely naked women and men was entirely modest. There was never an indecent look or a consciously indecent gesture.

They had no blankets or hammocks, and when night came, simply lay down in the sand. Colonel Rondon stated that they never wore a covering by night or by day, and if it was cool, slept one on each side of a small fire. Their huts were merely slight shelters against the rain.

The moon was nearly full, and after nightfall, a few of the Indians suddenly held an improvised dance for us in front of our house. There were four men, a small boy, and two young women or grown girls. Two of the men had been doing some work for the commission and were dressed, one completely and one partially, in ordinary clothes. Two of the men and the boy were practically naked, and the two young women were absolutely so. All of them danced in a circle, without a touch of embarrassment or impropriety. The two girls kept hold of each other's hands throughout, dancing among the men as modestly as possible, and with the occasional interchange of a laugh or jest, in as good taste and temper as in any dance in civilization. The dance consisted in slowly going round in a circle, first one way then the other, rhythmically beating time with the feet to the music of the song they were chanting. The chants—there were three of them, all told—were measured and rather slowly uttered melodies, varied with an occasional half-subdued shrill cry. The women continually uttered a kind of long-drawn wailing or droning; I am not enough of a musician to say whether it was an over-tone or the sustaining of the burden of the ballad. The young boy sang better than any of the others. It was a strange and interesting sight to see these utterly wild, friendly savages circling in their slow dance and chanting their immemorial melodies, in the brilliant tropical moonlight, with the river rushing by in the background, through the lonely heart of the wilderness.

The Indians stayed with us, feasting, dancing, and singing until the early hours of the morning. They then suddenly and silently disappeared in the darkness and did not return. In the morning, we discovered that they had gone off with one of Colonel Rondon's dogs. Probably the temptation had proved irresistible to one of their number, and the others had been afraid to interfere and also afraid to stay in or return to our neighborhood. We had not time to go after them; but Rondon remarked that

A Nhambiquara family

as soon as he again came to the neighborhood, he would take some soldiers, hunt up the Indians, and reclaim the dog. It has been his mixture of firmness, good nature, and good judgment that has enabled him to control these bold, warlike savages, and even to reduce the warfare between them and the Paresis. In spite of their good nature and laughter, their fearlessness and familiarity showed how necessary it was not to let them get the upper hand. They are always required to leave all their arms a mile or two away before they come into the encampment. They are much wilder and more savage, and at a much lower cultural level, than the Paresis.

In the afternoon of the day following our arrival, there was a heavy rainstorm which drove into the unglazed windows, and here and there came through the roof and walls of our daub-and-wattle house. The heat was intense, and there was much moisture in this valley. During the downpour, I looked out at the dreary little houses, showing through the driving rain, while the sheets of muddy water slid past their doorsills, and I felt a sincere respect for the lieutenant and his soldiers who were holding this desolate outpost of civilization. It is an unhealthy spot; there has been much malarial fever and beriberi—an obscure and deadly disease.

Next morning we resumed our march. It soon began to rain, and we were drenched when, some fifteen miles on, we reached the river where we were to camp. After the great heat, we felt quite cold in our wet clothes and gladly crowded round a fire which was kindled under a thatched shed, beside the cabin of the ferryman. This ferryboat was so small that it could only take one mule, or at most two, at a time. The mules and a span of six oxen dragging an ox cart, which we had overtaken, were ferried slowly to the farther side that afternoon, as there was no feed on the hither bank, where we ourselves camped. The ferryman was a soldier in the employ of the Telegraphic Commission. His good-looking, pleasant-mannered wife, evidently of both Indian and Negro blood, was with him and was doing all she could do as a housekeeper in the comfortless little cabin, with its primitive bareness of furniture and fittings.

After leaving the Juruena, the ground became somewhat more hilly, and the scrubby forest was less open, but otherwise there was no change in the monotonous, and yet to me rather attractive, landscape. The anthills, and the ant houses in the trees—arboreal anthills, so to speak—were as conspicuous as ever. The architects of some were red ants; of others, black ants; and others, which were on the whole the largest, had been built by the white ants, the termites. The latter were not infrequently taller than a horseman's head.

[Cherrie and Miller] were short of literature, by the way—a party such as ours always needs books—and as Kermit's reading matter consisted chiefly of Camoens [sic] and other Portuguese, or else Brazilian, writers, I strove to supply the deficiency with spare volumes of Gibbon. At the end of our march, we were usually far ahead of the mule train, and the rain was also usually falling. Accordingly we would sit about under trees or under a shed or lean-to, if there was one, each solemnly reading a volume of Gibbon—and no better reading can be found. In my own case, as I had been having rather a steady course of Gibbon, I varied him now and then with a volume of Arsène Lupin lent me by Kermit.

There were many swollen rivers to cross at this point of our journey. Some we waded at fords. Some we crossed by rude bridges. The larger ones, such as the Juína, we crossed by ferry, and when the approaches were swampy and the river broad and swift, many hours might be consumed in getting the mule train, the loose bullocks, and the ox cart over. We had few accidents, although we once lost a ferry-load of provisions, which was quite a misfortune in a country where they could not be replaced. The pasturage was poor, and it was impossible to make long marches with our weakened animals.

At one camp, three Nhambiquaras paid us a visit at breakfast time. They left their weapons behind them before they appeared and shouted loudly while they were still hid by the forest, and it was only after repeated answering calls of welcome that they approached. Always in the wilderness friends proclaim their presence; a silent advance marks a foe. Our visitors were men, and stark-naked, as usual. One seemed sick; he was thin, and his back was scarred with marks of the grub of the loathsome berni fly. Indeed, all of them showed scars, chiefly from insect wounds. But the other two were in good condition, and, although they ate greedily of the food offered them, they had with them a big manioc cake, some honey, and a little fish. One of them wore a high helmet of puma skin, with the tail hanging down his back—handsome headgear, which he gladly bartered for several strings of bright coral-red beads. Around the upper arms of two of them were bands bound so tightly as to cut into and deform the muscles—a singular custom, seemingly not only purposeless but mischievous, which is common among this tribe and many others.

The Nhambiquaras are a numerous tribe, covering a large region. But they have no general organization. Each group of families acts for itself. Half a dozen years previously, they had been very hostile, and Colonel Rondon had to guard his camp and exercise every precaution to guarantee his safety, while at the same time successfully endeavoring to avoid the necessity of himself shedding blood. Now they are, for the most part, friendly. But there are groups or individuals that are not. Several soldiers have been killed at these little lonely stations; and while in some cases, the attack may have been due to the soldiers' having meddled with Nhambiquara women, in other cases, the killing was entirely wanton and unprovoked. Sooner or later these criminals or outlaws will have to be brought to justice; it will not do to let their crimes go unpunished. Twice soldiers have deserted and fled to the Nhambiquaras. The runaways were well received, were given wives, and adopted into the tribe.

I have touched above on the insect pests. Men

unused to the South American wilderness speak with awe of the danger therein from jaguars, crocodiles, and poisonous snakes. In reality, the danger from these sources is trivial, much less than the danger of being run down by an automobile at home. But at times, the torment of insect plagues can hardly be exaggerated. There are many different species of mosquitoes, some of them bearers of disease. There are many different kinds of small, biting flies and gnats, loosely grouped together under various titles. The ones more especially called piums by my companions were somewhat like our northern black flies. They gorged themselves with blood. At the moment, their bites did not hurt, but they left an itching scar. Head nets and gloves are a protection but are not very comfortable in stifling hot weather. It is impossible to sleep without mosquito bars. At the camp of the piums, a column of the carnivorous foraging ants made its appearance before nightfall, and for a time, we feared it might put us out of our tents, for it went straight through camp, between the kitchen tent and our own sleeping tents. However, the column turned neither to the right nor the left, streaming uninterruptedly past for several hours and doing no damage except to the legs of any incautious man who walked near it.

On the afternoon of February 15, we reached Campos Novos. This place was utterly unlike the country we had been traversing. It was a large basin, several miles across, traversed by several brooks. The brooks ran in deep, swampy valleys, occupied by a matted growth of tall tropical forest. Between them, the ground rose in bold hills, bare of forest and covered with grass, on which our jaded animals fed eagerly. On one of these rounded hills, a number of buildings were ranged in a quadrangle, for the pasturage at this spot is so good that it is permanently occupied.

There were milk cows, and we got delicious fresh milk; and there were goats, pigs, turkeys, and chickens. Most of the buildings were made of upright poles with roofs of palm thatch. One or two were of native brick, plastered with mud, and before these, there was an enclosure with a few ragged palms and some pineapple plants. Here we halted. Our attendants made two kitchens: one was out in the open air; one was under a shelter of ox hide. The view over the surrounding grassy hills, riven by deep wooded valleys, was lovely. The air was cool and fresh. We were not bothered by insects, although mosquitoes swarmed in every belt of timber. Yet there has been much fever at this beautiful and seemingly healthy place. Doubtless when settlement is sufficiently advanced, a remedy will be developed.

Here we found Amilcar and Mello, who had waited for us with the rear guard of their pack train, and we enjoyed our meeting with the two fine fellows, than whom no military service of any nation could

produce more efficient men for this kind of difficult and responsible work. Next morning they mus-
tered their soldiers, muleteers, and pack-ox men and
marched off. We left the oxcart at Campos Novos;
from thence on, the trail was only for pack animals.

Two days after leaving Campos Novos, we reached
Vilhena, where there is a telegraph station. We
camped once at a small river named by Colonel Rondon the "Twelfth of October," because he reached it
on the day Columbus discovered America—I had
never before known what day it was!—and once at
the foot of a hill which he had named after Lyra, his
companion in the exploration. The two days'
march—really one full day and part of two others—
was through beautiful country, and we enjoyed it
thoroughly, although there were occasional driving
rainstorms, when the rain came in almost level sheets
and drenched everyone and everything.

For these forty-eight hours, the trail climbed into
and out of steep valleys and broad basins and up
and down hills. In the deep valleys were magnificent
woods, in which giant rubber trees towered, while
the huge leaves of the low-growing *pacova*, or wild
banana, were conspicuous in the undergrowth.
Great azure butterflies flitted through the open,
sunny glades, and the bellbirds, sitting motionless,
uttered their ringing calls from the dark stillness of
the columned groves. The hillsides were grassy pastures or else covered with low, open forest.

From Vilhena, we traveled in a generally north-ward direction. For a few leagues, we went across the *chapadão*, the sands or clays of the nearly level upland plateau, grassy or covered with thin, stunted forest, the same type of country that had been predominant ever since we ascended the Paresis tableland on the morning of the third day after leaving the Sepotuba. Then, at about the point where the trail dipped into a basin containing the headsprings of the Ananás, we left this type of country and began to march through thick forest, not very high. There was little feed for the animals on the *chapadão*. There was less in the forest. Moreover, the continual heavy rains made the traveling difficult and laborious for them, and they weakened. However, a couple of marches before we reached Tres Buritis where there is a big ranch with hundreds of cattle, we were met by ten fresh pack oxen, and our serious difficulties were over.

The third night out from Vilhena, we emerged for a moment from the endless close-growing forest in which our poor animals got such scanty pickings and came to a beautiful open country, where grassy slopes, dotted with occasional trees, came down on either side of a little brook which was one of the headwaters of the Dúvida. It was a pleasure to see the mules greedily bury their muzzles in the pasturage. Our tents were pitched in the open, near a shady tree, which sent out its low branches on every side.

Here Kermit, while a couple of miles from our tents, came across an encampment of Nhambiquaras. There were twenty or thirty of them—men, women, and a few children. Kermit, after the manner of honest folk in the wilderness, advanced ostentatiously in the open, calling out to give warning of his coming. The Nhambiquaras received Kermit with the utmost cordiality and gave him pineapple wine to drink. They were stark-naked as usual; they had no hammocks or blankets, and their huts were flimsy shelters of palm branches. Yet they were in fine condition.

Half a dozen of the men and a couple of boys accompanied Kermit back to our camp, paying no slightest heed to the rain which was falling. They were bold and friendly, good-natured—at least superficially—and very inquisitive. In feasting, the long reeds thrust through holes in their lips did not seem to bother them, and they laughed at the suggestion of removing them; evidently to have done so would have been rather bad manners—like using a knife as an aid in eating ice cream. They held two or three dances, and we were again struck by the rhythm and weird, haunting melody of their chanting. After supper, they danced beside the campfire; and finally, to their delight, most of the members of our own party, Americans and Brazilians, enthusiastically joined the dance, while the colonel and I furnished an appreciative and applauding audience.

Next morning, when we were awakened by the chattering and screaming of the numerous macaws, parrots, and parakeets, we found that nearly all the Indians, men and women, were gathered outside the tent. As far as clothing was concerned, they were in the condition of Adam and Eve before the fall. One of the women carried a little squirrel monkey. She put it up the big tree some distance from the tents; and when she called, it came scampering to her across the grass, ran up her, and clung to her neck. They would have liked to pilfer; but as they had no clothes, it was difficult for them to conceal anything. One of the women was observed to take a fork; but as she did not possess a rag of clothing of any kind, all she did do was to try to bury the fork in the sand and then sit on it, and it was reclaimed without difficulty. One or two of the children wore necklaces and bracelets made of the polished wood of the tucum palm, and of the molars of small rodents.

Next day's march led us across a hilly country of good pastureland. The valleys were densely wooded, palms of several kinds being conspicuous among the other trees; and the brooks at the bottoms we crossed at fords or by the usual rude pole bridges. On the open pastures were occasional trees, usually slender bacaba palms, with heads which the winds had disheveled until they looked like mops. It was evidently a fine natural cattle country, and we soon began to see scores, perhaps hundreds, of the cattle belonging to the government ranch at Tres Buritis, which we reached in the early afternoon. It is beautifully situated: the view roundabout is lovely, and certainly the land will prove healthy when settlements have been definitely established. Here we reveled in abundance of good fresh milk and eggs; and for dinner we had chicken *canja* [soup] and fat beef roasted on big wooden spits; and we even had watermelons. The latter were from seeds brought down by the American engineers who built the Madeira-Mamoré Railroad—a work which stands honorably distinguished among the many great and useful works done in the development of the tropics of recent years.

Amilcar's pack oxen, which were nearly worn out, had been left in these fertile pastures. Most of the fresh oxen which he took in their places were unbroken, and there was a perfect circus before they were packed and marched off; in every direction, said the gleeful narrators, there were bucking oxen and loads strewed on the ground. This cattle ranch is managed by the colonel's uncle, his mother's brother, a hale old man of seventy, white-haired but as active and vigorous as ever; with a fine, kindly, intelligent face. His name is Miguel Evangelista. He is a native of Mato Grosso, of practically pure Indian blood, and was dressed in the ordinary costume of the *caboclo*—hat, shirt, trousers, and no shoes or stockings. Within the last year he had killed three jaguars, which had been living on the mules; as long as they could get mules, they did not at this station molest the cattle.

It was with this uncle's father, Colonel Rondon's own grandfather, that Colonel Rondon as an orphan spent the first seven years of his life. His father died before he was born, and his mother when he was only a year old. He lived on his grandfather's cattle ranch, some fifty miles from Cuiabá. Then he went to live in Cuiabá with a kinsman on his father's side, from whom he took the name of Rondon; his own father's name was Da Silva. He studied in the Cuiabá Government School, and at sixteen was inscribed as one of the instructors. Then he went to Rio, served for a year in the army as an enlisted man in the ranks, and succeeded finally in getting into the military school. After five years as pupil, he served three years as professor of mathematics in this school; and then, as a lieutenant of engineers in the Brazilian army, he came back to his home in Mato Grosso and began his lifework of exploring the wilderness.

Next day we journeyed to the telegraph station at José Bonifácio, through alternate spells of glaring sunshine and heavy rain. On the way, we stopped at an *aldéia*—village—of Nhambiquaras. We first met a couple of men going to hunt, with bows and arrows longer than themselves. A rather comely young woman, carrying on her back a wickerwork basket, or creel, supported by a forehead band, and accompanied by a small child, was with them. At the village, there were a number of men, women, and children. Although as completely naked as the others we had met, the members of this band were more ornamented with beads and wore earrings made from the inside of mussel shells or very big snail shells. They were more hairy than the ones we had so far met. The women, but not the men, completely remove the hair from their bodies—and look more, instead of less, indecent in consequence. The chief, whose body was painted red with the juice of a fruit, had what could fairly be styled a mustache and imperial [pointed beard on lower lip and chin]; and one old man looked somewhat like a hairy Ainu [first people of Japan], or perhaps even more like an Australian black fellow. My companion told me that this probably represented an infusion of Negro blood, and possibly of mulatto blood, from runaway slaves of the old days, when some of the Mato Grosso mines were worked by slave labor. They also thought it possible that this infiltration of African Negroes might be responsible for the curious shape of the bigger huts, which were utterly unlike their flimsy, ordinary shelters, and bore no resemblance in shape to those of the other Indian tribes of this region, whereas they were not unlike the ordinary beehive huts of the agricultural African Negroes.

Nhambiquara shelters

There were in this village several huts or shelters open at the sides, and two of the big huts. These were of closely woven thatch, circular in outline, with a rounded dome, and two doors a couple of feet high opposite each other, and no other open-ing. There were fifteen or twenty people to each hut. Inside were their implements and utensils, such as wicker baskets (some of them filled with pineap-ples), gourds, fire sticks, wooden knives, wooden mortars, and a board for grating manioc, made of a thick slab of wood, inset with sharp points of a harder wood. From the Brazilians one or two of them had obtained blankets, and one a hammock; and they had also obtained knives, which they sorely needed, for they are not even in the Stone Age. One woman shielded herself from the rain by holding a green palm branch down her back. An-other had on her head what we at first thought to be a monkey-skin headdress. But it was a little, live, black monkey. It stayed habitually with its head above her forehead, and its arms and legs spread so that it lay molded to the shape of her head; but both woman and monkey showed some reluctance about having their photographs taken.

José Bonifácio consisted of several thatched one-room cabins, connected by a stockade which was extended to form an enclosure behind them. A number of tame parrots and parakeets, of several different species, scrambled over the roofs and en-

Nhambiquara archers

tered the houses. In the open pastures nearby were the curious, extensive burrows of a gopher rat, which ate the roots of grass, not emerging to eat the grass but pulling it into the burrows by the roots. In looks it closely resembled our pocket gophers, but it had no pockets. This was one of the most interesting small mammals that we secured.

From José Bonifácio we went about seven miles, across a rolling prairie dotted with trees and clumps of shrub. There, on February 24, we joined Amilcar, who was camped by a brook which flowed into the Dúvida. We were only some six miles from our place of embarkation on the Dúvida, and we divided our party and our belongings. Amilcar, Miller, Mello, and Oliveira were to march three days to the Ji-Paraná, and then descend it, and continue down the Madeira to Manaus. Rondon, Lyra, the doctor, Cherrie, Kermit, and I, with sixteen paddlers, in seven canoes, were to descend the Dúvida, and find out whether it led into the Ji-Paraná; our purpose was to return and descend the Ananás, whose outlet was also unknown.

Having this in view, we left a fortnight's provisions for our party of six at José Bonifácio. We took with us provisions for about fifty days, not full rations, for we hoped in part to live on the country—on fish, game, nuts, and palm tops. Our personal baggage was already well cut down: Cherrie, Kermit, and I took the naturalist's fly to sleep under,

Making ready for the start down the River of Doubt

and a very light little tent extra for anyone who might fall sick. Rondon, Lyra, and the doctor took one of their own tents. The things that we carried were necessities—food, medicines, bedding, instruments for determining the altitude and longitude and latitude—except a few books, each in small compass: Lyra's were in German, consisting of two tiny volumes of Goethe and Schiller; Kermit's were in Portuguese; mine, all in English, included the last two volumes of Gibbon, the plays of Sophocles, More's *Utopia*, Marcus Aurelius, and Epictetus, the two latter lent me by a friend, Major Shipton of the regulars, our military attaché at Buenos Aires.

If our canoe voyage was prosperous, we would

gradually lighten the loads by eating the provisions. If we met with accidents, such as losing canoes and men in the rapids, or losing men in encounters with Indians, or if we encountered overmuch fever and dysentery, the loads would lighten themselves. We were all armed. We took no cartridges for sport. Cherrie had some to be used sparingly for collecting specimens. The others were to be used—unless in the unlikely event of having to repel an attack—only to procure food. The food and the arms we carried represented all reasonable precautions against suffering and starvation; but, of course, if the course of the river proved very long and difficult, if we lost our boats over falls or in rapids, or had to make too many and too long portages, or were brought to a halt by impassable swamps, then we would have to reckon with starvation as a possibility. Anything might happen. We were about to go into the unknown, and no one could say what it held.

NOTES

1. Enoerey: probably a reference to ritual objects connected to "enore nawe" a realm of spirits who live in a village in the sky.

VIII. The River of Doubt

On February 27, 1914, shortly after midday, we started down the River of Doubt into the unknown. We were quite uncertain whether after a week we should find ourselves in the Ji-Paraná, or after six weeks in the Madeira, or after three months we knew not where. That was why the river was rightly christened the Dúvida.

We had been camped close to the river, where the trail that follows the telegraph line crosses it by a rough bridge. As our laden dugouts swung into the stream, Amilcar and Miller and all the others of the Ji-Paraná party were on the banks and the bridge to wave farewell and wish us goodbye and good luck. It was the height of the rainy season, and the swollen torrent was swift and brown. Our camp was at about 12° 1′ latitude south and 60° 15′ longitude west of Greenwich. Our general course was to be northward toward the equator, by waterway through the vast forest.

We had seven canoes, all of them dugouts. One was small, one was cranky, and two were old, water-logged, and leaky. The other three were good. The two old canoes were lashed together, and the cranky one was lashed to one of the others. Kermit with two paddlers went in the smallest of the good canoes; Colonel Rondon and Lyra with three other paddlers in the next largest; and the doctor, Cherrie,

Colonel Roosevelt's sketch map of the River of Doubt

and I in the largest with three paddlers. The remaining eight *camaradas*—there were sixteen in all—were equally divided between our two pairs of lashed canoes. Although our personal baggage was cut down to the limit necessary for health and efficiency, yet on such a trip as ours, where scientific work has to be done and where food for twenty-two men for an unknown period of time has to be carried, it is impossible not to take a good deal of stuff; and the seven dugouts were too heavily laden.

The paddlers were a strapping set. They were expert rivermen and men of the forest, skilled veterans in wilderness work. They were lithe as panthers and brawny as bears. They swam like waterdogs. They were equally at home with pole and paddle, with axe and machete; and one was a good cook, and others were good men around camp. They looked like pirates in the pictures of Howard Pyle or Maxfield Parrish; one or two of them were pirates, and one worse than a pirate; but most of them were hardworking, willing, and cheerful. They were white—or, rather, the olive of southern Europe—black, copper-colored, and of all intermediate shades. In my canoe Luiz the steersman, the headman, was a Mato Grosso Negro; Julio the bowsman was from Bahia and of pure Portuguese blood; and the third man, Antonio, was a Paresi Indian.

The actual surveying of the river was done by Colonel Rondon and Lyra, with Kermit as their as-

Launching the canoes down the River of Doubt

sistant. Kermit went first in his little canoe with the sighting rod, on which two disks, one red and one white, were placed a meter apart. He selected a place which commanded as long vistas as possible upstream and down, and which therefore might be at the angle of a bend; landed; cut away the branches which obstructed the view; and set up the sighting pole—incidentally encountering marabunta wasps and swarms of biting and stinging ants. Lyra, from his station upstream, with his telemeter [range-finding instrument] established the distance, while Colonel Rondon, with the compass took the direction, and made the records. Then they moved on to the point Kermit had left, and Kermit established a new point within their sight. The first half-day's work was slow. The general course of the stream was a trifle east of north, but at short intervals it bent and curved literally toward every point of the compass. Kermit landed nearly a hundred times, and we made but 9⅓ kilometers.

My canoe ran ahead of the surveying canoes. The height of the water made the going easy, for most of the snags and fallen trees were well beneath the surface. Now and then, however, the swift water hurried us toward ripples that marked ugly spikes of sunken timber, or toward uprooted trees that stretched almost across the stream. Then the muscles stood out on the backs and arms of the paddlers as stroke on stroke they urged us away from and past the obstacle. If the leaning or fallen trees were the thorny, slender-stemmed boritana palms, which love the wet, they were often, although plunged beneath the river, in full and vigorous growth, their stems curving upward, and their frond-crowned tops shaken by the rushing water.

It was interesting work, for no civilized man, no white man, had ever gone down or up this river or seen the country through which we were passing. The lofty and matted forest rose like a green wall on either hand. The trees were stately and beautiful. The looped and twisted vines hung from them like great ropes. Masses of epiphytes grew both on the

Drifting into the unknown wilderness

dead trees and the living; some had huge leaves like elephants' ears. Now and then fragrant scents were blown to us from flowers on the banks. There were not many birds, and for the most part, the forest was silent; rarely we heard strange calls from the depths of the woods or saw a cormorant or ibis.

My canoe ran only a couple of hours. Then we halted to wait for the others. After a couple of hours more, as the surveyors had not turned up, we landed and made camp at a spot where the bank rose

226

sharply for a hundred yards to a level stretch of ground. Our canoes were moored to trees. The axe men cleared a space for the tents; they were pitched, the baggage was brought up, and fires were kindled. The woods were almost soundless. Through them ran old tapir trails, but there was no fresh sign. Before nightfall the surveyors arrived. There were a few piums and gnats, and a few mosquitoes after dark, but not enough to make us uncomfortable. The small stingless bees, of slightly aromatic odor, swarmed while daylight lasted and crawled over our faces and hands; they were such tame, harmless little things that when they tickled too much, I always tried to brush them away without hurting them. But they became a great nuisance after a while. It had been raining at intervals, and the weather was overcast; but after the sun went down, the sky cleared. The stars were brilliant overhead, and the new moon hung in the west. It was a pleasant night, the air almost cool, and we slept soundly.

Next morning, the two surveying canoes left immediately after breakfast. An hour later, the two pairs of lashed canoes pushed off. I kept our canoe to let Cherrie collect, for in the early hours, we could hear a number of birds in the woods nearby. The most interesting birds he shot were a cotinga, brilliant turquoise-blue with a magenta-purple throat, and a big woodpecker, black above and cinnamon below with an entirely red head and neck.

It was almost noon before we started. We saw a few more birds; there were fresh tapir and paca [a large rodent] tracks at one point where we landed; once we heard howler monkeys from the depth of the forest; and once we saw a big otter in midstream. As we drifted and paddled down the swirling brown current, through the vivid rain-drenched green of the tropic forest, the trees leaned over the river from both banks. When those that had fallen in the river at some narrow point were very tall, or where it happened that two fell opposite each other, they formed barriers which the men in the leading canoes cleared with their axes. There were many palms, both the buriti with its stiff fronds like enormous fans, and a handsome species of bacaba, with very long, gracefully curving fronds. In places the palms stood close together, towering and slender, their stems a stately colonnade, their fronds an arched fretwork against the sky. Butterflies of many hues fluttered over the river. The day was overcast, with showers of rain. When the sun broke through rifts in the clouds, his shafts turned the forest to gold.

In mid-afternoon, we came to the mouth of a big and swift affluent entering from the right. It was undoubtedly the Bandeira, which we had crossed well toward its head, some ten days before, on our road to José Bonifácio.

The Nhambiquaras had then told Colonel Ron-

Colonel Roosevelt's and Colonel Rondon's canoes at the mouth of the Bandeira River

don that it flowed into the Dúvida. After its junction, with the added volume of water, the river widened without losing its depth. It was so high that it had overflowed and stood among the trees on the lower levels. Only the higher stretches were dry. On the sheer banks where we landed, we had to push the canoes for yards or rods through the branches of the submerged trees, hacking and hewing. There were occasional bays and oxbows [U-shaped river bends] from which the current had shifted. In these, the coarse marsh grass grew tall.

This evening, we made camp on a flat of dry ground, densely wooded, of course, directly on the edge of the river and five feet above it. It was fine to see the speed and sinewy ease with which the choppers cleared an open space for the tents. Next morning, when we bathed before sunrise, we dived into deep water right from the shore and from the moored canoes. This second day we made 16½ kilometers along the course of the river, and nine kilometers in a straight line almost due north.

The following day, March 1, there was much rain—sometimes showers, sometimes vertical sheets of water. Our course was somewhat west of north, and we made 20½ kilometers. We passed signs of Indian habitation. There were abandoned palm-leaf shelters on both banks. On the left bank, we came to two or three old Indian fields, grown up with coarse fern and studded with the burned skeletons of trees. At the mouth of a brook which entered from the right, some sticks stood in the water, marking the site of an old fish trap.

At one point, we found the tough vine handrail of an Indian bridge running right across the river, a couple of feet above it. Evidently the bridge had been built at low water. Three stout poles had been driven into the streambed in a line at right angles to the current. The bridge had consisted of poles fastened to these supports, leading between them and from the support at each end to the banks. The rope of tough vines had been stretched as a handrail, necessary with such precarious footing. The rise of the river had swept away the bridge, but the props and the rope handrail remained. In the afternoon, from the boat, Cherrie shot a large dark-gray monkey with a prehensile tail. It was very good eating.

We camped on a dry level space, but a few feet above, and close beside, the river—so that our swimming bath was handy. The trees were cleared, and camp was made with orderly hurry. One of the men almost stepped on a poisonous coral snake, which would have been a serious thing, as his feet were bare. But I had on stout shoes, and the fangs of these serpents—unlike those of the pit vipers—are too short to penetrate good leather. I promptly put my foot on him, and he bit my shoe with harmless venom.

We were still in the Brazilian highlands. The for-

*George Cherrie and Colonel Roosevelt swimming near the
primitive bridge*

est did not teem with life. It was generally rather
silent; we did not hear such a chorus of birds and
mammals as we had occasionally heard even on our
overland journey, when more than once we had
been awakened at dawn by the howling, screaming,
yelping, and chattering of monkeys, toucans, macaws, parrots, and parakeets. There were, however,
from time to time, queer sounds from the forest,
and after nightfall, different kinds of frogs and insects uttered strange cries and calls. In volume and
frequency these seemed to increase until midnight.
Then they died away, and before dawn everything
was silent

At this camp the *carregadores* ants completely devoured the doctor's undershirt and ate holes in his mosquito net; and they also ate the strap of Lyra's gun case. The little stingless bees, of many kinds, swarmed in such multitudes, and were so persevering, that we had to wear our head nets when we wrote or skinned specimens.

The following day was almost without rain. It was delightful to drift and paddle slowly down the beautiful tropical river. Until mid-afternoon the current was not very fast, and the broad, deep, placid stream bent and curved in every direction, although the general course was northwest. The country was flat, and more of the land was under than above water. Continually we found ourselves traveling between stretches of marshy forest, where for miles the water stood or ran among the trees. Once we passed a hillock. We saw brilliantly colored parakeets and trogons. At last the slow current quickened. Faster it went, and faster, until it began to run like a millrace and we heard the roar of rapids ahead. We pulled to the right bank, moored the canoes, and while most of the men pitched camp, two or three of them accompanied us to examine the rapids. We had made twenty kilometers.

We soon found that the rapids were a serious obstacle. There were many curls and one or two regular falls, perhaps six-feet high. It would have been impossible to run them, and they stretched for nearly a mile. The carry, however, which led through woods and over rocks in a nearly straight line, was somewhat shorter. It was not an easy portage over which to carry heavy loads and drag heavy dugout canoes. At the point where the descent was steepest, there were great naked flats of friable sandstone and conglomerate. Over parts of these, where there was a surface of fine sand, there was a growth of coarse grass. Other parts were bare and had been worn by the weather into fantastic shapes—one projection looked like an old-fashioned beaver hat upside down. In this place, where the naked flats of rock showed the projection of the ledge through which the river had cut its course, the torrent rushed down a deep, sheer-sided, and extremely narrow channel. At one point, it was less than two yards across, and for quite a distance, not more than five or six yards. Yet only a mile or two above the rapids, the deep, placid river was at least a hundred yards wide. It seemed extraordinary, almost impossible, that so broad a river could in so short a space of time contract its dimensions to the width of the strangled channel through which it now poured its entire volume.

This has for long been a station where the Nhambiquaras at intervals built their ephemeral villages and tilled the soil with the rude and destructive cultivation of savages. There were several abandoned old fields, where the dense growth of rank fern hid the tangle of burnt and fallen logs. Nor had the Nhambiquaras been long absent. In one trail we found what gypsies would have called a *pateran*, a couple of branches arranged crosswise, eight leaves to a branch; it had some special significance, belonging to that class of signals, each with some peculiar and often complicated meaning, which are commonly used by many wild peoples. The Indians had thrown a simple bridge, consisting of four long poles, without a handrail, across one of the narrowest parts of the rock gorge through which the river foamed in its rapid descent. This sub-tribe of Indians was called the Navaïté; we named the rapids after them, Navaïté Rapids.

We spent March 3 and 4 and the morning of the 5th in portaging around the rapids. The first night we camped in the forest beside the spot where we had halted. Next morning, we moved the baggage to the foot of the rapids, where we intended to launch the canoes, and pitched our tents on the open sandstone flat. It rained heavily. The little bees were in such swarms as to be a nuisance. Many small stinging bees were with them, which stung badly. We were bitten by huge horseflies, the size of bumblebees. More serious annoyance was caused by the pium and *borrachudo* flies during the hours of daylight, and by the *pólvora*, the sand flies, after dark. There were a few mosquitoes. The *borrachudos* were the worst pests; they brought the blood at once and left marks that lasted for weeks. I did my writing in head net and gauntlets. Fortunately we had with us several bottles of "fly dope" [insect repellent]—so named on the label—put up, with the rest of our medicine, by Doctor Alexander Lambert;[1] he had tested it in the north woods and found it excellent. I had never before been forced to use such an ointment and had been reluctant to take it with me; but now I was glad enough to have it, and we all of us found it exceedingly useful. I would never again go into mosquito or sand-fly country without it. The effect of an application wears off after half an hour or so, and under many conditions, as when one is perspiring freely, it is of no use; but there are times when minute mosquitoes and gnats get through head nets and under mosquito bars, and when the ointment occasionally renewed may permit one to get sleep or rest which would otherwise be impossible of attainment. The termites got into our tent on the sand flat, ate holes in Cherrie's mosquito net and poncho, and were starting to work at our duffel bags, when we discovered them.

Packing the loads across was simple. Dragging the heavy dugouts was labor. The biggest of the two waterlogged ones was the heaviest. Lyra and Kermit did the job. All the men were employed at it except the cook and one man who was down with fever. A road was chopped through the forest, and a couple of hundred stout six-foot poles, or small logs, were

Colonel Roosevelt writing, protected from insects with netting and gloves

cut as rollers and placed about two yards apart. With block and tackle, the seven dugouts were hoisted out of the river up the steep banks and up the rise of ground until the level was reached. Then the men harnessed themselves two by two on the dragrope, while one of their number pried behind with a lever, and the canoe, bumping and sliding, was twitched through the woods. Over the sandstone flats there were some ugly ledges, but on the whole, the course was downhill and relatively easy.

Looking at the way the work was done, at the goodwill, the endurance, and the bull-like strength of the *camaradas*, and at the intelligence and the unwearied efforts of their commanders, one could but wonder at the ignorance of those who do not realize the energy and the power that are so often possessed by, and that may be so readily developed in, the men of the tropics. Another subject of perpetual wonder is the attitude of certain men who stay at home, and still more the attitude of certain men who travel under easy conditions and who belittle the achievements of the real explorers of, the real adventurers in, the great wilderness. The impostors and romancers among explorers or would-be explorers and wilderness wanderers have been unusually prominent in connection with South America (although the conspicuous ones are not South Americans, by the way); and these are fit subjects for condemnation and derision. But the work of the genuine explorer and wilderness wanderer is fraught with fatigue, hardship, and danger.

Many of the men of little knowledge talk glibly of portaging as if it were simple and easy. A portage over rough and unknown ground is always a work of difficulty and of some risk to the canoe; and in the untrodden, or even in the unfrequented, wilderness, risk to the canoe is a serious matter. This particular portage at Navaïté Rapids was far from being unusually difficult; yet it not only cost 2½ days of severe and incessant labor, but it cost something in damage to the canoes. One in particular, the one in which I had been journeying, was split in a manner

Dragging the canoes over a portage with ropes and logs

which caused us serious uneasiness as to how long, even after being patched, it would last. Where the canoes were launched, the bank was sheer, and one of the waterlogged canoes filled and went to the bottom; and there was more work in raising it.

We were still wholly unable to tell where we were going or what lay ahead of us. Round the campfire, after supper, we held endless discussions and hazarded all kinds of guesses on both subjects. The river might bend sharply to the west and enter the Ji-Paraná high up or low down, or go north to the Madeira, or bend eastward and enter the Tapajós, or fall into the Canumá and finally through one of its mouths enter the Amazon direct. Lyra inclined to the first, and Colonel Rondon to the second, of these propositions. We did not know whether we had one hundred or eight hundred kilometers to go, whether the stream would be fairly smooth or whether we would encounter waterfalls, or rapids, or even some big marsh or lake. We could not tell whether or not we would meet hostile Indians, although no one of us ever went ten yards from camp without his rifle. We had no idea how much time the trip would take. We had entered a land of unknown possibilities.

We started downstream again early in the afternoon of March 5. Our hands and faces were swollen from the bites and stings of the insect pests at the sand-flat camp, and it was a pleasure once more to be in the middle of the river, where they did not come, in any numbers, while we were in motion. The current was swift, but the river was so deep that there were no serious obstructions. Twice we went down over slight riffles, which in the dry season were doubtless rapids; and once we struck a spot where many whirlpools marked the presence underneath of boulders which would have been above water had not the river been so swollen by the rains. The distance we covered in a day going downstream would have taken us a week if we had been going up. The course wound hither and thither, sometimes in sigmoid curves; but the general direction was east of north. As usual, it was very beautiful; and we never could tell what might appear around any curve. In the forest that rose on either hand were tall rubber trees. The surveying canoes, as usual, went first, while I shepherded the two pairs of lashed cargo canoes. I kept them always between me and the surveying canoes—ahead of me until I passed the surveying canoes, then behind me until, after an hour or so, I had chosen a place to camp. There was so much overflowed ground that it took us some little time this afternoon before we found a flat place high enough to be dry.

Just before reaching camp, Cherrie shot a jacu, a handsome bird somewhat akin to, but much smaller than, a turkey; after Cherrie had taken its skin, its body made an excellent *canja*. We saw parties of monkeys; and the false bellbirds uttered their ringing whistles in the dense timber around our tents. The giant ants, an inch and a quarter long, were rather too plentiful around this camp; one stung Kermit; it was almost like the sting of a small scorpion and pained severely for a couple of hours. This half-day we made twelve kilometers.

On the following day, we made nineteen kilometers, the river twisting in every direction, but in its general course running a little west of north. Once we stopped at a bee tree, to get honey. The tree was a towering giant, of the kind called milk tree, because a thick milky juice runs freely from any cut. Our *camaradas* eagerly drank the white fluid that flowed from the wounds made by their axes. I tried it. The taste was not unpleasant, but it left a sticky feeling in the mouth. The helmsman of my boat, Luiz, a powerful Negro, chopped into the tree, balancing himself with springy ease on a slight scaffolding. The honey was in a hollow and had been made by medium-sized stingless bees. At the mouth of the hollow, they had built a curious entrance of their own, in the shape of a spout of wax about a foot long. At the opening, the walls of the spout showed the wax formation, but elsewhere it had become in color and texture indistinguishable from the bark of the tree. The honey was delicious, sweet and yet with a tart flavor.

At about three o'clock, I was in the lead, when

the current began to run more quickly. We passed over one or two decided ripples, and then heard the roar of rapids ahead, while the stream began to race. We drove the canoe into the bank and then went down a tapir trail, which led alongside the river, to reconnoiter. A quarter of a mile's walk showed us that there were big rapids, down which the canoes could not go; and we returned to the landing. All the canoes had gathered there, and Rondon, Lyra, and Kermit started downstream to explore. They returned in an hour, with the information that the rapids continued for a long distance, with falls and steep pitches of broken water, and that the portage would take several days. We made camp just above the rapids. Ants swarmed, and some of them bit savagely. Our men, in clearing away the forest for our tents, left several very tall and slender accashy [likely means *açaí*] palms; the bole of this palm is as straight as an arrow and is crowned with delicate, gracefully curved fronds. We had come along the course of the river almost exactly a hundred kilometers; it had twisted so that we were only about fifty-five kilometers north of our starting point. The rock was porphyritic [having larger crystals in a fine background].

The 7th, 8th, and 9th we spent in carrying the loads and dragging and floating the dugouts past the series of rapids at whose head we had stopped.

The first day, we shifted camp a kilometer and a

half to the foot of this series of rapids. This was a charming and picturesque camp. It was at the edge of the river, where there was a little, shallow bay with a beach of firm sand. In the water, at the middle point of the beach, stood a group of three buriti palms, their great trunks rising like columns. Round the clearing in which our tents stood were several very big trees; two of them were rubber trees. Kermit went downstream five or six kilometers and returned, having shot a jacu and found that at the point which he had reached, there was another rapids, almost a fall, which would necessitate our again dragging the canoes over a portage. Antonio, the Paresi, shot a big monkey; of this I was glad because portaging is hard work, and the men appreciated the meat. So far Cherrie had collected sixty birds on the Dúvida, all of them new to the collection, and some probably new to science. We saw the fresh sign of paca, agouti [rodent that looks like a large guinea pig], and the small peccary; and Kermit, with the dogs, roused a tapir, which crossed the river right through the rapids; but no one got a shot at it.

Except at one or perhaps two points, a very big dugout, lightly loaded, could probably run all these rapids. But even in such a canoe, it would be silly to make the attempt on an exploring expedition, where the loss of a canoe or of its contents means disaster; and, moreover, such a canoe could not be taken, for it would be impossible to drag it over the portages on the occasions when the portages became inevitable. Our canoes would not have lived half a minute in the wild water.

On the second day, the canoes and loads were brought down to the foot of the first rapids. Lyra cleared the path and laid the logs for rollers, while Kermit dragged the dugouts up the bank from the water with block and tackle, with strain of rope and muscle. Then they joined forces, as over the uneven ground it needed the united strength of all their men to get the heavy dugouts along. Meanwhile, the colonel with one attendant measured the distance and then went on a long hunt but saw no game. I strolled down beside the river for a couple of miles but also saw nothing. In the dense tropical forest of the Amazonian basin, hunting is very difficult, especially for men who are trying to pass through the country as rapidly as possible. On such a trip as ours, getting game is largely a matter of chance.

On the following day, Lyra and Kermit brought down the canoes and loads, with hard labor, to the little beach by the three palms where our tents were pitched. Many *pacovas* grew round about. The men used their immense leaves, some of which were twelve feet long and 2½ feet broad, to roof the flimsy shelters under which they hung their hammocks. I went into the woods, but in the tangle of vegetation, it would have been a mere hazard had I seen any big animal. Generally the woods were silent and empty. Now and then little troops of birds of many kinds passed—wood-hewers, ant-thrushes, tanagers, flycatchers—as in the spring and fall similar troops of warblers, chickadees, and nuthatches pass through our northern woods. On the rocks and on the great trees by the river grew beautiful white and lilac orchids—the sobralia of sweet and delicate fragrance. For the moment, my own books seemed a trifle heavy, and perhaps I would have found the day tedious if Kermit had not lent me the *Oxford Book of French Verse*. Eustache Deschamps, Joachim du Bellay, Ronsard, the delightful La Fontaine, the delightful but appalling Villon, Victor Hugo's "Guitare," Madame Desbordes-Valmore's lines on the little girl and her pillow, as dear little verses about a child as ever were written—these and many others comforted me much, as I read them in head net and gauntlets, sitting on a log by an unknown river in the Amazonian forest.

On the 10th, we again embarked and made a kilometer and a half, spending most of the time in getting past two more rapids. Near the first of these, we saw a small caiman, a *jacaré-tinga*. At each set of rapids, the canoes were unloaded and the loads borne past on the shoulders of the *camaradas*; three of the canoes were paddled down by a couple of naked paddlers apiece; and the two sets of double canoes were let down by ropes, one of one couple being swamped but rescued and brought safely to shore on each occasion. One of the men was upset while working in the swift water, and his face was cut against the stones. Lyra and Kermit did the actual work with the *camaradas*. Kermit, dressed substantially like the *camaradas* themselves, worked in the water, and, as the overhanging branches were thronged with crowds of biting and stinging ants, he was marked and blistered over his whole body. Indeed, we all suffered more or less from these ants, while the swarms of biting flies grew constantly more numerous. The termites ate holes in my helmet and also in the cover of my cot. Everyone else had a hammock.

At this camp, we had come down the river about 102 kilometers, according to the surveying records, and in height had descended nearly 100 meters, as shown by the aneroid [barometer]—although the figure in this case is only an approximation, as an aneroid cannot be depended on for absolute accuracy of results.

Next morning, we found that during the night we had met with a serious misfortune. We had halted at the foot of the rapids. The canoes were moored to trees on the bank, at the tail of the broken water. The two old canoes, although one of them was our biggest cargo carrier, were waterlogged and heavy, and one of them was leaking. In the night, the river rose. The leaky canoe, which at best was too low in the water, must have gradually filled from the wash of the waves. It sank, dragging down the other; they began to roll, bursting their moorings; and in the morning, they had disappeared.

A canoe was launched to look for them; but, rolling over the boulders on the rocky bottom, they had at once been riven asunder, and the big fragments that were soon found, floating in eddies, or along the shore, showed that it was useless to look farther. We called these rapids Broken Canoe Rapids.

It was not pleasant to have to stop for some days; thanks to the rapids, we had made slow progress, and with our necessarily limited supply of food, and no knowledge whatever of what was ahead of us, it was important to make good time. But there was no alternative. We had to build either one big canoe or two small ones. It was raining heavily as the men started to explore in different directions for good canoe trees. Three—which ultimately proved not very good for the purpose—were found close to camp, splendid-looking trees, one of them five feet in diameter three feet from the ground. The axe men immediately attacked this one under the superintendence of Colonel Rondon. Lyra and Kermit started in opposite directions to hunt. Lyra killed a jacu for us, and Kermit killed two monkeys for the men. Toward nightfall it cleared. The moon was nearly full, and the foaming river gleamed like silver.

On the 12th, the men were still hard at work hollowing out the hard wood of the big tree, with axe and adze, while watch and ward were kept over them to see that the idlers did not shirk at the expense of the industrious. Kermit and Lyra again hunted; the former shot a curassow, which was welcome, as we were endeavoring in all ways to economize our food supply. We were using the tops of palms also. I spent the day hunting in the woods, for the most part by the river, but saw nothing. In the season of the rains, game is away from the river and fish are scarce and turtles absent. Yet it was pleasant to be in the great silent forest. Here and there grew immense trees, and on some of them mighty buttresses sprang from the base. The lianas and vines were of every size and shape. Some were twisted and some were not. Some came down straight and slender from branches a hundred feet above. Others curved like long serpents around the trunks. Others were like knotted cables. In the shadow, there was little noise. The wind rarely moved the hot, humid air. There were few flowers or birds. Insects were altogether too abundant, and even when traveling slowly, it was impossible always to avoid them—not to speak of our constant companions the bees, mosquitoes, and especially the *borrachudos*, or bloodsucking flies.

Now while bursting through a tangle, I disturbed a nest of wasps, whose resentment was active; now

I heedlessly stepped among the outliers of a small party of the carnivorous foraging ants; now, grasping a branch as I stumbled, I shook down a shower of fire ants; and among all these my attention was particularly arrested by the bite of one of the giant ants, which stung like a hornet, so that I felt it for three hours. The *camaradas* generally went barefoot or only wore sandals; and their ankles and feet were swollen and inflamed from the bites of the *borrachudos* and ants, some being actually incapacitated from work. All of us suffered more or less, our faces and hands swelling slightly from the *borrachudo* bites; and in spite of our clothes, we were bitten all over our bodies, chiefly by ants and the small forest ticks. Because of the rain and the heat, our clothes were usually wet when we took them off at night, and just as wet when we put them on again in the morning.

All day on the 13th, the men worked at the canoe, making good progress. In rolling and shifting the huge, heavy tree trunk, everyone had to assist now and then. The work continued until ten in the evening, as the weather was clear. After nightfall, some of the men held candles and the others plied axe or adze, standing within or beside the great, half-hollowed logs, while the flicker of the lights showed the tropic forest rising in the darkness round about. The night air was hot and still and heavy with moisture. The men were stripped to the waist. Olive and copper and ebony, their skins glistened as if oiled and rippled with the ceaseless play of the thews [strong muscles] beneath.

On the morning of the 14th, the work was resumed in a torrential tropic downpour. The canoe was finished, dragged down to the water, and launched soon after midday, and another hour or so saw us under way. The descent was marked, and the swollen river raced along. Several times we passed great whirlpools, sometimes shifting, sometimes steady. Half a dozen times we ran over rapids, and, although they were not high enough to have been obstacles to loaded Canadian canoes, two of them were serious to us. Our heavily laden, clumsy dugouts were sunk to within three or four inches of the surface of the river, and, although they were buoyed on each side with bundles of buriti-palm branch stems, they shipped a great deal of water in the rapids.

The two biggest rapids we only just made, and after each, we had hastily to push ashore in order to bail. In one set of big ripples or waves, my canoe was nearly swamped. In a wilderness, where what is ahead is absolutely unknown, alike in terms of time, space, and method—for we had no idea where we would come out, how we would get out, or when we would get out—it is of vital consequence not to lose one's outfit, especially the provisions; and yet it is of only less consequence to go as rapidly as possible lest all the provisions be exhausted and the final stages of the expedition be accomplished by men weakened from semi-starvation, and therefore ripe for disaster.

On this occasion, of the two hazards, we felt it necessary to risk running the rapids, for our progress had been so very slow that unless we made up the time, it was probable that we would be short of food before we got where we could expect to procure any more except what little the country in the time of the rains and floods might yield. We ran until after five, so that the work of pitching camp was finished in the dark. We had made nearly sixteen kilometers in a direction slightly east of north. This evening the air was fresh and cool.

The following morning, the 15th of March, we started in good season. For six kilometers we drifted and paddled down the swift river without incident. At times we saw lofty Brazil nut trees rising above the rest of the forest on the banks; and back from the river, these trees grow to enormous proportions, towering like giants. There were great rubber trees also, their leaves always in sets of threes. Then the ground on either hand rose into boulder-strewn, forest-clad hills, and the roar of broken water announced that once more our course was checked by dangerous rapids. Round a bend we came on them; a wide descent of white water, with an island in the middle, at the upper

The island in the center of the rapids

edge. Here grave misfortune befell us, and graver misfortune was narrowly escaped.

Kermit, as usual, was leading in his canoe. It was the smallest and least seaworthy of all. He had in it little except a week's supply of our boxed provisions and a few tools, fortunately none of the food for the *camaradas*. His dog Trigueiro was with him. Besides himself, the crew consisted of two men: João, the helmsman, or pilot, as he is called in Brazil, and Simplicio, the bowman [oarsman nearest the bow]. Both were Negroes and exceptionally good men in every way. Kermit halted his canoe on the left bank, above the rapids, and waited for the colonel's canoe.

Then the colonel and Lyra walked down the bank to see what was ahead. Kermit took his canoe across to the island to see whether the descent could be better accomplished on the other side. Having made his investigation, he ordered the men to return to the bank he had left, and the dugout was headed upstream accordingly.

Before they had gone a dozen yards, the paddlers digging their paddles with all their strength into the swift current, one of the shifting whirlpools of which I have spoken came downstream, whirled them around, and swept them so close to the rapids that no human power could avoid going over them. As they were drifting into them broadside on, Kermit yelled to the steersman to turn her head, so as to take them in the only way that offered any chance whatever of safety. The water came aboard, wave after wave, as they raced down. They reached the bottom with the canoe upright, but so full as barely to float, and the paddlers urged her toward the shore. They had nearly reached the bank, when another whirlpool or whirling eddy tore them away and hurried them back to midstream, where the dugout filled and turned over. João, seizing the rope, started to swim ashore; the rope was pulled from his hand, but he reached the bank. Poor Simplicio must have been pulled under at once and his life beaten out on the boulders beneath the racing torrent. He never rose again, nor did we ever recover his body.

Kermit clutched his rifle, his favorite 405 Winchester with which he had done most of his hunting both in Africa and America, and climbed on the bottom of the upset boat. In a minute he was swept into the second series of rapids and whirled away from the rolling boat, losing his rifle. The water beat his helmet down over his head and face and drove him beneath the surface; and when he rose at last, he was almost drowned, his breath and strength almost spent. He was in swift but quiet water and swam toward an overhanging branch. His jacket hindered him, but he knew he was too nearly gone to be able to get it off, and, thinking with the curious calm one feels when death is but a moment away, he realized that the utmost his failing strength could do was to reach the branch. He reached, and clutched it, and then almost lacked strength to haul himself out on the land.

Good Trigueiro had faithfully swum alongside him through the rapids, and now himself scrambled ashore. It was a very narrow escape. Kermit was a great comfort and help to me on the trip; but the fear of some fatal accident befalling him was always a nightmare to me. He was to be married as soon as the trip was over, and it did not seem to me that I could bear to bring bad tidings to his betrothed and to his mother.

Simplicio was unmarried. Later we sent to his mother all the money that would have been his had he lived. The following morning we put on one side of the post erected to mark our camping spot the following inscription, in Portuguese:

"IN THESE RAPIDS DIED POOR SIMPLICIO."

On an expedition such as ours, death is one of the accidents that may at any time occur, and narrow escapes from death are too common to be felt as they would be felt elsewhere. One mourns sincerely, but mourning cannot interfere with labor. We immediately proceeded with the work of the portage. From the head to the tail of this series of rapids, the distance was about six hundred yards. A path was cut along the bank, over which the loads were brought. The empty canoes ran the rapids without mishap, each with two skilled paddlers. One of the canoes almost ran into a swimming tapir at the head of the rapids; it went down the rapids and then climbed out of the river.

Kermit, accompanied by João, went three or four miles down the river, looking for the body of Simplicio and for the sunk canoe. He found neither. But he found a box of provisions and a paddle and salvaged both by swimming into midstream after them. He also found that a couple of kilometers below, there was another stretch of rapids, and following them on the left-hand bank to the foot, he found that they were worse than the ones we had just passed and impassable for canoes on this left-hand side.

The morning of the 16th was dark and gloomy. Through sheets of blinding rain, we left our camp of misfortune for another camp where misfortune also awaited us. Less than half an hour took our dugouts to the head of the rapids below. As Kermit had already explored the left-hand side, Colonel Rondon and Lyra went down the right-hand side and found a channel which led round the worst part, so that they deemed it possible to let down the canoes by ropes from the bank. The distance to the foot of the rapids was about a kilometer.

While the loads were being brought down the left bank, Luiz and Antonio Correa, our two best watermen, started to take a canoe down the right side, and Colonel Rondon walked ahead to see anything he could about the river. He was accompanied by one of our three dogs, Lobo. After walking about a kilometer, he heard ahead a kind of howling noise, which he thought was made by spider monkeys. He walked in the direction of the sound, and Lobo ran ahead. In a minute, he heard Lobo yell with pain, and then, still yelping, come toward him, while the creature that was howling also approached, evidently in pursuit. In a moment, a second yell from Lobo, followed by silence, announced that he was dead; and the sound of the howling when near convinced Rondon that the dog had been killed by an

Indian, doubtless with two arrows. Probably the Indian was howling to lure the spider monkeys toward him.

Rondon fired his rifle in the air, to warn off the Indian or Indians, who in all probability had never seen a civilized man and certainly could not imagine that one was in the neighborhood. He then returned to the foot of the rapids, where the portage was still going on, and, in company with Lyra, Kermit, and Antonio Paresi, the Indian, walked back to where Lobo's body lay. Sure enough, he found him, slain by two arrows. One arrowhead was in him, and nearby was a strange stick used in the very primitive method of fishing of all these Indians. Antonio recognized its purpose. The Indians, who were apparently two or three in number, had fled. Some beads and trinkets were left on the spot to show that we were not angry and were friendly.

Meanwhile Cherrie stayed at the head and I at the foot of the portage as guards. Luiz and Antonio Correa brought down one canoe safely. The next was the new canoe, which was very large and heavy, being made of wood that would not float. In the rapids the rope broke, and the canoe was lost, Luiz being nearly drowned.

It was a very bad thing to lose the canoe, but it was even worse to lose the rope and pulleys. This meant that it would be physically impossible to hoist big canoes up even small hills or rocky hill-

258

ocks, such as had been so frequent beside the many rapids we had encountered. It was not wise to spend the four days necessary to build new canoes where we were, in danger of attack from the Indians. Moreover, new rapids might be very near, in which case the new canoes would hamper us. Yet the four remaining canoes would not carry all the loads and all the men, no matter how we cut the loads down; and we intended to cut everything down at once.

We had been gone eighteen days. We had used over a third of our food. We had gone only 125 kilometers, and it was probable that we had at least five times, perhaps six or seven times, this distance still to go. We had taken a fortnight to descend rapids amounting in the aggregate to less than seventy yards of fall; a very few yards of fall makes a dangerous rapid when the river is swollen and swift and there are obstructions. We had only one aneroid to determine our altitude, and therefore could make merely a loose approximation to it, but we probably had between two and three times this descent in the aggregate of rapids ahead of us. So far, the country had offered little in the way of food except palm tops. We had lost four canoes and one man. We were in the country of wild Indians, who shot well with their bows. It behooved us to go warily, but also to make all speed possible, if we were to avoid serious trouble.

The best plan seemed to be to march thirteen

men down along the bank, while the remaining canoes, lashed two and two, floated down beside them. If after two or three days we found no bad rapids, and there seemed a reasonable chance of going some distance at decent speed, we could then build the new canoes—preferably two small ones, this time, instead of one big one. We left all the baggage we could. We were already down as far as comfort would permit, but we now struck off much of the comfort. Cherrie, Kermit, and I had been sleeping under a very light fly; and there was another small light tent for one person, kept for possible emergencies. The last was given to me for my cot, and all five of the others swung their hammocks under the big fly. This meant that we left two big and heavy tents behind. A box of surveying instruments was also abandoned. Each of us got his personal belongings down to one box or duffel bag—although there was only a small diminution thus made because we had so little that the only way to make a serious diminution was to restrict ourselves to the clothes on our backs.

The biting flies and ants were to us a source of discomfort and at times of what could fairly be called torment. But to the *camaradas*, most of whom went barefoot or only wore sandals—and they never did or would wear shoes—the effect was more serious. They wrapped their legs and feet in pieces of canvas or hide, and the feet of three of them became so swollen that they were crippled and could not walk any distance. The doctor, whose courage and cheerfulness never flagged, took excellent care of them. Thanks to him, there had been among them hitherto but one or two slight cases of fever. He administered to each man daily a half-gram—nearly eight grains—of quinine, and every third or fourth day a double dose.

The following morning Colonel Rondon, Lyra, Kermit, Cherrie, and nine of the *camaradas* started in single file down the bank, while the doctor and I went in the two double canoes, with six *camaradas*, three of them the invalids with swollen feet. We halted continually, as we went about three times as fast as the walkers; and we traced the course of the river. After forty minutes' actual going in the boats, we came to some rapids; the unloaded canoes ran them without difficulty, while the loads were portaged. In an hour and a half, we were again underway, but in ten minutes came to other rapids, where the river ran among islands and there were several big curls.

The clumsy, heavily laden dugouts, lashed in couples, were unwieldy and hard to handle. The rapids came just round a sharp bend, and we got caught in the upper part of the swift water and had to run the first set of rapids in consequence. We in the leading pair of dugouts were within an ace of coming to grief on some big boulders against which we were swept by a crosscurrent at the turn. All of us paddling hard—scraping and bumping—we got through by the skin of our teeth and managed to make the bank and moor our dugouts. It was a narrow escape from grave disaster. The second pair of lashed dugouts profited by our experience and made the run—with risk, but with less risk—and moored beside us. Then all the loads were taken out, and the empty canoes were run down through the least dangerous channels among the islands.

This was a long portage, and we camped at the foot of the rapids, having made nearly seven kilometers. Here a little river, a rapid stream of volume equal to the Dúvida at the point where we first embarked, joined from the west. Colonel Rondon and Kermit came to it first, and the former named it Rio Kermit. There was in it a waterfall about six or eight feet high, just above the junction. Here we found plenty of fish. Lyra caught two pacu, good-sized, deep-bodied fish. They were delicious eating.

Antonio the Paresi said that these fish never came up heavy rapids in which there were falls they had to jump. We could only hope that he was correct, as in that case, the rapids we would encounter in the future would rarely be so serious as to necessitate our dragging the heavy dugouts overland. Passing the rapids we had hitherto encountered had meant severe labor and some danger. But the event showed that he was mistaken. The worst rapids were ahead of us.

While our course as a whole had been almost due north, and sometimes east of north, yet where there were rapids, the river had generally, although not always, turned westward. This seemed to indicate that to the east of us there was a low northward projection of the central plateau across which we had traveled on muleback. This is the kind of projection that appears on the maps of this region as a sierra. Probably it sent low spurs to the west, and the farthest points of these spurs now and then caused rapids in our course (for the rapids generally came where there were hills) and for the moment deflected the river westward from its general downhill trend to the north.

There was no longer any question that the Dúvida was a big river, a river of real importance. It was not a minor affluent of some other affluent. But we were still wholly in the dark as to where it came out. It was still possible, although exceedingly improbable, that it entered the Ji-Paraná, as another river of substantially the same size, near its mouth. It was much more likely, but not probable, that it entered the Tapajós. It was probable, although far from certain, that it entered the Madeira low down, near its point of junction with the Amazon. In this event, it was likely, although again far from certain, that its

The Rio Roosevelt

mouth would prove to be the Aripuanã. The Aripuanã does not appear on the maps as a river of any size; on a good standard map of South America which I had with me, its name does not appear at all, although a dotted indication of a small river or creek at about the right place probably represents it.

Nevertheless, from the report of one of his lieutenants who had examined its mouth, and from the stories of the rubber gatherers, or *seringueiros,* Colonel Rondon had come to the conclusion that this was the largest affluent of the Madeira, with such a body of water that it must have a big drainage basin. He thought that the Dúvida was probably one of its head streams—although every existing map represented the lay of the land to be such as to render impossible the existence of such a river system and drainage basin. The rubber gatherers reported that they had gone many days' journey up the river, to a point where there was a series of heavy rapids, with above them, the junction point of two large rivers, one entering from the west. Beyond this, they had difficulties because of the hostility of the Indians, and where the junction point was no one could say. On the chance, Colonel Rondon had directed one of his subordinate officers, Lieutenant Pirineus [de Sousa Belém], to try to meet us, with boats and provisions, by ascending the Aripuanã to the point of entry of its first big affluent. This was the course followed when Amilcar had been directed to try to meet the explorers who in 1909 came down the Ji-Paraná. At that time, the effort was a failure, and the two parties never met; but we might have better luck, and in any event, the chance was worth taking.

On the morning following our camping by the mouth of the Rio Kermit, Colonel Rondon took a good deal of pains in getting a big post set up at the entry of the smaller river into the Dúvida. Then he summoned me, and all the others, to attend the ceremony of its erection. We found the *camaradas* drawn up in line, and the colonel preparing to read aloud "the orders of the day." To the post was nailed a board with "Rio Kermit" on it; and the colonel read the orders reciting that by the direction of the

Brazilian government, and inasmuch as the unknown river was evidently a great river, he formally christened it the Rio Roosevelt. This was a complete surprise to me. Both Lauro Müller and Colonel Rondon had spoken to me on the subject, and I had urged, and Kermit had urged, as strongly as possible, that the name be kept as Rio da Dúvida. We felt that the "River of Doubt" was an unusually good name, and it is always well to keep a name of this character. But my kind friends insisted otherwise, and it would have been churlish of me to object longer. I was much touched by their action, and by the ceremony itself.

At the conclusion of the reading, Colonel Rondon led in cheers for the United States and then for me and for Kermit; and the *camaradas* cheered with a will. I proposed three cheers for Brazil and then for Colonel Rondon, and Lyra, and the doctor, and then for all the *camaradas*. Then Lyra said that everybody had been cheered except Cherrie; and so we all gave three cheers for Cherrie, and the meeting broke up in high good humor.

Immediately afterward, the walkers set off on their march downstream, looking for good canoe trees. In a quarter of an hour, we followed with the canoes. As often as we overtook them, we halted until they had again gone a good distance ahead. They soon found fresh Indian sign, and actually heard the Indians; but the latter fled in panic. They

The camaradas gathered around the monument at the naming ceremony for the Rio Roosevelt

came on a little Indian fishing village, just abandoned. The three low, oblong huts, of palm leaves,
had each an entrance for a man on all fours, but no
other opening. They were dark inside, doubtless as
a protection against the swarms of biting flies. On
a pole in this village, an axe, a knife, and some
strings of red beads were left, with the hope that the
Indians would return, find the gifts, and realize that
we were friendly. We saw further Indian sign on
both sides of the river.

After about two hours and a half, we came on a
little river entering from the east. It was broad but
shallow, and at the point of entrance rushed down,
green and white, over a sharply inclined sheet of
rock. It was a lovely sight, and we halted to admire
it. Then on we went, until, when we had covered
about eight kilometers, we came on a stretch of rapids. The canoes ran them with about a third of the
loads, the other loads being carried on the men's
shoulders. At the foot of the rapids, we camped, as
there were several good canoe trees near, and we had
decided to build two rather small canoes. After
dark, the stars came out; but in the deep forest, the
glory of the stars in the night of the sky, the serene
radiance of the moon, the splendor of sunrise and
sunset, are never seen as they are seen on the vast
open plains.

The following day, the 19th, the men began work
on the canoes. The ill-fated big canoe had been

made of wood so hard that it was difficult to work, and so heavy that the chips sank like lead in the water. But these trees were *araputangas* [mahogany trees], with wood which was easier to work, and which floated. Great buttresses, or flanges, jutted out from their trunks at the base, and they bore big, hard nuts or fruits which stood erect at the ends of the branches. The first tree felled proved rotten, and moreover it was chopped so that it smashed a number of lesser trees into the kitchen, overthrowing everything, but not inflicting serious damage. Hardworking, willing, and tough though the *camaradas* were, they naturally did not have the skill of northern lumberjacks.

We hoped to finish the two canoes in three days. A space was cleared in the forest for our tents. Among the taller trees grew huge-leafed *pacovas*, or wild bananas. We bathed and swam in the river, although in it we caught piranhas. *Carregadores* ants swarmed all around our camp. As many of the nearest of their holes as we could we stopped with fire, but at night some of them got into our tents and ate things we could ill spare. In the early morning, a column of foraging ants appeared, and we drove them back, also with fire. When the sky was not overcast, the sun was very hot, and we spread out everything to dry. There were many wonderful butterflies round about, but only a few birds. Yet in the early morning and late afternoon, there was some

269

attractive bird music in the woods. The two best performers were our old friend the false bellbird, with its series of ringing whistles, and a shy, attractive ant thrush. The latter walked much on the ground, with dainty movements, curtseying and raising its tail; and in accent and sequence, although not in tone or time, its song resembled that of our white-throated sparrow.

It was three weeks since we had started down the River of Doubt. We had come along its winding course about 140 kilometers, with a descent of somewhere in the neighborhood of 124 meters. It had been slow progress. We could not tell what physical obstacles were ahead of us, nor whether the Indians would be actively hostile. But a river normally describes in its course a parabola, the steep descent being in the upper part; and we hoped that in the future we should not have to encounter so many and such difficult rapids as we had already encountered, and that, therefore, we would make better time—a hope destined to failure.

NOTES

1. Alexander Lambert (1861–1939), personal friend and family physician of Theodore Roosevelt.

IX. Down an Unknown
River into the Equatorial Forest

THE MIGHTIEST RIVER in the world is the Amazon. It runs from west to east, from the sunset to the sunrise, from the Andes to the Atlantic. The main stream flows almost along the equator, while the basin which contains its affluents extends many degrees north and south of the equator. The gigantic equatorial river basin is filled with an immense forest, the largest in the world, with which no other forest can be compared save those of western Africa and Malaysia. We were within the southern boundary of this great equatorial forest, on a river which was not merely unknown but unguessed at, no geographer having ever suspected its existence. This river flowed northward toward the equator, but whither it would go, whether it would turn one way or another, the length of its course, where it would come out, the character of the stream itself, and the character of the dwellers along its banks—all these things were yet to be discovered.

One morning while the canoes were being built, Kermit and I walked a few kilometers down the river and surveyed the next rapids below. The vast, still forest was almost empty of life. We found old Indian signs. There were very few birds, and these in the tops of the tall trees. We saw a recent tapir track; and under a *cajazeira* tree by the bank, there were the tracks of capybaras which had been eating the fallen fruit. This fruit is delicious and would make a valuable addition to our orchards.

There were tremendous downpours of rain, lasting for a couple of hours and accompanied by thunder and lightning. But on the whole, it seemed as if the rains were less heavy and continuous than they had been. We all of us had to help in building the canoes now and then. Kermit, accompanied by Antonio the Paresi and João, crossed the river and walked back to the little river that had entered from the east, so as to bring back a report of it to Colonel Rondon. Lyra took observations, by the sun and by the stars. The river had wound so that we had gone two miles for every one we made northward. Our progress had been very slow; and until we got out of the region of incessant rapids, with their attendant labor and hazard, it was not likely that we should go much faster.

On the morning of March 22, we started in our six canoes. We made ten kilometers. Twenty minutes after starting, we came to the first rapids. Here everyone walked except the three best paddlers, who took the canoes down in succession—an hour's job. Soon after this, we struck a bees' nest in the top of a tree overhanging the river; our steersman climbed out and robbed it, but, alas! lost the honey on the way back. We came to a small, steep fall which we did not dare run in our overladen, clumsy, and cranky dugouts. Fortunately, we were able to follow a deep canal which led off for a kilometer, returning just below the falls, fifty yards from where it had started. Then, having been in the boats and in motion only one hour and a half, we came to a long stretch of rapids, which it took us six hours to descend, and we camped at the foot. Everything was taken out of the canoes, and they were run down in succession. At one difficult and perilous place they were let down by ropes; and, even thus, we almost lost one.

We went down the right bank. On the opposite bank was an Indian village, evidently inhabited only during the dry season. The marks on the stumps of trees showed that these Indians had axes and knives; and there were old fields in which maize, beans, and cotton had been grown. The forest dripped and steamed. Rubber trees were plentiful. At one point in the stream, to our great surprise, we saw a flying fish. It skimmed the water like a swallow for over twenty yards.

Although we made only ten kilometers, we worked all day. The last canoes were brought down and moored to the bank at nightfall. Our tents were pitched in the darkness.

Next day, we made thirteen kilometers. We ran, all told, a little over an hour and three-quarters. Seven hours were spent in getting past a series of rapids at which the portage, over rocky and difficult ground, was a kilometer long. The canoes were run down empty—a hazardous run, in which one of them upset.

Yet while we were actually on the river, paddling and floating downstream along the reaches of swift, smooth water, it was very lovely. When we started in the morning, the day was overcast and the air was heavy with vapor. Ahead of us the shrouded river stretched between dim walls of forest, half seen in the mist. Then the sun burned up the fog and loomed through it in a red splendor that changed first to gold and then to molten white. In the dazzling light, under the brilliant blue of the sky, every detail of the magnificent forest was vivid to the eye: the great trees, the network of bush ropes, the caverns of greenery, where thick-leaved vines covered all things else. Wherever there was a hidden boulder, the surface of the current was broken by waves. In one place, in midstream, a pyramidal rock thrust itself six feet above the surface of the river. On the banks we found fresh Indian sign.

In the morning, just before leaving this camp, a tapir swam across stream a little way above us; but unfortunately we could not get a shot at it. An ample supply of tapir beef would have meant much to us. We had started with fifty days' rations; but this by no means meant full rations, in the sense of giving every man all he wanted to eat. We had

two meals a day and were on rather short com-
mons [meager rations]—both our mess and the
camaradas'—except when we got plenty of palm
tops. For our mess we had the boxes chosen by
Fiala, each containing a day's rations for six men,
our number. But we made each box last a day and
a half, or at times two days, and, in addition, we
gave some of the food to the *camaradas*. It was only
on the rare occasions when we had killed some
monkeys or curassows, or caught some fish, that
everybody had enough. We would have welcomed
that tapir. So far the game, fish, and fruit had been
too scarce to be an element of weight in our food
supply. In an exploring trip like ours, through a difficult and utterly unknown country, especially if
densely forested, there is little time to halt, and
game cannot be counted on. It is only in lands like
our own West thirty years ago, like South Africa in
the middle of the last century, like East Africa today,
that game can be made the chief food supply. On
this trip, our only substantial food supply from the
country hitherto had been that furnished by the
palm tops. Two men were detailed every day to cut
down palms for food.

A kilometer and a half after leaving this camp, we
came on a stretch of big rapids. The river here twists
in loops, and we had heard the roaring of these rapids the previous afternoon. Then we passed out of
earshot of them; but Antonio Correa, our best wa-

terman, insisted all along that the roaring meant rapids worse than any we had encountered for some days. "I was brought up in the water, and I know it like a fish, and all its sounds," said he. He was right. We had to carry the loads nearly a kilometer that afternoon, and the canoes were pulled out on the bank so that they might be in readiness to be dragged overland next day. Rondon, Lyra, Kermit, and Antonio Correa explored both sides of the river. On the opposite or left bank, they found the mouth of a considerable river, bigger than the Rio Kermit, flowing in from the west and making its entrance in the middle of the rapids. This river we christened the Taunay,[1] in honor of a distinguished Brazilian, an explorer, a soldier, a senator, who was also a writer of note. Kermit had with him two of his novels, and I had read one of his books dealing with a disastrous retreat during the Paraguayan war.

Next morning, the 25th, the canoes were brought down. A path was chopped for them and rollers laid; and halfway down the rapids, Lyra and Kermit, who were overseeing the work as well as doing their share of the pushing and hauling, got them into a canal of smooth water, which saved much severe labor. As our food supply lowered, we were constantly more desirous of economizing the strength of the men. One day more would complete a month since we had embarked on the Dúvida—as we had started in February, the lunar and calendar months coincided. We had used up over half our provisions. We had come only a trifle over 160 kilometers, thanks to the character and number of the rapids. We believed we had three or four times the distance yet to go before coming to a part of the river where we might hope to meet assistance, either from rubber gatherers, or from Pirineus, if he were really coming up the river which we were going down. If the rapids continued to be as they had been, it could not be much more than three weeks before we were in straits for food, aside from the ever-present danger of accident in the rapids; and if our progress were no faster than it had been—and we were straining to do our best—we would in such event still have several hundreds of kilometers of unknown river before us. We could not even hazard a guess at what was in front.

The river was now a really big river, and it seemed impossible that it could flow either into the Ji-Paraná or the Tapajós. It was possible that it went into the Canumá, a big affluent of the Madeira low down, and next to the Tapajós. It was more probable that it was the headwaters of the Aripuanã, a river which, as I have said, was not even named on the excellent English map of Brazil I carried. Nothing but the mouth had been known to any geographer; but the lower course had long been known to rubber gatherers, and recently a commission from the government of Amazonas [a Brazilian state] had

277

partway ascended one branch of it—not as far as the rubber gatherers had gone, and, as it turned out, not the branch we came down. Two of our men were down with fever. Another man, Julio, a fellow of powerful frame, was utterly worthless, being an inborn, lazy shirk with the heart of a ferocious cur in the body of a bullock. The others were good men, some of them very good indeed. They were under the immediate supervision of Pedrinho Craveiro, who was first-class in every way.

This camp was very lovely. It was on the edge of a bay, into which the river broadened immediately below the rapids. There was a beach of white sand, where we bathed and washed our clothes. All around us, and across the bay, and on both sides of the long water street made by the river, rose the splendid forest. There were flocks of parakeets colored green, blue, and red. Big toucans called overhead, lustrous green-black in color, with white throats, red gorgets [throats], red-and-yellow tail coverts [feathers that cover other feathers], and huge black-and-yellow bills.

Here the soil was fertile; it will be a fine site for a coffee plantation when this region is open to settlement. Surely such a rich and fertile land cannot be permitted to remain idle, to lie as a tenantless wilderness, while there are such teeming swarms of human beings in the overcrowded, over-peopled countries of the Old World. The very rapids and waterfalls which now make the navigation of the river so difficult and dangerous would drive electric trolleys up and down its whole length and far out on either side, and run mills and factories, and lighten the labor on farms. With the incoming of settlement and with the steady growth of knowledge how to fight and control tropical diseases, fear of danger to health would vanish. A land like this is a hard land for the first explorers, and perhaps for their immediate followers, but not for the people who come after them.

In mid-afternoon we were once more in the canoes; but we had paddled with the current only a few minutes, we had gone only a kilometer, when the roar of rapids in front again forced us to haul up to the bank. As usual, Rondon, Lyra, and Kermit, with Antonio Correa, explored both sides while camp was being pitched. The rapids were longer and of steeper descent than the last, but on the opposite, or western, side there was a passage down which we thought we could get the empty dugouts at the cost of dragging them only a few yards at one spot. The loads were to be carried down the hither bank, for a kilometer, to the smooth water. The river foamed between great rounded masses of rock, and at one point, there was a sheer fall of six or eight feet. We found and ate wild pineapples. Wild beans were in flower. At dinner, we had a toucan and a couple of parrots, which were very good.

All next day was spent by Lyra in superintending our three best watermen as they took the canoes down the west side of the rapids, to the foot, at the spot to which the camp had meantime been shifted. In the forest, some of the huge *cipós*, or rope vines, which were as big as cables, bore clusters of fragrant flowers. The men found several honey trees, and fruits of various kinds, and small coconuts; they chopped down an ample number of palms, for the palm cabbage; and, most important of all, they gathered a quantity of big Brazil nuts, which when roasted tasted like the best of chestnuts and are nutritious; and they caught a number of big piranhas, which were good eating. So we all had a feast, and everybody had enough to eat and was happy.

By these rapids, at the fall, Cherrie found some strange carvings on a bare mass of rock. They were evidently made by men a long time ago. As far as is known, the Indians thereabouts make no such figures now. They were in two groups, one on the surface of the rock facing the land; the other on that facing the water. The latter were nearly obliterated. The former were in good preservation, the figures sharply cut into the rock. They consisted, upon the upper flat part of the rock, of four multiple circles with a dot in the middle (◉), very accurately made and about a foot and a half in diameter; and below them, on the side of the rock, four multiple m's or inverted w's (〰). What these curious symbols represented, or who made them, we could not, of course, form the slightest idea. It may be that in a very remote past some Indian tribes of comparatively advanced culture had penetrated to this lovely river, just as we had now come to it. Before white men came to South America, there had already existed therein various semi-civilizations, some rude, others fairly advanced, which rose, flourished, and persisted through immemorial ages, and then vanished.

The vicissitudes in the history of humanity during its stay on this southern continent have been as strange, varied, and inexplicable as paleontology shows to have been the case, on the same continent, in the history of the higher forms of animal life during the age of mammals. Colonel Rondon stated that such figures as these are not found anywhere else in Mato Grosso where he has been, and, therefore, it was all the more strange to find them in this one place on the unknown river never before visited by white men, which we were descending.

Next morning we went about three kilometers before coming to some steep hills, beautiful to look upon, clad as they were in dense, tall, tropical forest, but ominous of new rapids. Sure enough, at their foot we had to haul up and prepare for a long portage. The canoes we ran down empty. Even so, we were within an ace of losing two, the lashed couple in which I ordinarily journeyed. In a sharp bend of the rapids, between two big curls, they were swept among the boulders and under the matted branches which stretched out from the bank. They filled, and the racing current pinned them where they were, one partly on the other.

All of us had to help get them clear. Their fastenings were chopped asunder with axes. Kermit and half a dozen of the men, stripped to the skin, made their way to a small rock island in the little falls just above the canoes and let down a rope which we tied to the outermost canoe. The rest of us, up to our armpits and barely able to keep our footing as we slipped and stumbled among the boulders in the swift current, lifted and shoved while Kermit and his men pulled the rope and fastened the slack to a half-submerged tree. Each canoe in succession was hauled up the little rock island, baled, and then taken down in safety by two paddlers. It was nearly four o'clock before we were again ready to start, having been delayed by a rainstorm so heavy that we could not see across the river.

Ten minutes' run took us to the head of another series of rapids; the exploring party returned with the news that we had an all-day's job ahead of us; and we made camp in the rain, which did not matter much, as we were already drenched through. It was impossible, with the wet wood, to make a fire sufficiently hot to dry all our soggy things, for the rain was still falling. A tapir was seen from our boat,

George Cherrie measuring a narrow rapids with his rifle

but, as at the moment we were being whisked round in a complete circle by a whirlpool, I did not myself see it in time to shoot.

Next morning we went down a kilometer, and then landed on the other side of the river. The canoes were run down and the loads carried to the other side of a little river coming in from the west, which Colonel Rondon christened Cherrie River. Across this, we went on a bridge consisting of a huge tree felled by Macario, one of our best men.

Here we camped, while Rondon, Lyra, Kermit, and Antonio Correa explored what was ahead. They were absent until mid-afternoon. Then they returned with the news that we were among ranges of low mountains, utterly different in formation from the high plateau region to which the first rapids, those we had come to on the 2nd of March, belonged. Through the first range of these mountains, the river ran in a gorge, some three kilometers long, immediately ahead of us. The ground was so rough and steep that it would be impossible to drag the canoes over it and difficult enough to carry the loads; and the rapids were so bad, containing several falls, one of at least ten meters in height, that it was doubtful how many of the canoes we could get down them. Kermit, who was the only man with much experience of rope work, was the only man who believed we could get the canoes down at all; and it was, of course, possible that we should have to build new ones at the foot to supply the place of any that were lost or left behind. In view of the length and character of the portage, and of all the unpleasant possibilities that were ahead, and of the need of keeping every pound of food, it was necessary to reduce weight in every possible way and to throw away everything except the barest necessities.

We thought we had reduced our baggage before, but now we cut to the bone. We kept the fly for all six of us to sleep under. Kermit's shoes had gone,

284

thanks to the amount of work in the water which he had been doing; and he took the pair I had been wearing, while I put on my spare pair. In addition to the clothes I wore, I kept one set of pajamas, a spare pair of drawers, a spare pair of socks, half a dozen handkerchiefs, my wash kit, my pocket medicine case, and a little bag containing my spare spectacles, gun grease, some adhesive plaster, some needles and thread, the "fly dope," and my purse and letter of credit, to be used at Manaus. All of these went into the bag containing my cot, blanket, and mosquito net. I also carried a cartridge bag containing my cartridges, head net, and gauntlets. Kermit cut down even closer; and the others about as close.

The last three days of March we spent in getting to the foot of the rapids in this gorge. Lyra and Kermit, with four of the best watermen, handled the empty canoes. The work was not only difficult and laborious in the extreme, but hazardous, for the walls of the gorge were so sheer that at the worst places they had to cling to narrow shelves on the face of the rock, while letting the canoes down with ropes. Meanwhile, Rondon surveyed and cut a trail for the burden bearers and superintended the portage of the loads. The rocky sides of the gorge were too steep for laden men to attempt to traverse them. Accordingly, the trail had to go over the top of the mountain, both the ascent and the descent of the rock-strewn, forest-clad slopes being very steep. It was hard work to carry loads over such a trail.

From the top of the mountain, through an opening in the trees on the edge of a cliff, there was a beautiful view of the country ahead. All around and in front of us there were ranges of low mountains about the height of the lower ridges of the Alleghenies. Their sides were steep, and they were covered with the matted growth of the tropical forest. Our next camping place, at the foot of the gorge, was almost beneath us, and from thence the river ran in a straight line, flecked with white water, for about a kilometer. Then it disappeared behind and between mountain ridges, which we supposed meant further rapids. It was a view well worth seeing, but, beautiful although the country ahead of us was, its character was such as to promise further hardships, difficulty, and exhausting labor, and especially further delay; and delay was a serious matter to men whose food supply was beginning to run short, whose equipment was reduced to the minimum, who for a month, with the utmost toil, had made very slow progress, and who had no idea of either the distance or the difficulties of the route in front of them.

There was not much life in the woods, big or little. Small birds were rare, although Cherrie's unwearied efforts were rewarded from time to time by a species new to the collection. There were tracks of tapir, deer, and agouti; and if we had taken two or three days to devote to nothing else than hunting them, we might perchance have killed something; but the chance was much too uncertain, the work we were doing was too hard and wearing, and the need of pressing forward altogether too great to permit us to spend any time in such manner. The hunting had to come in incidentally.

This type of well-nigh impenetrable forest is the one in which it is most difficult to get even what little game exists therein. A couple of curassows and a big monkey were killed by the colonel and Kermit. On the day the monkey was brought in, Lyra, Kermit, and their four associates had spent from sunrise to sunset in severe and at moments dangerous toil among the rocks and in the swift water, and the fresh meat was appreciated. The head, feet, tail, skin, and entrails were boiled for the gaunt and ravenous dogs. The flesh gave each of us a few mouthfuls, and how good those mouthfuls tasted!

Cherrie, in addition to being out after birds in every spare moment, helped in all emergencies. He was a veteran in the work of the tropic wilderness. We talked together often, and of many things, for our views of life, and of a man's duty to his wife and children, to other men, and to women, and to the state in peace and war, were in all essentials the same. His father had served all through the Civil War, entering an Iowa cavalry regiment as a private and coming out as a captain; his breastbone was shattered by a blow from a musket butt in hand-to-hand fighting at Shiloh.

During this portage, the weather favored us. We were coming toward the close of the rainy season. On the last day of the month, when we moved camp to the foot of the gorge, there was a thunderstorm; but on the whole, we were not bothered by rain until the last night, when it rained heavily, driving under the fly so as to wet my cot and bedding. However, I slept comfortably enough, rolled in the damp blanket. Without the blanket I should have been uncomfortable; a blanket is a necessity for health. On the third day, Lyra and Kermit, with their daring and hard-working watermen, after wearing labor, succeeded in getting five canoes through the worst of the rapids to the chief fall. The sixth, which was frail and weak, had its bottom beaten out on the jagged rocks of the broken water. On this night, although I thought I had put my clothes out of reach, both the termites and the *carregadores* ants got at them, ate holes in one boot, ate one leg of my drawers, and riddled my handkerchief; and I now had nothing to replace anything that was destroyed.

Next day, Lyra, Kermit, and their *camaradas* brought the five canoes that were left down to camp. They had in four days accomplished a work of incredible labor and of the utmost importance, for at the first glance it had seemed an absolute impossibility to avoid abandoning the canoes when we found that the river sank into a cataract-broken torrent at the bottom of a canyon-like gorge between steep mountains.

On April 2, we once more started, wondering how soon we should strike other rapids in the mountains ahead and whether in any reasonable time we should, as the aneroid indicated, be so low down that we should necessarily be in a plain where we could make a journey of at least a few days without rapids.

We had been exactly a month going through an uninterrupted succession of rapids. During that month we had come only about 110 kilometers and had descended nearly 150 meters—the figures are approximate but fairly accurate. We had lost four of the canoes with which we started, and one other, which we had built, and the life of one man, and the life of a dog, which by its death, had in all probability saved the life of Colonel Rondon. In a straight line northward, toward our supposed destination, we had not made more than a mile and a quarter a day, at the cost of bitter toil for most of the party, of much risk for some of the party, and of some risk and some hardship for all the party. Most of the *camaradas* were downhearted, naturally enough, and occasionally asked one of us if we really believed that we should ever get out alive; and we had to cheer them up as best we could.

289

There was no change in our work for the time being. We made but three kilometers that day. Most of the party walked all the time, but the dugouts carried the luggage until we struck the head of the series of rapids which were to take up the next two or three days. The river rushed through a wild gorge, a chasm or canyon, between two mountains. Its sides were very steep, mere rock walls, although in most places so covered with the luxuriant growth of the trees and bushes that clung in the crevices, and with green moss, that the naked rock was hardly seen. Rondon, Lyra, and Kermit, who were in front, found a small, level spot, with a beach of sand, and sent back word to camp there, while they spent several hours in exploring the country ahead. The canoes were run down empty, and the loads carried painfully along the face of the cliffs; so bad was the trail that I found it rather hard to follow, although carrying nothing but my rifle and cartridge bag.

The explorers returned with the information that the mountains stretched ahead of us and that there were rapids as far as they had gone. We could only hope that the aneroid was not hopelessly out of kilter and that we should, therefore, fairly soon find ourselves in comparatively level country. The severe toil, on a rather limited food supply, was telling on the strength as well as on the spirits of the men; Lyra and Kermit, in addition to their other work, performed as much actual physical labor as any of them.

Next day, the 3rd of April, we began the descent of these sinister rapids of the chasm. Colonel Rondon had gone to the summit of the mountain in order to find a better trail for the burden bearers, but it was hopeless, and they had to go along the face of the cliffs. Such an exploring expedition as that in which we were engaged, of necessity, involves hard and dangerous labor and perils of many kinds. To follow downstream an unknown river, broken by innumerable cataracts and rapids, rushing through mountains of which the existence has never been even guessed, bears no resemblance whatever to following even a fairly dangerous river which has been thoroughly explored and has become in some sort a highway, so that experienced pilots can be secured as guides, while the portages have been pioneered and trails chopped out, and every dangerous feature of the rapids is known beforehand. In this case, no one could foretell that the river would cleave its way through steep mountain chains, cutting narrow clefts in which the cliff walls rose almost sheer on either hand. Genuine wilderness exploration is as dangerous as warfare. The conquest of wild nature demands the utmost vigor, hardihood, and daring, and takes from the conquerors a heavy toll of life and health.

Lyra, Kermit, and Cherrie, with four of the men, worked the canoes halfway down the canyon. Again and again it was touch and go whether they could get by a given point. At one spot, the channel of the furious torrent was only fifteen yards across. One canoe was lost, so that of the seven with which we had started, only two were left. Cherrie labored with the other men at times and also stood as guard over them, for, while actually working, of course no one could carry a rifle. Kermit's experience in bridge building was invaluable in enabling him to do the rope work by which alone it was possible to get the canoes down the canyon.

He and Lyra had now been in the water for days. Their clothes were never dry. Their shoes were rotten. The bruises on their feet and legs had become sores. On their bodies some of the insect bites had become festering wounds, as indeed was the case with all of us. Poisonous ants, biting flies, ticks, wasps, bees were a perpetual torment. However, no one had yet been bitten by a venomous serpent, a scorpion, or a centipede, although we had killed all of the three within camp limits.

Under such conditions whatever is evil in men's natures comes to the front. On this day, a strange and terrible tragedy occurred. One of the *camaradas*, a man of pure European blood, was the man named Julio, of whom I have already spoken. He was a very powerful fellow and had been importunately eager to come on the expedition, and he had the reputation of being a good worker. But, like so many men of higher standing, he had had no idea of what such an expedition really meant, and under the strain of toil, hardship, and danger, his nature showed its true depths of selfishness, cowardice, and ferocity. He shirked all work. He shammed sickness. Nothing could make him do his share; and yet unlike his self-respecting fellows, he was always shamelessly begging for favors.

Kermit was the only one of our party who smoked; and he was continually giving a little tobacco to some of the *camaradas* who worked especially well under him. The good men did not ask for it; but Julio, who shirked every labor, was always, and always in vain, demanding it. Colonel Rondon, Lyra, and Kermit each tried to get work out of him, and in order to do anything with him, had to threaten to leave him in the wilderness. He threw all his tasks on his comrades; and, moreover, he stole their food as well as ours. On such an expedition, the theft of food comes next to murder as a crime and should by rights be punished as such. We could not trust him to cut down palms or gather nuts because he would stay out and eat what ought to have gone into the common store. Finally, the men on several occasions themselves detected him stealing their food. Alone of the whole party, and thanks to the stolen food, he had kept in full flesh and bodily vigor.

One of our best men was a huge Negro named [Corporal Manoel Vincente de] Paixão—

[pronounced] Paishon—a corporal and acting sergeant in the engineer corps. He had, by the way, literally torn his trousers to pieces, so that he wore only the tatters of a pair of old drawers until I gave him my spare trousers when we lightened loads. He was a stern disciplinarian. One evening he detected Julio stealing food and smashed him in the mouth. Julio came crying to us, his face working with fear and malignant hatred; but after investigation, he was told that he had gotten off uncommonly lightly. The men had three or four carbines, which were sometimes carried by those who were not their owners.

On this morning, at the outset of the portage, Pedrinho discovered Julio stealing some of the men's dried meat. Shortly afterward, Paixão rebuked him for, as usual, lagging behind. By this time, we had reached the place where the canoes were tied to the bank and then taken down one at a time. We were sitting down, waiting for the last loads to be brought along the trail. Pedrinho was still in the camp we had left. Paixão had just brought in a load, left it on the ground with his carbine beside it, and returned on the trail for another load. Julio came in, put down his load, picked up the carbine, and walked back on the trail, muttering to himself but showing no excitement. We thought nothing of it, for he was always muttering; and occasionally one of the men saw a monkey or big bird and tried to shoot it, so it was never surprising to see a man with a carbine.

In a minute we heard a shot; and in a short time, three or four of the men came up the trail to tell us that Paixão was dead, having been shot by Julio, who had fled into the woods. Colonel Rondon and Lyra were ahead; I sent a messenger for them, directed Cherrie and Kermit to stay where they were and guard the canoes and provisions, and started down the trail with the doctor—an absolutely cool and plucky man, with a revolver but no rifle—and a couple of the *camaradas*. We soon passed the dead body of poor Paixão. He lay in a huddle, in a pool of his own blood, where he had fallen, shot through the heart. I feared that Julio had run amuck and intended merely to take more lives before he died and that he would begin with Pedrinho, who was alone and unarmed in the camp we had left. Accordingly I pushed on, followed by my companions, looking sharply right and left; but when we came to the camp, the doctor quietly walked by me, remarking, "My eyes are better than yours, colonel; if he is in sight, I'll point him out to you, as you have the rifle." However, he was not there, and the others soon joined us with the welcome news that they had found the carbine.

The murderer had stood to one side of the path and killed his victim when a dozen paces off, with deliberate and malignant purpose. Then, evidently, his murderous hatred had at once given way to his innate cowardice; and, perhaps hearing someone coming along the path, he fled in panic terror into the wilderness. A tree had knocked the carbine from his hand. His footsteps showed that after going some rods, he had started to return, doubtless for the carbine, but had fled again, probably because the body had then been discovered. It was questionable whether or not he would live to reach the Indian villages, which were probably his goal. He was not a man to feel remorse—never a common feeling; but surely that murderer was in a living hell, as, with fever and famine leering at him from the shadows, he made his way through the empty desolation of the wilderness. Franca, the cook, quoted out of the melancholy proverbial philosophy of the people, the proverb: "No man knows the heart of any one," and then expressed with deep conviction a weird ghostly belief I had never encountered before: "Paixão is following Julio now, and will follow him until he dies; Paixão fell forward on his hands and knees, and when a murdered man falls like that, his ghost will follow the slayer as long as the slayer lives."

We did not attempt to pursue the murderer. We could not legally put him to death, although he was a soldier who in cold blood had just deliberately killed a fellow soldier. If we had been near civilization, we would have done our best to bring him in and turn him over to justice. But we were in the wilderness, and how many weeks' journey were ahead of us we could not tell. Our food was running low, sickness was beginning to appear among the men, and both their courage and their strength were gradually ebbing. Our first duty was to save the lives and the health of the men of the expedition who had honestly been performing, and had still to perform, so much perilous labor.

If we brought the murderer in, he would have to be guarded night and day on an expedition where there were always loaded firearms about and where there would continually be opportunity and temptation for him to make an effort to seize food and a weapon and escape, perhaps murdering some other good man. He could not be shackled while climbing along the cliff slopes; he could not be shackled in the canoes, where there was always chance of upset and drowning; and standing guard would be an additional and severe penalty on the weary, honest men already exhausted by overwork. The expedition was in peril, and it was wise to take every chance possible that would help secure success. Whether the murderer lived or died in the wilderness was of no moment compared with the duty of doing everything to secure the safety of the rest of the party.

For the two days following, we were always on the watch against his return, for he could have readily killed someone else by rolling rocks down on any of the men working on the cliff sides or in the bottom of the gorge. But we did not see him until the morning of the third day. We had passed the last of the rapids of the chasm, and the four boats were going downstream, when he appeared behind some trees on the bank and called out that he wished to surrender and be taken aboard; for the murderer was an arrant craven at heart, a strange mixture of ferocity and cowardice. Colonel Rondon's boat was far in advance; he did not stop nor answer. I kept on in similar fashion with the rear boats, for I had no intention of taking the murderer aboard, to the jeopardy of the other members of the party, unless Colonel Rondon told me that it would have to be done in pursuance of his duty as an officer of the army and a servant of the government of Brazil. At the first halt, Colonel Rondon came up to me and told me that this was his view of his duty, but that he had not stopped because he wished first to consult me as the chief of the expedition. I answered that for the reasons enumerated above, I did not believe that in justice to the good men of the expedition we should jeopardize their safety by taking the murderer along and that if the responsibility were mine I should refuse to take him; but that he, Colonel Rondon, was the superior officer of both the murderer and of all the other enlisted men and army officers on the expedition, and in return was responsible for his actions to his own governmental superiors and to the laws of Brazil and that in view of this responsibility, he must act as his sense of duty bade him. Accordingly, at the next camp, he sent back two men, expert woodsmen, to find the murderer and bring him in. They failed to find him.[2]

I have anticipated my narrative because I do not wish to recur to the horror more than is necessary. I now return to my story. After we found that Julio had fled, we returned to the scene of the tragedy. The murdered man lay with a handkerchief thrown over his face. We buried him beside the place where he fell. With axes and knives the *camaradas* dug a shallow grave while we stood by with bared heads. Then reverently and carefully we lifted the poor body which but half an hour before had been so full of vigorous life. Colonel Rondon and I bore the head and shoulders. We laid him in the grave, and heaped a mound over him, and put a rude cross at his head. We fired a volley for a brave and loyal soldier who had died doing his duty. Then we left him forever, under the great trees beside the lonely river.

That day we got only halfway down the rapids. There was no good place to camp. But at the foot of one steep cliff, there was a narrow, boulder-covered slope where it was possible to sling hammocks and cook; and a slanting spot was found for my cot, which had sagged until by this time it looked like a broken-backed centipede. It rained a little during the night, but not enough to wet us much. Next day, Lyra, Kermit, and Cherrie finished their job and brought the four remaining canoes to camp, one leaking badly from the battering on the rocks. We then went downstream a few hundred yards and camped on the opposite side; it was not a good camping place, but it was better than the one we left.

The men were growing constantly weaker under the endless strain of exhausting labor. Kermit was having an attack of fever, and Lyra and Cherrie had touches of dysentery, but all three continued to work. While in the water trying to help with an upset canoe, I had by my own clumsiness bruised my leg against a boulder; and the resulting inflammation was somewhat bothersome. I now had a sharp attack of fever, but thanks to the excellent care of the doctor, was over it in about forty-eight hours; but Kermit's fever grew worse, and he too was unable to work for a day or two. We could walk over the portages, however. A good doctor is an absolute necessity on an exploring expedition in such a country as that we were in, under penalty of a frightful mortality among the members; and the necessary risks and hazards are so great, the chances of disaster so large, that there is no warrant for increasing them by the failure to take all feasible precautions.

The next day we made another long portage round some rapids and camped at night still in the

Kermit Roosevelt in his canoe

hot, wet, sunless atmosphere of the gorge. The following day, April 6, we portaged past another set of rapids, which proved to be the last of the rapids of the chasm. For some kilometers we kept passing hills and feared lest at any moment we might again find ourselves fronting another mountain gorge, with, in such case, further days of grinding and perilous labor ahead of us, while our men were disheartened, weak, and sick. Most of them had already begun to have fever. Their condition was inevitable after over a month's uninterrupted work of the hardest kind in getting through the long series of rapids we had just passed; and a long further delay, accompanied by wearing labor, would have almost certainly meant that the weakest among our party would have begun to die. There were already two of the *camaradas* who were too weak to help the others, their condition being such as to cause us serious concern.

However, the hills gradually sank into a level plain, and the river carried us through it at a rate that enabled us during the remainder of the day to reel off thirty-six kilometers, a record that for the first time held out promise. Twice tapirs swam the river while we passed, but not near my canoe. However, the previous evening. Cherrie had killed two monkeys and Kermit one, and we all had a few mouthfuls of fresh meat; we had already had a good soup made out of a turtle Kermit had caught. We

had to portage by one short set of rapids, the unloaded canoes being brought down without difficulty. At last, at four in the afternoon, we came to
the mouth of a big river running in from the right.
We thought it was probably the Ananás, but, of
course, could not be certain. It was less in volume
than the one we had descended, but nearly as broad;
its breadth at this point being 95 yards as against 120
for the larger river. There were rapids ahead, immediately after the junction, which took place in
latitude 10° 58′ south. We had come 216 kilometers
all told and were nearly north of where we had
started.

We camped on the point of land between the
two rivers. It was extraordinary to realize that here,
about the eleventh degree, we were on such a big
river, utterly unknown to the cartographers and not
indicated by even a hint on any map. We named
this big tributary Rio Cardoso, after a gallant officer
of the commission who had died of beriberi just as
our expedition began. We spent a day at this spot,
determining our exact position by the sun, and afterward by the stars, and sending on two men to
explore the rapids in advance. They returned with
the news that there were big cataracts in them and
that they would form an obstacle to our progress.
They had also caught a huge siluroid fish, which
furnished an excellent meal for everybody in camp.
This evening at sunset, the view across the broad

river from our camp where the two rivers joined was very lovely; and for the first time, we had an open space in front of and above us, so that after nightfall, the stars and the great waxing moon were glorious overhead, and against the rocks in midstream, the broken water gleamed like tossing silver.

The huge catfish which the men had caught was over three feet and a half long, with the usual enormous head, out of all proportions to the body, and the enormous mouth, out of all proportion to the head. Such fish, although their teeth are small, swallow very large prey. This one contained the nearly digested remains of a monkey. Probably the monkey had been seized while drinking from the end of a branch; and once engulfed in that yawning cavern, there was no escape. We Americans were astounded at the idea of a catfish making prey of a monkey; but our Brazilian friends told us that in the lower Madeira and the part of the Amazon near its mouth, there is a still more gigantic catfish which in similar fashion occasionally makes prey of man. This is a grayish-white fish over nine feet long, with the usual disproportionately large head and gaping mouth, with a circle of small teeth; for the engulfing mouth itself is the danger, not the teeth. It is called the *piraíba*—pronounced in four syllables.

While stationed at the small city of Itacoatiara, on the Amazon, at the mouth of the Madeira, the doctor had seen one of these monsters which had been killed by the two men it had attacked. They were fishing in a canoe, when it rose from the bottom—for it is a ground fish—and raising itself half out of the water lunged over the edge of the canoe at them, with open mouth. They killed it with their *falcóns*, as machetes are called in Brazil. It was taken round the city in triumph in an ox cart; the doctor saw it, and said it was three meters long. He said that swimmers feared it even more than the big caiman, because they could see the latter, whereas the former lay hid at the bottom of the water. Colonel Rondon said that in many villages where he had been on the lower Madeira, the people had built stockaded enclosures in the water in which they bathed, not venturing to swim in the open water for fear of the *piraíba* and the big caiman.

Next day, April 8, we made five kilometers only, as there was a succession of rapids. We had to carry the loads past two of them but ran the canoes without difficulty, for on the west side were long canals of swift water through the forest. The river had been higher, but was still very high, and the current raced round the many islands that at this point divided the channel. At four, we made camp at the head of another stretch of rapids, over which the Canadian canoes would have danced without shipping a teaspoonful of water, but which our dugouts could only run empty. Cherrie killed three monkeys, and

Lyra caught two big piranhas, so that we were again all of us well provided with dinner and breakfast. When a number of men, doing hard work, are most of the time on half-rations, they grow to take a lively interest in any reasonably full meal that does arrive.

On the 10th, we repeated the proceedings: a short, quick run; a few hundred meters' portage, occupying, however, at least a couple of hours; again a few minutes' run; again other rapids. We again made less than five kilometers; in the two days we had been descending nearly a meter for every kilometer we made in advance; and it hardly seemed as if this state of things could last, for the aneroid showed that we were getting very low down. How I longed for a big Maine birch bark, such as that in which I once went down the Mattawamkeag at high water! It would have slipped down these rapids as a girl trips through a country dance. But our loaded dugouts would have shoved their noses under every curl.

The country was lovely. The wide river, now in one channel, now in several channels, wound among hills; the shower-freshened forest glistened in the sunlight; the many kinds of beautiful palm fronds and the huge *pacova* leaves stamped the peculiar look of the tropics on the whole landscape— it was like passing by water through a gigantic botanical garden. In the afternoon we got an elderly toucan, a piranha, and a reasonably edible side-necked river turtle, so we had fresh meat again. We slept as usual in earshot of rapids. We had been out six weeks, and almost all the time we had been engaged in wearily working our own way down and past rapid after rapid. Rapids are by far the most dangerous enemies of explorers and travelers who journey along these rivers.

Next day was a repetition of the same work. All the morning was spent in getting the loads to the foot of the rapids at the head of which we were encamped, down which the canoes were run empty. Then for thirty or forty minutes, we ran down the swift, twisting river, the two lashed canoes almost coming to grief at one spot where a swirl of the current threw them against some trees on a small submerged island. Then we came to another set of rapids, carried the baggage down past them, and made camp long after dark in the rain—a good exercise in patience for those of us who were still suffering somewhat from fever. No one was in really buoyant health. For some weeks, we had been sharing part of the contents of our boxes with the *cama-radas*; but our food was not very satisfying to them. They needed quantity and the mainstay of each of their meals was a mass of palmitos [hearts of palm]; but on this day, they had no time to cut down palms. We finally decided to run these rapids with the empty canoes, and they came down in safety.

On such a trip, it is highly undesirable to take any save necessary risks, for the consequences of disaster are too serious; and yet if no risks are taken, the progress is so slow that disaster comes anyhow; and it is necessary perpetually to vary the terms of the perpetual working compromise between rashness and overcaution. This night we had a very good fish to eat, a big silvery fellow called a *pescada* [whitefish], of a kind we had not caught before.

One day Trigueiro failed to embark with the rest of us, and we had to camp where we were next day to find him. Easter Sunday we spent in the fashion with which we were altogether too familiar. We only ran in a clear course for ten minutes all told and spent eight hours in portaging the loads past rapids down which the canoes were run; the balsa was almost swamped. This day we caught twenty-eight big fish, mostly piranhas, and everybody had all he could eat for dinner and for breakfast the following morning.

The forenoon of the following day was a repetition of this wearisome work; but late in the afternoon, the river began to run in long, quiet reaches. We made fifteen kilometers, and for the first time in several weeks, camped where we did not hear the rapids. The silence was soothing and restful. The following day, April 14, we made a good run of some thirty-two kilometers. We passed a little river which entered on our left. We ran two or three light rapids and portaged the loads by another. The river ran in long and usually tranquil stretches. In the morning when we started, the view was lovely. There was a mist, and for a couple of miles, the great river, broad and quiet, ran between the high walls of tropical forest, the tops of the giant trees showing dim through the haze. Different members of the party caught many fish and shot a monkey and a couple of *jacutinga*—birds kin to a turkey, but the size of a fowl—so we again had a camp of plenty. The dry season was approaching, but there were still heavy, drenching rains. On this day, the men found some new nuts of which they liked the taste; but the nuts proved unwholesome and half of the men were very sick and unable to work the following day. In the balsa, only two were left fit to do anything, and Kermit plied a paddle all day long.

Accordingly, it was a rather sorry crew that embarked the following morning, April 15. But it turned out a red-letter day. The day before, we had come across cuttings, a year old, which were probably, but not certainly, made by pioneer rubber men. But on this day—during which we made twenty-five kilometers—after running two hours and a half, we found on the left bank a board on a post, with the initials J. A., to show the farthest-up point which a rubber man had reached and claimed as his own. An hour farther down, we came on a newly built house in a little planted clearing; and we cheered heartily. No one was at home, but the house, of palm thatch, was clean and cool. A couple of dogs were on watch, and the belongings showed that a man, a woman, and a child lived there, and had only just left. Another hour brought us to a similar house where dwelt an old black man, who showed the innate courtesy of the Brazilian peasant. We came on these rubber men and their houses in about latitude 10° 24′.

In mid-afternoon, we stopped at another clean, cool, picturesque house of palm thatch. The inhabitants all fled at our approach, fearing an Indian raid, for they were absolutely unprepared to have anyone come from the unknown regions upstream. They returned and were most hospitable and communicative, and we spent the night there. Said Antonio Correa to Kermit: "It seems like a dream to be in a house again and hear the voices of men and women, instead of being among those mountains and rapids." The river was known to them as the Castanho and was the main affluent or rather the left or western branch, of the Aripuanã; the Castanho is a name used by the rubber gatherers only; it is unknown to the geographers. We were, according to our informants, about fifteen days' journey from the confluence of the two rivers; but there were many rubber men along the banks, some of whom had become permanent settlers. We had come over three hundred kilometers, in forty-eight

At the rubber man's house

days, over absolutely unknown ground; we had seen no human being, although we had twice heard Indians. Six weeks had been spent in steadily slogging our way down through the interminable series of rapids.

It was astonishing before, when we were on a river of about the size of the upper Rhine or Elbe, to realize that no geographer had any idea of its existence. But, after all, no civilized man of any grade had ever been on it. Here, however, was a river with people dwelling along the banks, some of whom had lived in the neighborhood for eight or ten years; and yet on no standard map was there a hint of the river's existence. We were putting on the map a river, running through between five and six

311

degrees of latitude—of between seven and eight if, as should properly be done, the lower Aripuanã is included as part of it—of which no geographer, in any map published in Europe, or the United States, or Brazil had even admitted the possibility of the existence; for the place actually occupied by it was filled, on the maps, by other—imaginary—streams, or by mountain ranges.

Before we started, the Amazonas Boundary Commission had come up the lower Aripuanã and then the eastern branch, or upper Aripuanã, following the course which for a couple of decades had been followed by the rubber men, but not going as high. The lower main stream, and the lower portion of its main affluent, the Castanho, had been commercial highways for rubber men and settlers for nearly two decades, and, as we speedily found, were as easy to traverse as the upper stream, which we had just come down, was difficult to traverse; but the governmental and scientific authorities, native and foreign, remained in complete ignorance; and the rubber men themselves had not the slightest idea of the headwaters, which were in country never hitherto traversed by civilized men. At this stage of the growth of world geography, I esteemed it a great piece of good fortune to be able to take part in such a feat—a feat which represented the capping of the pyramid which during the previous seven years had been built by the labor of the Brazilian Telegraphic Commission.

We had passed the period when there was a chance of peril, of disaster, to the whole expedition. There might be risk ahead to individuals, and some difficulties and annoyances for all of us, but there was no longer the least likelihood of any disaster to the expedition as a whole. We now no longer had to face continual anxiety, the need of constant economy with food, the duty of labor with no end in sight, and bitter uncertainty as to the future.

It was time to get out. The wearing work, under very unhealthy conditions, was beginning to tell on everyone. Half of the *camaradas* had been down with fever and were much weakened; only a few of them retained their original physical and moral strength. Cherrie and Kermit had recovered, but both Kermit and Lyra still had bad sores on their legs from the bruises received in the water work. I was in worse shape. The aftereffects of the fever still hung on; and the leg which had been hurt while working in the rapids with the sunken canoe had taken a turn for the bad and developed an abscess. The good doctor, to whose unwearied care and kindness I owe much, had cut it open and inserted a drainage tube; an added charm being given the operation, and the subsequent dressings, by the enthusiasm with which the piums and *borrachudos*

313

took part therein. I could hardly hobble and was
pretty well laid up. But "there aren't no 'stop, con-
ductor,' while a battery's changing ground."[3] No
man has any business to go on such a trip as ours
unless he will refuse to jeopardize the welfare of his
associates by any delay caused by a weakness or ail-
ment of his. It is his duty to go forward, if necessary
on all fours, until he drops.

Fortunately, I was put to no such test. I remained
in good shape until we had passed the last of the
rapids of the chasms. When my serious trouble
came, we had only canoe riding ahead of us. It is
not ideal for a sick man to spend the hottest hours
of the day stretched on the boxes in the bottom of
a small, open dugout, under the well-nigh intolerable heat of the torrid sun of the mid-tropics, varied
by blinding, drenching downpours of rain; but I
could not be sufficiently grateful for the chance.
Kermit and Cherrie took care of me as if they had
been trained nurses; and Colonel Rondon and Lyra
were no less thoughtful.

The north was calling strongly to the three men
of the north—Rocky Dell Farm to Cherrie, Sagamore Hill to me, and to Kermit the call was stron-
ger still. After nightfall, we could now see the
Dipper well above the horizon—upside down, with
the two pointers pointing to a north star below the
world's rim—but the Dipper, with all its stars. In
our home country, spring had now come, the won-

Colonel Roosevelt's covered canoe after he was taken ill

derful northern spring of long, glorious days, of brooding twilights, of cool delightful nights. Robin and bluebird, meadowlark and song sparrow, were singing in the mornings at home; the maple buds were red; windflowers and bloodroot were blooming, while the last patches of snow still lingered; the rapture of the hermit thrush in Vermont, the serene golden melody of the wood thrush on Long Island, would be heard before we were there to listen. Each man to his home, and to his true love! Each was longing for the homely things that were so dear to him, for the home people who were dearer still, and for the one who was dearest of all.

NOTES

1. Alfredo Maria Adriano d'Escragnolle Taunay, viscount of Taunay (1843–99), was a French Brazilian writer, musician, professor, military engineer, historian, politician, sociologist, and nobleman.

2. Author's note: The above account of all the circumstances connected with the murder was read to and approved as correct by all six members of the expedition.

3. From Kipling's poem "Snarleyow."

X. To the Amazon and Home

OUR ADVENTURES and our troubles were alike over. We now experienced the incalculable contrast between descending a known and traveled river and one that is utterly unknown. After four days, we hired a rubber man to go with us as guide. We knew exactly what channels were passable when we came to the rapids, when the canoes had to unload, and where the carry trails were. It was all child's play compared to what we had gone through. We made long days' journeys, for at night we stopped at some palm-thatched house, inhabited or abandoned, and, therefore, the men were spared the labor of making camp; and we bought ample food for them, so there was no further need of fishing and chopping down palms for the palm tops. The heat of the sun was blazing; but it looked as if we had come back into the rainy season, for there were many heavy rains, usually in the afternoon, but sometimes in the morning or at night. The mosquitoes were sometimes rather troublesome at night. In the daytime, the piums swarmed and often bothered us even when we were in midstream.

For four days, there were no rapids we could not run without unloading. Then, on the 19th, we got a canoe from Senhor Barboso. He was a most kind and hospitable man, who also gave us a duck and a chicken and some manioc and six pounds of rice,

The river widens beyond the rapids

and would take no payment; he lived in a roomy house with his dusky, cigar-smoking wife and his many children. The new canoe was light and roomy, and we were able to rig up a low shelter under which I could lie; I was still sick. At noon we passed the mouth of a big river, the Rio Branco, coming in from the left; this was about in latitude 9° 38′. Soon afterward, we came to the first serious rapids, the Panela. We carried the boats past, ran down the empty canoes, and camped at the foot in a roomy house. The doctor bought a handsome trumpeter bird, very friendly and confiding, which was thenceforth my canoe companion.

We had already passed many inhabited—and a still larger number of uninhabited—houses. The dwellers were rubber men, but generally they were permanent settlers also, home makers, with their wives and children. Some, both of the men and women, were apparently of pure Negro blood, or of pure Indian or south European blood; but in the great majority, all three strains were mixed in varying degrees. They were most friendly, courteous, and hospitable. Often they refused payment for what they could afford, out of their little, to give us. When they did charge, the prices were very high, as was but just, for they live back of the beyond, and everything costs them fabulously, save what they raise themselves.

The cool, bare houses of poles and palm thatch

contained little except hammocks and a few simple cooking utensils, and often a clock or sewing machine, or Winchester rifle, from our own country. They often had flowers planted, including fragrant roses. Their only livestock, except the dogs, were a few chickens and ducks. They planted patches of manioc, maize, sugarcane, rice, beans, squashes, pineapples, bananas, lemons, oranges, melons, pepper, and various purely native fruits and vegetables, such as the kniabo—a vegetable-fruit growing on the branches of a high bush—which is cooked with meat. They get some game from the forest, and more fish from the river. There is no representative of the government among them— indeed, even now their very existence is barely known to the governmental authorities; and the church has ignored them as completely as the state. When they wish to get married, they have to spend several months getting down to and back from Manaus or some smaller city; and usually the first christening and the marriage ceremony are held at the same time. They have merely squatter's right to the land and are always in danger of being ousted by unscrupulous big men who come in late, but with a title technically straight. The land laws should be shaped so as to give each of these pioneer settlers the land he actually takes up and cultivates, and upon which he makes his home. The small home maker, who owns the land which he tills with his own hands, is the greatest element of strength in any country.

These are real pioneer settlers. They are the true wilderness winners. No continent is ever really conquered, or thoroughly explored, by a few leaders or exceptional men, although such men can render great service. The real conquest, the thorough exploration and settlement, is made by a nameless multitude of small men of whom the most important are, of course, the home makers. Each treads most of the time in the footsteps of his predecessors, but for some few miles, at some time or other, he breaks new ground; and his house is built where no house has ever stood before. Such a man, the real pioneer, must have no strong desire for social life and no need, probably no knowledge, of any luxury or of any comfort save of the most elementary kind. The pioneer who is always longing for the comfort and luxury of civilization, and especially of great cities, is no real pioneer at all. These settlers whom we met were contented to live in the wilderness. They had found the climate healthy and the soil fruitful; a visit to a city was a very rare event, nor was there any overwhelming desire for it.

On the 20th, we stopped at the first store, where we bought, of course at a high price, sugar and tobacco for the *camaradas*. In this land of plenty, the *camaradas* overate, and sickness was as rife among them as ever. In Cherrie's boat, he himself and the steersman were the only men who paddled strongly and continuously. The storekeeper's stock of goods was very low, only what he still had left from that brought in nearly a year before; for the big boats, or *batelãos* [barges]—[pronounced] batelons—had not yet worked as far upstream. We expected to meet them somewhere below the next rapids, the Inferno. The trader or rubber man brings up his year's supply of goods in a *batelão*, starting in February and reaching the upper course of the river early in May, when the rainy season is over. The parties of rubber explorers are then equipped and provisioned; and the settlers purchase certain necessities and certain things that strike them as luxuries. This year the Brazil-nut crop on the river had failed, a serious thing for all explorers and wilderness wanderers.

On the 20th, we made the longest run we had made, fifty-two kilometers. At this camping place the great, beautiful river was a little over three hundred meters wide. We were in an empty house. The marks showed that in the high water, a couple of months back, the river had risen until the lower part of the house was flooded. The difference between the level of the river during the floods and in the dry season is extraordinary.

On the 21st, we made another good run, getting down to the Inferno Rapids. Until we reached the Cardoso, we had run almost due north; since then, we had been running a little west of north. Before we reached these rapids we stopped at a large, pleasant thatch house and got a fairly big and roomy as well as light boat, leaving both our two smaller dugouts behind. Above the rapids a small river, the Madeirinha, entered from the left. The rapids had a fall of over ten meters, and the water was very wild and rough. Met with for the first time, it would doubtless have taken several days to explore a passage and, with danger and labor, get the boats down. But we were no longer exploring, pioneering, over unknown country. It is easy to go where other men have prepared the way. We had a guide; we took our baggage down by a carry three-quarters of a kilometer long; and the canoes were run through known channels the following morning. At the foot of the rapids was a big house and store; and camped at the head were a number of rubber workers, waiting for the big boats of the head rubber men to work their way up from below. They were a reckless set of brown daredevils. These men lead hard lives of labor and peril; they continually face death themselves, and they think little of it in connection with others. It is small wonder that they sometimes have difficulties with the tribes of utterly wild Indians with whom they are brought in contact, although there is a strong Indian strain in their own blood.

The following morning, after the empty canoes had been run down, we started, and made a rather short afternoon's journey. We had to take the baggage by one rapids. We camped in an empty house, in the rain. Next day we ran nearly fifty kilometers, the river making a long sweep to the west. We met half a dozen *batelãos* making their way upstream, each with a crew of six or eight men, and two of them with women and children in addition. The crew were using very long poles, with crooks, or rather the stubs of cut branches which served as crooks, at the upper end. With these, they hooked into the branches and dragged themselves up along the bank, in addition to poling where the depth permitted it. The river was as big as the Paraguay at Corumbá; but, in striking contrast to the Paraguay, there were few water birds. We ran some rather stiff rapids, the Inferninho, without unloading, in the morning. In the evening we landed for the night at a large, open, shed-like house, where there were two or three pigs, the first livestock we had seen other than poultry and ducks. It was a dirty place, but we got some eggs.

The following day, the 24th, we ran down some fifty kilometers to the Carupaná Rapids. We met several *batelãos*, and the houses on the bank showed that the settlers were somewhat better off than was the case farther up. At the rapids was a big store, the property of Senhor Caripe, the wealthiest rubber man who works on this river; many of the men we met were in his employ. He has himself risen from the ranks. He was most kind and hospitable, and gave us another boat to replace the last of our shovel-nosed dugouts. The large, open house was cool, clean, and comfortable.

With these began a series of half a dozen sets of rapids, all coming within the next dozen kilometers, and all offering very real obstacles. At one we saw the graves of four men who had perished therein, and many more had died whose bodies were never recovered; the toll of human life had been heavy. Had we been still on an unknown river, pioneering our own way, it would doubtless have taken us at least a fortnight of labor and peril to pass. But it actually took only a day and a half. All the channels were known, all the trails cut. Senhor Caripe, a first-class waterman, cool, fearless, and brawny as a bull, came with us as guide. Half a dozen times the loads were taken out and carried down. At one cataract, the canoes were themselves dragged overland; else-where, they were run down empty, shipping a good deal of water.

At the foot of the cataract, where we dragged the canoes overland, we camped for the night. Here Kermit shot a big caiman. Our camp was alongside the graves of three men who at this point had per-ished in the swift water.

By mid-forenoon on April 26, we had passed the last dangerous rapids. The paddles were plied with hearty good will, Cherrie and Kermit, as usual, working like the *camaradas*, and the canoes went dancing down the broad, rapid river. The equatorial forest crowded on either hand to the water's edge; and, although the river was falling, it was still so high that in many places little islands were completely submerged and the current raced among the trunks of the green trees. At one o'clock, we came to the mouth of the Castanho proper, and in sight of the tent of Lieutenant Pirineus, with the flags of the United States and Brazil flying before it; and, with rifles firing from the canoes and the shore, we moored at the landing of the neat, soldierly, well-kept camp.

We had been two months in the canoes, from the 27th of February to the 26th of April. We had gone over 750 kilometers. The river from its source, near the thirteenth degree, to where it became navigable and we entered it, had a course of some 200 kilometers—probably more, perhaps 300 kilometers. Therefore we had now put on the map a river nearly 1,000 kilometers in length of which the existence was not merely unknown but impossible if the standard maps were correct. But this was not all. It seemed that this river of 1,000 kilometers in length was really the true upper course of the Aripuaná proper, in which case, the total length was nearly 1,500 kilometers. Pirineus had been waiting for us over a month, at the junction of what the rubber men called the Castanho and of what they called the upper Aripuaná. (He had no idea as to which stream we would appear upon, or whether we would appear upon either.)

We were glad indeed to see Pirineus and be at his attractive camp. We were only four hours above the little river hamlet of São João, a port of call for rubber steamers, from which the larger ones go to Manaus in two days. These steamers mostly belong to Senhor Caripe. From Pirineus we learned that Lauriadó and Fiala had reached Manaus on March 26. On the swift water in the gorge of the Papagaio, Fiala's boat had been upset and all his belongings lost, while he himself had narrowly escaped with his life. I was glad indeed that the fine and gallant fellow had escaped. The Canadian canoe had done very well. We were no less rejoiced to learn that Amilcar, the head of the party that went down the Ji-Paraná, was also all right, although his canoe too had been upset in the rapids and his instruments and all his notes lost. He had reached Manaus on April 10. Fiala had gone home. Miller was collecting near Manaus. He had been doing capital work.

The piranhas were bad here, and no one could bathe. Cherrie, while standing in the water close to the shore, was attacked and bitten; but with one bound, he was on the bank before any damage could be done.

We spent a last night under canvas, at Pirineus' encampment. It rained heavily. Next morning, we all gathered at the monument which Colonel Rondon had erected, and he read the orders of the day. These recited just what had been accomplished: set forth the fact that we had now by actual exploration and investigation discovered that the river whose upper portion had been called the Dúvida on the maps of the Telegraphic Commission and the unknown major part of which we had just traversed, and the river known to a few rubber men, but to no one else, as the Castanho, and the lower part of the river known to the rubber men as the Aripuanã (which did not appear on the maps save as its mouth was sometimes indicated, with no hint of its size) were all parts of one and the same river; and that by order of the Brazilian government, this river, the largest affluent of the Madeira, with its source near the 13th degree and its mouth a little south of the 5th degree, hitherto utterly unknown to cartographers and in large part utterly unknown to any save the local tribes of Indians, had been named the Rio Roosevelt.

We left Rondon, Lyra, and Pirineus to take observations, and the rest of us embarked for the last time on the canoes, and, borne swiftly on the rapid current, we passed over one set of not very important rapids and ran down to Senhor Caripe's little hamlet of São João, which we reached about one o'clock on April 27, just before a heavy afternoon rain set in. We had run nearly eight hundred kilometers during the sixty days we had spent in the

canoes. Here we found and boarded Pirineus's river
steamer, which seemed in our eyes extremely comfortable. In the senhor's pleasant house, we were
greeted by the senhora, and they were both more
than thoughtful and generous in their hospitality.
Ahead of us lay merely thirty-six hours by steamer
to Manaus. Such a trip as that we had taken tries
men as if by fire. Cherrie had more than stood every
test, and, in him, Kermit and I had come to recog-
nize a friend with whom our friendship would never
falter or grow less.

Early the following afternoon, our whole party,
together with Senhor Caripe, started on the steamer.
It took us a little over twelve hours' swift steaming
to run down to the mouth of the river on the upper
course of which our progress had been so slow and
painful; from source to mouth, according to our
itinerary and to Lyra's calculations, the course of the
stream down which we had thus come was about
1,500 kilometers in length—about 900 miles, perhaps nearly 1,000 miles—from its source near the
13th degree in the highlands to its mouth in the
Madeira, near the 5th degree.

Next morning, we were on the broad sluggish
current of the lower Madeira, a beautiful tropical
river. There were heavy rainstorms, as usual, although this is supposed to be the very end of the
rainy season. In the afternoon, we finally entered
the wonderful Amazon itself, the mighty river which

*The Palácio Rio Negro, the seat of the government and residence
of the governer of Manaus*

contains one tenth of all the running water of the globe. It was miles across where we entered it; and indeed we could not tell whether the farther bank, which we saw, was that of the mainland or an island. We went up it until about midnight; then steamed up the Rio Negro for a short distance, and at one in the morning of April 30, reached Manaus.

Manaus is a remarkable city. It is only three degrees south of the equator. Sixty years ago, it was a nameless little collection of hovels, tenanted by a few Indians and a few of the poorest class of Brazilian peasants. Now, it is a big, handsome modern city, with opera house, tramways, good hotels, fine squares and public buildings, and attractive private houses. The brilliant coloring and odd architecture give the place a very foreign and attractive flavor in northern eyes. Its rapid growth to prosperity was due to the rubber trade. This is now far less remunerative than formerly. It will undoubtedly in some degree recover; and in any event, the development of the immensely rich and fertile Amazonian valley is sure to go on, and it will be immensely quickened when closer connections are made with the Brazilian highland country lying south of it.

Here we found Miller, and glad indeed we were to see him. He had made good collections of mammals and birds on the Ji-Paraná, the Madeira, and in the neighborhood of Manaus; his entire collection of mammals was really noteworthy. Among them was the only sloth any of us had seen on the trip. The most interesting of the birds he had seen was the hoatzin. This is a most curious bird of very archaic type. Its flight is feeble, and the naked young have spurs on their wings, by the help of which they crawl actively among the branches before their feathers grow. They swim no less easily, at the same early age. Miller got one or two nests, and preserved specimens of the surroundings of the nests; and he made exhaustive records of the habits of the birds. Near Megasso [perhaps *Rio Barão de Melgaço*], a jaguar had killed one of the bullocks that were being driven along for food. The big cat had not seized the ox with its claws by the head, but had torn open its throat and neck.

Everyone was most courteous at Manaus, especially the governor of the state and the mayor of the city. Mr. Robiliard, the British consular representative, and also the representative of the Booth line of steamers, was particularly kind. He secured for us passages on one of the cargo boats of the line to Pará, and thence on one of the regular cargo-and-passenger steamers to Barbados and New York. The Booth people were most courteous to us.

I said goodbye to the *camaradas* with real friendship and regret. The parting gift I gave to each was in gold sovereigns; and I was rather touched to learn later that they had agreed among themselves each to keep one sovereign as a medal of honor and token that the owner had been on the trip. They were a fine set, brave, patient, obedient, and enduring. Now they had forgotten their hard times; they were fat from eating, at leisure, all they wished; they were to see Rio [de] Janeiro, always an object of ambition with men of their stamp; and they were very proud of their membership in the expedition.

Later, at Belém, I said goodbye to Colonel Rondon, Doctor Cajazeira, and Lieutenant Lyra. Together with my admiration for their hardihood, courage, and resolution, I had grown to feel a strong and affectionate friendship for them. I had become very fond of them, and I was glad to feel that I had been their companion in the performance of a feat which possessed a certain lasting importance.

On May 1, we left Manaus for Belém—Pará,[1] as until recently it was called. The trip was interesting. We steamed down through tempest and sunshine, and the towering forest was dwarfed by the giant river it fringed. Sunrise and sunset turned the sky to an unearthly flame of many colors above the vast water. It all seemed the embodiment of loneliness and wild majesty. Yet, everywhere, man was conquering the loneliness and wresting the majesty to his own uses. We passed many thriving, growing towns; at one, we stopped to take on cargo. Everywhere there was growth and development.

Miller, who was very fond of animals and always took much care of them, had a small collection which he was bringing back for the Bronx Zoo. An agouti was so bad-tempered that he had to be kept solitary; but three monkeys, big, middle-sized, and little, and a young peccary formed a happy family. The largest monkey cried, shedding real tears, when taken in the arms and pitied. The middle-sized monkey was stupid and kindly, and all the rest of the company imposed on it; the little monkey invariably rode on its back, and the peccary used it as a head pillow when it felt sleepy.

Belém, the capital of the state of Pará, was an admirable illustration of the genuine and almost startling progress which Brazil has been making of recent years. It is a beautiful city, nearly under the equator. But it is not merely beautiful. The docks, the dredging operations, the warehouses, the stores and shops, all tell of energy and success in commercial life. It is as clean, healthy, and well policed a city as any of the size in the North Temperate Zone. The public buildings are handsome; the private dwellings, attractive; there are a fine opera house, an excellent tramway system, and a good museum and botanical gardens. There are cavalry stables, where lights burn all night long to protect the horses from the vampire bats. The parks, the rows of palms and mango trees, the open-air restaurants, the gay life under the lights at night, all give the city its own special quality and charm. Belém and Manaus are very striking examples of what can be done in the mid-tropics. The governor of Pará and his charming wife were more than kind.

On May 7, we bade goodbye to our kind Brazilian friends and sailed northward for Barbados and New York.

NOTES

1. One early name for the city of Belém, capital of the state of Pará, was Nossa Senhora de Belém do Grão Pará (Our Lady of Bethlehem of the Great Pará).

334

Index

Note: Italicized page numbers refer to illustrations. Numbers after *n* refer to notes.

Index

Index

Index

Index

IMAGE CREDITS

DESIGNED, TYPESET, PRINTED, BOUND, AND DISTRIBUTED BY
R. R. DONNELLEY & SONS COMPANY

COMPOSITION:
ALLENTOWN, PENNSYLVANIA
CHENNAI, INDIA

SCANNING AND IMAGE PROOFING:
RR DONNELLEY
PREMEDIA TECHNOLOGIES
ELGIN, ILLINOIS

COMPUTER TO PLATES, PRINTING, AND BINDING:
CRAWFORDSVILLE, INDIANA

ADDRESSING AND MAILING:
RR DONNELLEY
RESPONSE MARKETING SERVICES

WORLDWIDE DISTRIBUTION:
RR DONNELLEY LOGISTICS

BODY TYPEFACE:
11/12.85 POINT ADOBE GARAMOND PRO

CLOTH:
ARRESTOX VELLUM, LAKESIDE GREEN,
BY HOLLISTON MILLS, INC.

PAPER STOCK:
50-POUND WHITE LAKESIDE CLASSIC
FROM LINDENMYER
BY GLATFELTER

LAKESIDE CLASSICS ARE PRINTED
ON A PERMANENT PAPER
FOR ENDURING QUALITY